ch

r

KANT'S
CRITICISM
OF METAPHYSICS

*

thoughts = produced by the
understanding

↑ ↓

intuitions - arise from the senses

necessity - a priori   }
universality

KANT'S
CRITICISM
OF METAPHYSICS

W. H. WALSH

The University of Chicago Press
Chicago

The University of Chicago Press, Chicago 60637

Published 1975 by Edinburgh University Press. Phoenix Edition 1976
Printed in the United States of America

International Standard Book Number: 0-226-87215-7

Contents

Chapter 5—*contd.*

Preface

The title of this work, which was also the title of my first philosophical article, is perhaps misleading. I offer not so much a specialist study of a particular aspect of Kant's philosophy as an essay on the central arguments of the *Critique of Pure Reason*. I am concerned to elucidate those arguments, display their connections and finally to assess them. Thus what appears here is by way of being a critical commentary on what I regard as the salient points of the *Critique*. I chose my title first because I wanted something short, and second because I believe that the problem of metaphysics, genuine and spurious, is the key problem with which Kant was concerned in this his major work. But it will soon be obvious that I by no means confine myself to his explicit pronouncements about metaphysics, or even to these and his implied views on the subject.

There are now a number of excellent books in English about the first *Critique*. My excuse for trying to add to their number is that I find that, with rare exceptions, those that are scholarly are not philosophically satisfying, whilst those which are philosophically stimulating tend to take too cavalier an attitude to the difficulties of Kant's text. I have tried to combine patience with Kant's way of expressing himself with interest in whether his arguments are sound and his conclusions true or false, enlightening or the reverse. I agree that in many respects he is a clumsy and irritating writer; I agree again that he wrote in the mistaken belief that no philosophical work could be respectable unless presented in technical terms and inside what purported to be a scientific framework. But I do not think we are entitled to set aside large portions of his work as unworthy of serious examination just because of these facts.

I owe debts to many previous commentators, and think it the more necessary to say this because other works on Kant are rarely mentioned in this book. I learned a lot about Kant from H. J. Paton; I have also found the work of my distinguished predecessor Norman Kemp Smith increasingly stimulating the more I have studied the *Critique*. Teaching Kant, at Edinburgh and elsewhere, over many years has alerted me to all sorts of simplicities in the views about him I originally held, and I am grateful to my students for having made some of these clear. I am also, paradoxically, indebted to myself, in so far as I here draw extensively on papers and articles on Kant of my own. Mostly I have restated the arguments, or rather those of them I continue to accept, in fresh ways, but sometimes I have transcribed passages more or less intact where I have not known how to improve on what I first said. In one instance (the part about the Antinomies) what appears here is substantially, though not completely, identical with what was presented in my recent paper on the subject. It may therefore be useful to list the articles concerned. They are:

'Categories', *Kantstudien*, 1954;

'Schematism', *Kantstudien*, 1957;

'Kant's Moral Theology', *Proceedings of the British Academy*, 1963;

'Philosophy and Psychology in Kant's *Critique*', *Kantstudien*, 1966;

'Kant on the Perception of Time', *The Monist*, 1967;

'Kant's Concept of Practical Reason', in S. Körner (ed.), *Practical Reason*, 1974;

'Intuition, Judgment, Appearance', *Akten des 4. Internationalen Kant-Kongresses* (forthcoming);

'The Structure of Kant's Antinomies', *Proceedings of the 1974 Ottawa Kant Congress* (forthcoming).

Mr A. R. Turnbull, Secretary to the Edinburgh University Press, has done me and my readers a major service by insisting that, even in what purports to be a philosophical work, there is no room for dubious grammar, gratuitously ugly expressions and relative pronouns with ambiguous antecedents. I have done what I could to remove defects of this kind he pointed out. It is salutary to reflect that, had an earlier Mr Turnbull been able to do the same for Kant, there might well have been no occasion for a book like this.

W.H.W.

References

The *Critique of Pure Reason* is referred to by the paging of the two original editions, A and B. Where a passage appears in both editions, the B reference is given first. The translation used is that of Norman Kemp Smith, with occasional minor alterations.

Kant's other works are mostly quoted according to the paging of the Berlin Academy edition, though section references are sometimes given when there are section divisions in the original (e.g. for the *Prolegomena* and the *Critique of Judgment*). To avoid confusion with references to the present work (e.g. section 27), Kant citations are printed in italic, thus: section *27*. The following English translations have been used or referred to:

Enquiry concerning the Clarity of the Principles of Natural Theology and Ethics, G. B. Kerferd and D. E. Walford, in *Kant: Selected Pre-Critical Writings*, Manchester 1968.

Dreams of a Spirit-Seer, E. F. Goerwitz, London and New York, 1900.

Inaugural Dissertation, John Handyside, in *Kant's Inaugural Dissertation and Early Writings on Space*, Chicago and London, 1929.

Prolegomena, P. G. Lucas, Manchester 1953.

Groundwork of the Metaphysic of Morals, translated as *The Moral Law*, H. J. Paton, London n.d.

Metaphysical Foundations of Natural Science, James Ellington, Indianapolis and New York, 1970.

Critique of Practical Reason, L. W. Beck, Chicago 1949.

Critique of Judgment, J. C. Meredith, Oxford 1911 and 1928.

First Introduction to the Critique of Judgment, James Haden, Indianapolis 1965.

Kant's letters are quoted in the translation by Arnulf Zweig, *Kant: Philosophical Correspondence*, Chicago 1967.

Cogito creations, a priori

form – being
Idea & representation

language is being

Preliminaries

§ 1. *Criticism, Scepticism and Metaphysics.* § 2.'A priori', '*analytic*', '*synthetic*'. § 3.*Intuitions and Concepts.*

§1 *Criticism, Scepticism and Metaphysics*

The word 'critique' means 'criticism' or 'critical examination', and the *Critique of Pure Reason* is a critical examination of the powers of the human intelligence, considered as operating on its own. When he began his enquiries some years before the *Critique* was published, Kant may have meant it to investigate the capacities of reason as they bear on action as well as on knowledge; in the event he separated off the first of these tasks and dealt with it in a further work, the *Critique of Practical Reason.* Apart from a few passages near the end, the first *Critique* is devoted exclusively to the question of the cognitive powers of reason; as Kant himself puts it in the preface to the first edition (A xvii), the chief question to which it addresses itself is 'what and how much can the understanding and reason know apart from all experience?'. 'The understanding' and 'reason' are Kant's names for two distinct sets of intellectual abilities, considered here as exercised in the search for knowledge, and Kant is interested in the question, not of whether these faculties, as they were traditionally called, have *any* part to play in human cognition (he takes it for granted that they have at least a logical role), but of whether they, or either of them, can be said to be a source of knowledge *on its own account.* His problem is whether the human intellect can produce truths out of its own unaided resources, as opposed to when it co-operates with the senses. And his principal aim in the *Critique* is to demonstrate that the problem must be given a negative solution: the intellect can produce from its own resources only analytic truths, apart from principles which bear directly on the sense world or govern the search for knowledge of that world.

It may seem odd that a great philosopher should have puzzled himself so long with a question to which the answer is so apparently obvious. To understand Kant here we must take account of the wider context in which he philosophised. The two prefaces to the *Critique* testify to Kant's preoccupation with two major issues, that of the nature and possibility of metaphysics, and that of the countering of scepticism. The issues were closely connected in Kant's mind, for the history of metaphysics (which was also the history of philosophy) began for him with a stage in which confident claims were asserted on the strength of what purported to be unassailably rational considerations, proceeded to a period of 'intestine wars' (A ix) in which rival parties advanced incompatible theses without being able to establish them definitively or drive their opponents from the field, and culminated in a general scepticism about the possibility of metaphysical knowledge. Kant was inclined to regard this outcome as disastrous for two main reasons. First, it seemed to him that the failure of reason in metaphysics must cast a shadow on its pretensions in other spheres, notably that of science. It is important to remember in this connection that Kant saw Hume not as an empiricist, but as a sceptic, one who declared that there was no rational basis for our beliefs about the world, including our scientific beliefs. Hume's scepticism was certainly encouraged, as he made clear himself in the Introduction to the *Treatise*, by the spectacle of unceasing and intractable disputes among philosophers; Kant hoped to counter Hume, in part at any rate, by showing that there was no need for such disputes to continue. Metaphysics as 'a completely isolated speculative science of reason, which soars far above the teachings of experience' (B xiv) must be abandoned. But this could be done without giving up what a page or two later (B xviii–xix) was called 'metaphysics in its first part', i.e. metaphysics as a foundation for science. Investigation of the empirical world proceeds on a basis which is rational; it is governed by principles which can be dispensed with only at the cost of losing all pretence to arrive at objective truth. The sceptic can formulate his position only by assuming what he attempts to deny, and hence Hume's doubts can be answered. It is not the case that we think as we do because custom and habit have so determined us, but that we must think on these lines if our thought is to be of any effect.

When the general issue of scepticism is uppermost in his mind Kant is apt to speak of the need for metaphysics to be *reformed*, not *abolished*. The Copernican Revolution which Kant proposed in his second edition preface was meant to put metaphysics on 'the secure path of a science' (B xix), by introducing a methodological change to which, Kant alleged, there were parallels in the successful development of mathematics and physics. But the metaphysics whose uncertainties were thus to be cleared up once and for all was not that with which previous philosophers had been concerned. What these had hoped to do was not just establish a necessary framework for what falls within experience, but provide an account of the essential nature of things as they are in themselves. They wanted to go behind the appearances of the senses to the realities which underlay them, and so to pronounce on the existence of God, the immortality of the soul and the freedom of the will. Their failure to make good their claims seemed to Kant to raise fresh problems about metaphysics, problems which, unlike those previously mentioned, affected not just the academic world but also the plain man. That metaphysics was in disorder not only threatened science, by fostering a general scepticism; it further undermined morals and religion, by suggesting that all attempted proofs of such theses as the existence of God and the freedom of the will must break down, and thus that continued belief in God and human responsibility was unfounded. Perhaps Kant's most important claim for his philosophy was that it cleared up these difficulties by the double expedient of demonstrating the total unknowability of the traditional metaphysical sphere and showing that a different foundation could be provided for the simple man's conviction that he is a free agent acting in a world which is created and governed by a just and beneficent God. As Kant said himself (B xxx), it denied knowledge in order to make room for faith. Kant's whole philosophical enterprise cannot be understood unless these wider considerations are borne in mind. There is a sense in which, like the positivists of our own time, he wanted to eliminate metaphysics, and leave the intellectual field clear for the empirical and mathematical sciences. But it was never his ambition to dispense with metaphysical *beliefs*: in his view a certain set of such beliefs was indispensable for moral practice. And that men are moral agents confronted by obligations and duties was a central fact about the human condition, which no amount of sophistry could remove or even disguise.

There are commentators today who insist that Kant was an opponent not of metaphysics as such but only of a certain type of metaphysics: he was a critic of the dogmatic metaphysics of the dry-as-dust Wolffian school, but advanced his criticisms in the interest of a practical or ethically-centred metaphysics of his own (see e.g. Heinz Heimsoeth in Moltke S. Gram's *Kant: Disputed Questions*). It is pointed out in support of this view that Kant himself was deeply engaged in metaphysical controversy throughout the pre-critical period (in 1763, for instance, he wrote an essay purporting to give an *a priori* proof of God's existence distinct from and superior to the ontological proof, of whose shortcomings he was already aware). It is further argued that, despite the requirements of logic, he was never prepared even at the time of the *Critiques* to jettison the thing in itself, but hung on to it as a reality which was unknowable but for all that undoubtedly there. The inference that the true nature of this reality is accessible in moral experience seems in these circumstances natural. Yet, given the arguments of the *Critique of Pure Reason*, Kant was simply not in a position to claim *knowledge* of a non-empirical reality, as a result of moral experience or indeed on any other basis. His doctrine of the Postulates of Pure Practical Reason enabled him to put forward the claim that the existence of God, the immortality of the soul and the freedom of the will are matters of justified moral belief. But he had already in the first *Critique* (cf. B 848/A 820 ff.) gone out of his way to show the profound differences between belief of this kind on the one hand and knowledge and everyday opinion on the other; as he argued there (see especially B 857/A 829) moral belief has a personal quality and a connection with first-hand moral experience which differentiates it entirely from knowledge proper. In the strict sense of the term no-one can *know* that there is a God, nor acquire the conviction of God's existence at second hand. It follows that the beliefs which Kant connects with pure practical faith and which he regards as indispensable for sustained moral action do not and cannot amount to a metaphysics. Formally the claim that Kant argued against a metaphysics modelled on science or mathematics only to plump for a metaphysics based on morals is a false one. The Neo-Kantians were right to see him as an outright opponent of metaphysical knowledge, except for that contained in his own metaphysics of experience. Kant was not a positivist before his time, for though he had a tremendous respect for science and mathematics he did not think of them as containing everything that could be said significantly. In his view statements about God, the soul and the will were certainly meaningful, even if they got their meaning in ways different from those in which scientific or everyday empirical statements acquired theirs. In one passage (B 491/A 463) he wrote that the mathematician 'would gladly exchange the whole of his science' for the solution of a number of metaphysical problems, namely those discussed in the Antinomies. But he went on to argue that all existing solutions must be dismissed as inadequate, and that the only proper conclusion to draw from their failure is that the world of things in space and time is a merely phenomenal world, one which can be an object of knowledge to the scientist but is not independently existent. As for the reality which lay behind such appearances, the very nature of their cognitive apparatus precluded knowledge of it for mere human beings. We could know things supersensible neither directly nor by description.

Kant differed from later critics of metaphysics not just in allowing sense to metaphysical statements, but further in being totally out of sympathy with any sort of naturalism: the doctrine of the omnicompetence of science had no attraction for him. He saw it as a merit in his own philosophy that it vindicated the claims of science without sacrificing the rights of morality, a result achieved by distinguishing sharply between the phenomenal and noumenal orders and associating science with the first, morals with the second. Given this analysis no scientific discovery could threaten human freedom or challenge the validity of the other postulates of practical reason: whatever the state of human knowledge, morals remains autonomous. This is the basis of Kant's assertion in the second edition preface that 'criticism alone can sever the root of *materialism, fatalism, atheism, free-thinking, fanaticism* and *superstition*' (B xxxiv). It is important to stress that Kant thought of himself as engaged in discrediting these views and attitudes; the fact not only differentiates him from many other opponents of metaphysics, but also serves to bring out vividly the wider interest of his philosophy. Those who say that he was not a mere epistemologist are correct in so far as he undertook epistemological enquiries with other purposes in mind. But those purposes were not strictly metaphysical: it is not true that he threw over one set of metaphysical doctrines only to embrace another. Leaving aside the necessary framework of experience, he did not believe in the possibility of any metaphysical knowledge.

§ 2 'A priori', *'analytic'*, *'synthetic'*

In a passage already quoted from the preface to his first edition (A xvii) Kant wrote that 'the chief question is always simply this: what and how much can understanding and reason know apart from all experience?'. In the Introduction to the *Critique* he reformulates his question, and at the same time makes a start towards answering it, in the celebrated words 'How are *a priori* synthetic judgments possible?', now said to contain 'the proper problem of pure reason' (B 19).

To make this formula intelligible we must first examine Kant's conception of the *a priori* and then consider the grounds for his distinction of analytic and synthetic judgments. These topics were treated by Kant himself in sections II and IV respectively of the second edition version of the Introduction. It must be conceded from the first that the treatment is both informal and unsatisfactory: too many loose ends are left for even the most indulgent Kantian to be entirely happy with what emerges. Nor did the fact that Kant recast the whole introduction for his second edition improve his account in any vital way, for what he did was really little more than to incorporate in it passages lifted bodily from the *Prolegomena*, passages which for the most part have little bearing on the main issue.

In the very first section of the Introduction Kant makes the by now familiar observation that though all our knowledge begins with experience, it does not follow that it all arises out of experience (B 1). If we had no experience at all, we should have no ideas and no knowledge, not even any *a priori* knowledge. No ideas or items of knowledge are literally innate. This is a position which Kant had taken up as early as the *Dissertation* (section *8*), but neither there nor in the *Critique* would he allow that it carried the Lockean consequence that all ideas are empirical. In the *Critique* itself he argues that we can draw a distinction between the empirical and non-empirical elements in our knowledge by considering our respective attitudes to them. We treat the former as contingent, the latter as necessary.

What conditions have to be fulfilled if we are to describe an item of knowledge, or more specifically a proposition we are ready to accept, as '*a priori*'? Kant says we use two criteria to pick out such propositions; he adds that they are both 'sure' and that they are 'inseparable from one another' (B 4), though they can be used separately and sometimes must be for convenience' sake. Each is thus a sufficient condition of apriority in a proposition, and perhaps both are thought of as necessary conditions, though Kant does not say this. The features concerned are (1) necessity, and (2) universality. Kant's treatment of both is on any estimate hasty. 'First, then', he writes (B 3), 'if we have a proposition which in being thought is thought as *necessary*, it is an *a priori* judgment'. And a little later: 'Experience never confers on its judgments true or strict, but only assumed and comparative *universality*, through induction. . . . If then a judgment is thought with strict universality, that is, in such a manner that no exception is allowed as possible, it is not derived from experience, but is valid absolutely *a priori*' (B 4). What it means to 'think' a proposition 'as necessary', and what the circumstances are in which we can properly allow no exception to a universal truth, get no further explanation at this stage of Kant's exposition.

The full inadequacy of his informal explanation of these points becomes apparent only when we pass on to his further distinction between analytic and synthetic judgments. Kant introduces this distinction not so much for its own sake as with a view to under-lining the difference between analytic judgments, which are *a priori* but in Locke's language 'trifling' or uninformative, and another class of judgment, all-important for Kant, which is at once *a priori* and instructive. Let us grant for the sake of argument that this distinction is genuine; let us assume that, for instance, *Every effect has a cause* and *Every event has a cause* are both *a priori* judgments, the first being analytic, the second not. We might just suppose that we could say of both that they hold with strict universality, no exception being allowed as possible in either case; we might further say of each that in being thought it is thought as necessary. But could we say that the grounds on which we refuse to allow exceptions are the same in the two cases, or that the two judgments are characterised by the same type of necessity? It is evident that we could not. The necessity which attaches to *Every effect has a cause* is logical necessity; given the accepted meanings of the words 'cause' and 'effect' it cannot be denied without logical absurdity. It is logic which backs up our refusal to allow any exception in this sort of case. But things are entirely different when we pass to *Every event has a cause*, whose denial, as Hume insisted and Kant himself emphasises, involves no contradiction, there being no connection of meaning between the notions of *cause* and *event*. If necessity attaches to this judgment, it must be necessity of a kind quite distinct from logical necessity. Similarly our refusal to allow exceptions to this judgment, if we do indeed take this attitude, must rest on something other than logic. That Kant in this preliminary passage fails to draw attention to this asymmetry, and so to bring into focus the all-important question of what sort of necessity it is which characterises his synthetic *a priori* judgments is a serious weakness in his exposition.

I pass now to Kant's treatment of the analytic/synthetic distinction itself. The first point to discuss is how widely he intended the distinction to apply. His initial definition of 'analytic' and 'synthetic' is in terms of the relationship of containment between subject and predicate concepts in a judgment, which would imply that only propositions of the subject-predicate type can be analytic or synthetic. In his discussion of the Ontological Proof, however, Kant himself says that 'every reasonable person' must admit that all existential propositions are synthetic, and he lays down in the same passage that '*being* is obviously not a real predicate' (B 626/A 598). It thus appears that the restricted way in which Kant first states the distinction is not to be taken too seriously, though what is to be put in its place is not immediately apparent. There are serious difficulties in any case about applying Kant's initial criterion, for who, after all, is to say what is contained in a concept and what is not? In this connection it is worth pointing out that Kant himself in an interesting discussion in the Discipline of Pure Reason says that empirical concepts 'cannot be defined at all, but only made explicit', at least if we accept the view that 'to define . . . means to present the complete, original concept of a thing within the limits of its concept' (B 755/A 727). The context shows that what Kant has in mind here is Locke's discussion of real and nominal definitions; the point he is making is the Lockean one that there is always something arbitrary in the definition of such a concept as *gold*, since 'we make use of certain characteristics only so long as they are adequate for the purpose of making distinctions; new observations remove some properties and add others; and thus the limits of the concept are never assured' (B 756/A 728). Our understanding of empirical concepts is in fact liable to shift from context to context, even from person to person; in modern terminology their texture is open. Similarly Kant says in the same passage that 'no concept given *a priori*, such as substance, cause, right, equity, etc. can, strictly speaking, be defined', the reason being that the concept may, as given, 'include many obscure representations, which we overlook in our analysis' (ibid.). Here again in place of strict definition we have to be content with a *pis aller*, which Kant calls 'exposition' and which consists in setting out the constituent marks of a concept as completely as we can. We can elucidate or clarify empirical or 'given *a priori*' concepts, but we cannot define them. In fact, the only concepts which admit of definition in the proper sense of the word are those which are 'arbitrarily invented', among which mathematical concepts alone are truly significant. 'Consequently mathematics is the only science which has definitions' (B 757/A 729).

The context in which this discussion appears is one where Kant is drawing a general contrast between thinking in philosophy and thinking in mathematics, a subject he had already treated at length in his pre-critical study *Enquiry concerning the Clarity of the Principles of Natural Theology and Ethics* (1763). It may be because he was following this early work, written before he made the analytic/synthetic distinction, that Kant in the *Critique* overlooked the implications for that distinction of what he has to say about definition. That it has serious implications can hardly be denied. In introducing the analytic/synthetic distinction Kant draws a contrast between the judgment *all bodies are extended* and the judgment *all bodies have weight*, describing the first as 'analytic', the second 'synthetic'. He says of the first (B 11–12):

> That a body is extended is a proposition that holds *a priori* and is not empirical. For, before appealing to experience, I have already in the concept of body all the conditions required for my judgment. I have only to extract from it, in accordance with the principle of contradiction, the required predicate, and in so doing can at the same time become conscious of the necessity of the judgment.

When it comes to *all bodies have weight*, however, 'I do not include in the concept of a body in general the predicate *weight*', the reason for connecting weight with bodies being only that there is an invariable empirical connection between weight and the defining characters of body—'extension, impenetrability, figure, etc.' (B 12). But *body*, after all, is an empirical concept, and if empirical concepts cannot be strictly defined we cannot say for certain what is contained in them and what not. May it not turn out some time in the future that weight is after all a constituent part of the concept of body? Or that extension or impenetrability are not?

This difficulty also affects the alternative account of the analytic/ synthetic distinction put forward by Kant. 'The principle of contradiction', he writes in a section entitled 'The Highest Principle of all Analytic Judgments' (B 191/A 151), 'must . . . be recognised as being the universal and completely sufficient principle of all analytic knowledge'. If a proposition is such that its denial involves one in self-contradiction, it is analytic; if its contradictory is not self-contradictory it is synthetic. I argued in a previous discussion of this topic (*Reason and Experience*, ch. 3) that this account is too narrow to cover all cases, for though it might, at a pinch, show the analyticity of *No bachelor is married*, it would not allow us to say that the complex proposition *If all men are mortal and Socrates is a man, then Socrates is mortal* has the same status, since its truth depends not just on the principle of contradiction but also on that of a certain type of syllogism. In fact, as Waismann made clear in the first of his 'Analytic/Synthetic' articles, to give an account of 'analytic' on these lines you need to make reference not just to a single logical principle, but to logical laws generally. Analytic judgments, on this account of the matter, are judgments which true in virtue of purely logical considerations, synthetic judgments those whose truth or falsehood cannot be so decided. But are analytic judgments true *solely* in virtue of logical considerations, as I was inclined to say in my previous discussion? It is obvious that their truth depends not just on logic, but also on the meaning of the terms of which they consist. *No bachelor is married* is analytic if and only if we mean by 'bachelor' a man who is not married. In other words, correct definitions are taken for granted on this account of the matter just as they were in the previous account. And that means that Kant's uncompromising denial of the possibility of finding true definitions outside mathematics has the consequence that only in mathematics, together with any other spheres in which we employ 'arbitrarily invented' concepts, will it be possible to say unequivocally whether or not a proposition is analytic.

If the analytic/synthetic distinction is only dubiously applicable, is Kant justified in relying on it as he does? The obvious answer would seem to be 'no'. But perhaps to insist on that conclusion is unduly harsh. It is notable that many modern critics of the analytic/synthetic distinction tend, despite their doubts, to use the distinction when it comes to confuting their opponents: they take it that the notion of an analytic proposition is sufficiently clear to be applicable in standard cases, even if there are others in which its application is controversial. In particular instances you can get an opponent to declare whether he intends what he says to be analytically true; the very fact that the question is sometimes seen as embarrassing shows that it is not misplaced. Thus the positivist challenge to the speculative metaphysician to say whether the propositions he puts forward are meant to be broad factual truths open to confutation in future experience or mere consequences of initial definitions, unshakeable because lacking in genuine factual content, remains impressive despite everything that has been said about the problem of analyticity. True, the metaphysician need not agree that the only alternative to his being an armchair scientist is that he is engaged in working out the consequences of arbitrarily assumed definitions; he can and would say that his definitions have a foundation in fact. The first principles of a metaphysical system might be suggested or supported by experience, even if what follows from them has a different logical status. Both Kant and the positivists made things too easy for themselves by assuming that metaphysical speculation is a game and nothing more. But they were not wrong to think of the analytic/synthetic distinction as being highly relevant to the whole question of the possibility of metaphysics.

If this is correct, Kant's formal shortcomings in his discussions of the distinction are less important than might at first be thought. It should be noticed, however, that to allow its general viability is by no means to confer respectability on the notion of the synthetic *a priori*. Even if it is agreed that there are propositions which are unquestionably synthetic, it will not follow that there have to be propositions which are synthetic and necessary. We have already seen that the necessity which would characterise synthetic propositions cannot be logical necessity; the question what sort of necessity it could be must be an urgent one for Kant. As Mr Richard Robinson pertinently asked, are synthetic *a priori* propositions simply those we can't help believing? Kant must surely have an alternative to this account. More important, he must, if his theories are to be worth serious consideration, present an account of the synthetic *a priori* which is unitary; that is, which applies equally to all cases falling under the concept. Professor Strawson has said that Kant 'really has no clear and general conception of the synthetic *a priori* at all' (*The Bounds of Sense*, p. 43). If this criticism can be sustained it is certainly damning. But whether it can be sustained can be decided only after Kant's ideas on the subject have been considered in detail.

§ 3 *Intuitions and Concepts*

In the Introduction to the *Critique*, section v, Kant announces cheerfully that 'in all theoretical sciences of reason synthetic *a priori* judgments are contained as principles' (B 14). He goes on to claim, first that mathematical judgments ('without exception', he says originally, though later he takes that back) are at once synthetic and necessary, then much more briefly that 'natural science (physics) contains *a priori* synthetic judgments as principles', finally that metaphysics, since its business is to extend our *a priori* knowledge, 'ought to' contain or consist of such propositions (B 14–18). This discussion leads up to the posing of the general question 'How are *a priori* synthetic judgments possible?', itself to be tackled by first answering a series of subordinate though still very difficult questions:

How is pure mathematics possible?
How is pure science of nature possible?
How is metaphysics, as natural disposition, possible?
How is metaphysics, as science, possible?

I shall revert to these questions later, but meantime want to concentrate on an important difference Kant finds between the propositions of pure mathematics and those which belong to 'pure science of nature'. The former, it turns out, depend on pure intuition, the latter on pure concepts. Before these notions can be clarified we need to consider the distinction between intuitions and concepts as such.

On this subject Kant wrote as follows (B 74/A 50):

> Our knowledge springs from two fundamental sources of the mind; the first is the capacity for receiving impressions (receptivity for impressions), the second is the power of knowing an object through these representations (spontaneity of concepts). Through the first an object is *given* to us, through the second the object is *thought* in relation to that representation (which is a mere determination of the mind). Intuition and concepts constitute, therefore, the elements of all our knowledge, so that neither concepts without an intuition in some way corresponding to them, nor intuition without concepts, can yield knowledge.

As the point is put a little later, 'Thoughts without content are empty, intuitions without concepts are blind' (B 75/A 51). What precisely are 'thoughts' and 'intuitions' in this context?

The process of intuiting, for Kant, is the process by which we become aware of particulars; the process of thought that by which we 'think' and so comprehend such particulars under a certain description. The term 'intuition' is itself ambiguous: it stands both for the general procedure involved and for its products, appearing in the singular when the first is in question and in the plural when the second. It was a central tenet of Kant's epistemology that intuitions and thoughts are both required for human knowledge, and that neither can replace, or be reduced to, the other. Thoughts as he saw it are produced by the understanding, intuitions as far as we are concerned arise only from the senses. 'The understanding can intuit nothing, the senses can think nothing' (ibid.).

For Kant it was a contingent fact that there are, as he put it elsewhere, 'two stems of human knowledge, namely *sensibility* and *understanding*', which are sharply separate even though they 'perhaps spring from a common, but to us unknown, root' (B 29/A 15). We can conceive of a mind in which there would be no such separation. An intuitive understanding, such as God is supposed to have, would apprehend particulars and conceptualise them in a single act; it would not need to go through the double process of first, as it were, getting in touch with its object and then making it out. Nor would it be under the disadvantage of being able to characterise the data of its experience, if such language is allowed, only in abstract general terms: each of its descriptions would fit one and one situation only, and that without reliance on a special set of individuating expressions. If such a mind could be said to possess concepts they would be self-specifying down to the level of individuals: the concepts themselves would determine what particulars fell under them, rather than wait around for application to any suitable particulars that might turn up. Concepts of this kind would be what Kant in the *Critique of Judgment* (section 77) called 'synthetic universals', as opposed to the 'analytic universals' which belong to our human understanding. But though we can form this idea, we can easily see that it has no application to our own case. With us, all concepts are general; to possess a concept is merely to contemplate a possibility. For knowledge we want something more, namely the power of apprehending particulars, and that belongs to a different faculty altogether.

Two questions can be asked about this doctrine of the separate nature of concepts and intuitions. The first and more serious is whether the notion of intuition can itself be made intelligible. In the passage from B 74/A 50 quoted above Kant says that through our capacity for receptivity for impressions an object is given to us, which object is then 'thought in relation to that representation' through the intellectual faculty. The difficulty here concerns the suggestion that intuition results in the grasping of an *object*, for if it does it would seem to be not just a component in knowledge, but a form of knowledge on its own. There are many passages in the *Critique of Pure Reason*, especially in the first edition, in which Kant seems to be accepting the empiricist account according to which the senses convey to us impressions or sense-data, which are objects on their own account though private to particular percipients; the person who confronts these objects must then on the strength of them determine the state of affairs in the public world. The trick is supposed to be done by importing what Kant calls 'concepts of an object in general', which serve to single out privileged groups of impressions entitled to special attention because having counterparts in many minds (see e.g. B 124/A 92 ff.). Fortunately for his reputation Kant offers an entirely different theory elsewhere in the *Critique*, arguing for a tight connection between awareness of objects and the making of judgments (e.g. B 140–2); on this view the objective world is descried on the basis of sensation, but the latter does not in the strict sense produce any objects of its own. What then is the status of the contents of sensation? I have myself spoken of them as 'particulars', but the term 'particular' is itself a correlate of 'universal': a particular is an instance of a universal. According to the theory stated above, intuitions need to be brought under concepts in order to be comprehended; if they are particulars they already stand under concepts. The only way I can see out of

this difficulty is to say that sensation is not strictly a form of awareness, since it has no true objects, but a mode of experience which is
sui generis; without it experience of particulars would be impossible,
though it is false to describe it as presenting particulars for description. Sensory content—'intuitions', as Kant calls them—are not
objects of any sort, public or private. It follows that the puzzling
question on which empiricism founders, namely how we get from
the world of private experience to the public world of common
objects, need not even arise.

I shall have more to say about this at a later stage in the book (see
especially section 17). Meantime, I turn to my second question, which
is whether Kant simply takes his doctrine of the heterogeneity of concepts and intuitions for granted, or advances arguments in its support. It looks at first sight as if he were laying down the doctrine by
fiat, but this impression is mistaken. There are in fact at least three
sets of passages in his writings from 1770 onwards where Kant offers
what amounts to a defence of this fundamental assumption. First,
there are those in which he analyses the idea of an intuitive understanding, especially the passage already referred to in the *Critique
of Judgment*. Kant's primary aim in undertaking this analysis is
plainly to illuminate the human cognitive situation, and in particular
to bring out the limitations of the human intellect which, unlike an
intuitive intelligence, needs to draw content from another source
and so must co-operate with a faculty distinct from itself. The fact
that the human understanding 'in its cognition . . . moves from
the analytic universal to the particular' and so 'determines nothing
in respect of the multiplicity of the particular' (*Critique of Judgment*,
section 77) is one piece of evidence in favour of this view. Another is
the distinction we draw between actuality and possibility, a distinction
of which Kant says in *Critique of Judgment*, section 76 that it is 'merely
valid for human understanding' (this is false: it is valid for any
discursive intelligence). If our understanding were intuitive or, as
Kant sometimes expresses it, 'archetypal', whatever it thought of
would be actual; that this is not so for us is due to the heterogeneity
of concepts and intuitions. Next come the passages in which Kant
insists that space and time are not concepts but intuitions, and must
hence be apprehended by sense rather than conceived by thought. I
intend to discuss the most important of these in the next section;
meantime it will be enough to mention the argument from incongruous counterparts, strangely omitted in the *Critique* but used in
the *Dissertation* (section *15C*) and the *Prolegomena* (section *13*), according to which the internal differences between, say, a hand and its image

in a mirror (the fact that if the first is a right hand, the second will be a left) can be indicated but not described. Finally, there are the passages in which Kant criticises, either directly or by implication, the Leibnizian thesis that sensing is merely a confused form of thinking. He argues, for example, that the doctrine of the identity of indiscernibles, 'which is valid only of concepts of things in general', is inapplicable to empirical objects like drops of water. 'A location *b* can contain a thing which is completely similar and equal to another in a location *a*, just as easily as if the things were inwardly ever so different' (B 328/A 272): difference of spatial and temporal position is enough to differentiate otherwise indiscernible entities. And this again shows that sensing and thinking are radically different in kind.

The upshot of this discussion must be that though the concept of intuition contains many obscurities (it can be described as awareness of particulars only proleptically, since strictly it is not a species of acquaintance), there are good grounds for thinking that intuition of the Kantian kind is indispensable to human knowledge as we have it. A mind which could think but not intuit might perhaps formulate certain general propositions, but could certainly not know whether or not they were true in particular instances. If we had only senses we might know, or more properly feel, that certain particulars existed (we could perhaps feel their presence), but could say nothing determinate about them. The 'two stems' of human knowledge are thus irreducible one to another, and the speculation that they spring from a common, though to us unknown, root is essentially idle. The fact that both would disappear in the experience of an intuitive intelligence lends no support to this speculation.

However, it is one thing to distinguish intuitions and concepts, another altogether to separate 'pure' intuitions from 'pure' concepts. We must now turn to Kant's grounds for thinking that the human mind contains pure intuitions in the shape of the ideas of space and time and pure concepts in the shape of the categories and ideas of reason. Space and time are dealt with comparatively briefly in the Transcendental Aesthetic, the categories and ideas of reason at enormous length in the two divisions of Transcendental Logic, Transcendental Analytic and Transcendental Dialectic, and our discussion must reflect this discrepancy. It may be worth saying in advance that use of the adjective 'transcendental' in this context need cause no particular alarm. It is simply a term of art invented by Kant as part of the vocabulary of epistemology; a transcendental enquiry is an enquiry into the possibility of knowledge, directed particularly to the question of *a priori* knowledge (cf. B 25, B 80–1 / A 56). Thus Transcendental Aesthetic is an enquiry into possible *a priori* elements in sensibility ('aesthesis' being the Greek for 'sensation'), Transcendental Logic an enquiry into possible *a priori* elements in thought ('logos' being the Greek for 'concept'). There may of course be no such elements, but at least it makes sense to enquire if there are.

Space, Time and Mathematics

§ 4. *Space and Time as* 'a priori *intuitions*'. § 5.'*Constructing*' *Mathematical Concepts.* § 6. *Empirical Realism and Transcendental Idealism.*

§ 4 *Space and Time as* 'a priori *intuitions*'

After a brief and confusing passage in which he introduces some of the key terms he is to use in the following discussion, Kant in the Aesthetic plunges straight into the task of showing that the ideas of space and time have a peculiar status. They are, he argues, intuitions and not concepts; they are also *a priori* and hence pure rather than empirical intuitions. They belong to the form of intuition rather than its matter, and it is this which explains how they can be known *a priori*. The detailed content of intuition is something given which can only come to light in experience, but the form of intuition may as it were lie ready in the mind or sensibility and thus be such that we can know it independently of experience. Kant claims that we have such knowledge of the essential properties of space and time, and argues on this basis that they 'belong to the form of intuition, and therefore to the subjective constitution of our mind' (B 37–8/A 23).

An immediate difficulty about this whole question is whether Kant is discussing space and time or the ideas of space and time. He introduces the subject in section 2 of the Aesthetic as if it were an enquiry about the ontological status of the former:

> What then are space and time? Are they real existences? Or are they only determinations or relations of things, yet such as would belong to things even if they were not intuited? Or are space and time such that they belong only to the form of intuition, and therefore to the subjective constitution of our mind, apart from which they could not be ascribed to anything whatsoever?

But when he begins to go into detail he talks about the 'concept' or 'representation' of space (e.g. B 38/A 24: 'Space is a necessary *a priori* representation'; B 39/A 24: 'Space is not a discursive or as we say general concept'), and similarly with time. The explanation of this discrepancy is, I think, that Kant's ultimate interest is in the ontological question, but that he believes the way to answer this is through an examination of the logical status of the *ideas* concerned.

His first task is to show that the idea of space, for example, is an *a priori* intuition and not, as is commonly assumed, an empirical concept. It should be obvious that space itself cannot be described as an intuition (a 'representation') or concept of any sort, since on any account it is a feature of experienced reality rather than an item in consciousness. It may be, as Kant claims, 'the subjective condition of sensibility' and belong to 'the receptivity of the subject' (B 42/A 26), but that will make it part of the apparatus of cognition and not, as intuitions and concepts are, a product of the working of that apparatus.

Does Kant show that the idea of space is an *a priori* intuition? His case for saying it is an intuition is a strong one. At the centre of it lies the simple observation that the relationship between particular spaces and space as a whole is entirely different from that between, say, particular red things and the concept of red. Different red things all instantiate redness, but different spaces simply belong together *in* space. Different spatial regions are in fact carved out of a wider space, which in turn is thought of as falling within something wider. The notion of space as a whole is not arrived at by building up from particular spaces, but is logically prior to the latter; it is indeed fundamental to our whole experience of the external world. Further, 'we can represent to ourselves only one space' (B 39/A 25): all spatial situations fall within a *single* spatial system. It follows that space is a special kind of individual, that the word 'space' is not a general term but a proper name, and that the idea of space is, in Kant's language, an intuition and not a concept. The same is true, *mutatis mutandis*, of the idea of time as well.

Kant has supplementary arguments for his thesis that the idea of space is an intuition. One is the powerful argument from incongruous counterparts, already briefly summarised. Another is found in the puzzling claim (B 39/A 25) that 'space is represented as an infinite *given* magnitude', which refers, I think, to the infinite divisibility of space and invokes once more the contrast between the way in which a given space contains an infinite number of parts *in* itself and that in which a given concept may have *under* itself an infinite number of instances. As the discussions of the Antinomies show, Kant was a firm believer in the infinite divisibility of space, though not of the infinite divisibility of material substance. But even if he was wrong here, he has enough grounds to support his claim that the idea of space is an intuition.

But is it also an *a priori* intuition? Kant adduces three sets of consideration in favour of saying that it is. First, he maintains that empiricist attempts to argue that we might derive the idea of space from reflection on particular spatial situations beg the question at issue. To say for example that we are presented in experience with things which are adjacent to or distant from one another, and get the idea of space by abstraction from such situations, will not do for the simple reason that 'adjacent to one another' means 'adjacent to one another *in space*'. Only someone who already *had* the idea of space could say that two things were adjacent to, or distant from, one another. Secondly, he argues that 'space is a necessary *a priori* representation' on the ground that 'we can never represent to ourselves the absence of space, though we can quite well think it as empty of objects' (B 38/A 24). Here the appeal seems to be to a sort of internal experiment: we could not, Kant seems to be saying, imagine what it would be like to live in a non-spatial world, as opposed to, say, a world without smell or colour. What makes this difficult is not only the dubious status of such a psychological appeal, but also the fact that Kant believes that the phenomena of inner sense have temporal but not spatial relations: for him as for many others the mental world is, strictly, non-spatial. Against that we can set the fact that Kant constantly stresses that we can make determinate statements about the mental world only if we present it in spatial imagery and against a spatial background; this is what lies behind the reiterated claim (e.g. B 156) that we 'cannot obtain for ourselves a representation of time . . . except under the image of a line'. It may well be, therefore, that Kant's doctrine of the inner life does not constitute an objection to his view here, though that still leaves the unsatisfactory appeal to what we can 'think' without proper defence.

These first two arguments show that the idea of space is fundamental rather than *a priori*: they demonstrate the basic character of the experience of being in space, but claim no insight into its properties. The third argument is more ambitious. In its more modest form it proceeds from the premise that we know, independently of experience, that certain axioms are true of space, e.g. that space has three dimensions (B 41). We do not regard it as a real possibility that we might wake up tomorrow and find that space has changed the number of its dimensions (cf. *Dissertation*, section 15 D). A stronger form of the argument rests on the contention that 'geometry is a science which determines the properties of space synthetically, and yet *a priori*' (B 40): it holds that we are sure in advance of experience that any space we come across will conform to Euclidean requirements. We do not have to look about the world to be sure that there are no two-sided figures enclosing a space, though the proposition is evidently not analytic. It is in fact at once synthetic and necessary, and the very fact that it is shows that the idea of space must be a pure intuition.

It is instructive in this connection to observe that though Kant's arguments about time run closely parallel to his arguments about space, he can find in the case of time no true counterpart to this argument about geometry. The 'apodeictic principles concerning the relations of time, or axioms of time in general' of which he speaks in B 47/A 31 belong to no particular science; they amount in fact to nothing more than that time has only one dimension and that different times are not simultaneous but successive. It is not even clear here that more than a single proposition is concerned. But even if Kant is correct and the two are independent, the amount of insight they offer into the properties of time is not impressive. To claim that time is an *a priori* intuition on the strength of this evidence will hardly seem reasonable to independent opinion.

Much therefore turns on whether we can accept what Kant says about space and geometry, and here the omens are not favourable to Kant in view of developments in mathematics since his day. However, before pronouncing on this we need to consider in some detail his account of the part played by pure intuition in geometrical and indeed in mathematical thinking generally. I shall therefore devote the next section to Kant's philosophy of mathematics.

§5 *'Constructing' Mathematical Concepts*

According to Kant, the distinctive feature of the concepts of mathematics is that they are capable of *construction*; they differ conspicuously in this respect from the concepts of philosophy. The latter necessarily handles abstract ideas, whereas mathematics, as Kant puts it (B 743–4/A 715–6),

> can achieve nothing by concepts alone but hastens at once to intuition, in which it considers the concept *in concreto*, though not empirically, but only in an intuition which it presents *a priori*, that is, which it has constructed, and in which whatever follows from the universal conditions of the construction must be universally valid of the object of the concept thus constructed.

Given the concept of a triangle and told to determine the relationship of the sum of its internal angles to a right angle, a philosopher will consider the meaning and possible interrelations of such concepts as *straight line*, *angle* and *three*, and will try in vain to solve the problem along these lines. A geometer, by contrast, will at once have recourse to a figure which represents or expresses the concept he is dealing with, will perform certain constructions on that figure and then, 'through a chain of inferences guided throughout by intuition', will arrive at 'a fully evident and universally valid solution of the problem' (B 744–5/A 716–7).

The first thing to be said about this doctrine is that it was not thought up with the express object of supporting the conclusions of the Transcendental Aesthetic. It is already present in essentials in a pre-critical work to which reference has already been made, the 1763 'prize essay' *Enquiry concerning the Clarity of the Principles of Natural Theology and Ethics*. There Kant writes that

> in geometry, in order to discover the properties of all circles, a circle is drawn; then, instead of drawing all the possible lines that intersect inside the circle, two lines only are drawn. From these two lines the relations are proved, and in them is observed, *in concreto*, the universal rule of the relations of intersecting lines inside any circle (op. cit., First Reflection, section 27; Berlin edition, II 278; Kerferd and Walford translation, p. 8).

The point here and above is that a geometrical problem begins to be solved only when recourse is had to a concrete instance. Kant is not saying that constructing a figure corresponding to the concept concerned is all that is involved in a geometrical proof; his remarks about further construction and about 'whatever follows from the universal conditions of the construction' show as much. But he is saying that constructing a figure is an indispensable part of proof in geometry; it is precisely on this point that his argument about the difference between proofs in philosophy and proofs in mathematics turns.

Jaakko Hintikka in a remarkable paper ('Kant on the Mathematical Method', in *Kant Studies Today*, ed. Lewis White Beck, 1969) has shown that this doctrine of Kant's relates very closely to procedures which were regularly followed in the geometry of Euclid. The structure of a typical Euclidean proof was as follows: *first*, an enunciation of what is to be proved (e.g., 'In any triangle the sum of the internal angles is equal to two right angles'); *second*, what was called the 'setting-out' or 'ecthesis', taking the form of recourse to a particular instance: 'Let ABC be a triangle'; *third*, the construction performed on the triangle taken as the instance: 'Produce the line BC to D, and at C draw a line CE parallel to BA'; *fourth*, the proof proper in which inferences were made on the basis of axioms and previously proved propositions about what was true of the figure as originally set down and extended by construction; *fifth*, reaffirmation of what was first enunciated as now proved.

It seems clear that the constructibility of geometrical concepts has to do with the second step here, the considering of the question by reference to a particular instance. But Kant did not believe that this procedure was peculiar to geometry. Indeed, in the 1763 essay he *introduced* the topic by talking about what goes on in arithmetic and algebra, where

> symbols are first of all supposed, instead of the things themselves, together with the special notations of their increase or decrease and their relations, etc. Afterwards, one proceeds with these signs, according to easy and certain rules, by means of substitution, combination or subtraction and many kinds of transformations, so that the things symbolised are here completely ignored, until, at the end, in the conclusion the meaning of the symbolical conclusion is interpreted (same reference).

This doctrine survives in the *Critique* in a passage (B 745/A 717; cf. B 762/A 734) where Kant speaks of algebra as constructing 'magnitude as such' and says

> It abstracts completely from the properties of the object that is to be thought in terms of such a concept of magnitude. It then chooses a certain notation for all constructions of magnitude as such (numbers), that is, for addition, subtraction, extraction of roots, etc. Once it has adopted a notation for the general concept of magnitude so far as their different relations are concerned, it exhibits in intuition, in accordance with certain universal rules, all the various operations through which the magnitudes are produced and modified.

Construction in algebra is thus 'symbolic', whereas in geometry it was 'ostensive' (ibid.). Kant does not make any separate pronouncement in the *Critique* about construction in arithmetic, though he does of course say notoriously (B 15) that in order to prove that the sum of seven and five is twelve, we have to 'go outside' these concepts and 'call in the aid of the intuition which corresponds to one of them, our five fingers, for instance, or, as Segner does in his *Arithmetic*, five points'. The seeming suggestion here that the arithmetician cannot calculate without counting on his fingers or consulting an abacus has done much to discredit Kant's whole theory.

However, the theory deserves to be taken more seriously than that, if only because of the evidence adduced by Hintikka. Let us therefore consider somewhat more fully the account of construction in geometry, asking first how it is supposed to work in its own terms. The important point to stress here is that the figure which is 'exhibited' or 'set out' in the process of ecthesis is specified only in a quite general way, or, as Kant himself says (B 742/A 714), is 'determined only by certain universal conditions of construction'. It is thus able to 'express' the concept without impairing its universality. We say 'Let ABC be a triangle', and at that point draw a particular triangle or imagine one. The only characteristics of the triangle in question which matter are those which make it a triangle. It must be a plane figure bounded by three straight lines; it cannot only be that (its angles, for example, must each be of a determinate size), but what more it is can be neglected. The triangle we draw enters into our consideration just as a triangle, and not as the fully determinate triangle it necessarily is. Because that is so we can take it as typical of triangles in general, without paying attention to any special qualities it has as an individual. Our procedure in all this is as follows. We want to know if a certain proposition holds of triangles as such. We take a particular triangle which is typical in all respects (because only so considered) and ask if the proposition is true in this case. Finding that it is we generalise, and so assert the content of the proposition as a universal truth.

It will be apparent from what has just been said that 'constructing' a geometrical concept on the lines explained is an entirely legitimate procedure. The principle which underlies it is, however, by no means peculiar to geometry, or even to mathematics. Proofs by ecthesis, i.e. by adducing some individual which comes into the argument as a typical instance, are common in modern predicate logic and are to be found even in the logic of Aristotle, where however they play only a very small part (see Lukasiewicz: *Aristotle's Syllogistic*, pp. 59 ff.). We have to do here, in fact, with a procedure which is not in the least 'extra-logical', but rather belongs to generally accredited logical practice. If so, any pretence that it has a special connection with pure intuition would seem singularly hard to sustain.

Before coming to that issue, however, it will be useful to consider the supposed parallel between 'ostensive' and 'symbolic' construction. The former, as we know, belongs to geometry, the latter to algebra (or according to the *Enquiry*, to arithmetic and algebra alike). Kant's reason for connecting them comes out clearly in the latter work, in a passage (same reference) which discusses the disadvantages of philosophical as compared with mathematical thinking. In philosophy, we read,

Neither figures nor visible signs can express either thoughts or their relations; nor can the transposition of symbols, according to rules, be substituted for abstract observation, so that the representation of the matters themselves is exchanged, in this procedure, for the clearer and easier representation of signs. Rather must the universal be considered in abstraction.

On this view the mathematician has the capacity to present his ideas and their connections in readily visualisable form, and this gives his thought a tremendous advantage over the abstract thought of the philosopher. We may agree with Kant that symbolism is all-important in mathematics, and even accept his thesis that mathematical symbols in a sense picture the objects and operations with which mathematics is concerned, without embracing his conclusion that the part played by figures in geometry is precisely parallel to that played by variables and symbols for addition, division, etc., in algebra. Recourse to a figure in geometry is a particular move in a geometrical proof, a move which Kant thought indispensable but one which could in principle be done without (as presumably it is in non-Euclidean geometries). Recourse to symbolism in algebra, by contrast, is of the essence of the subject; without it the subject would not exist. In a passage from the *Enquiry* quoted above Kant speaks of the student of algebra 'interpreting' the symbolical conclusions he comes to, presumably by moving from the abstract symbols to the things they symbolise. This suggests that we could, in principle at any rate, think that student's thoughts without having recourse to his symbols. But it is difficult to see precisely what this would mean: the world of pure algebra, like that of pure logic, has every appearance of being a self-contained or autonomous world, and questions about its relations to extra-mathematical objects are apt to be more confusing than enlightening. That algebra should change its symbols is certainly thinkable; that it should outgrow them altogether is surely impossible. Yet despite Kant it is by no means unthinkable that geometrical proofs should proceed without recourse to figures. Indeed, the algebraisation of geometry by Descartes and others would seem to have converted this possibility into a reality.

It might well be in Kant's interest to show that the cases of geometry and algebra are different if only to defend his story about pure intuition. If symbols in algebra perform the same function as figures in geometry Kant will be able to say that both sciences contain what he calls an intuitive element, an element of visualisation if we prefer to express it so. We shall have to admit that the intuitive component is weak (it will be present in just the same way in some purely logical thinking), but it will all the same be there. But what about its alleged *a priori* character? When he came to write the *Critique* (indeed, when he came to write the *Dissertation*) Kant had persuaded himself that the only explanation of our capacity to envisage concrete cases precisely in geometry was that we have special insight into the properties of space. As already noted, we do not have to look around the world to say that a diangle (a plane figure bounded by two straight lines) is impossible, although the concept of such a figure is not self-contradictory. It seemed to Kant that geometry was the science of the necessary properties of space, and that the fact that we can formulate such an impressive collection of geometrical propositions argued that space must have a quite unsuspected status. It must be a form of the human sensibility, rather than an independent existent or a property of anything independently existent. For the moment I do not wish to challenge this conclusion. My point in mentioning it is only to raise the question: what is the parallel doctrine about arithmetic and algebra?

The parallel doctrine we should expect is that arithmetic and algebra have a special connection with time, and are possible only because we have insight into its necessary properties. But Kant nowhere commits himself to this view. In the Aesthetic he says lamely that the concepts of alteration and motion are 'possible only through and in the representation of time': unless this representation were an *a priori* intuition the possibility of an alteration could not be made comprehensible (B 48). In the *Dissertation* (section *12*) we are told that 'pure mathematics considers space in geometry, time in pure mechanics', and something like this doctrine reappears in the *Prolegomena* (section *10*). In both works Kant adds a further claim about a connection between time and numerical concepts, arguing that the latter are formed 'by successive addition of units in time' (*Prolegomena*, loc. cit.). The *Dissertation* puts this thesis more persuasively if less effectively from Kant's point of view, when it says in the passage referred to that the concept of number, 'though itself indeed intellectual, yet demands for its actualisation in the concrete the auxiliary notions of space and time (in the successive addition and simultaneous juxtaposition of a plurality)'. In the *Critique* (B 182/A 142) number is said to be the 'pure schema' of magnitude as a pure concept of understanding; it is also described as 'a representation which comprises the successive addition of homogeneous units' (ibid.). It is unclear from this whether Kant thought that the connection between number and numbering was necessary or contingent. But whatever view he took on this point, what he has to say on the subject generally will not support any serious claim about arithmetic and algebra being possible only if time is a pure intuition. Whether or not time is known *a priori* is quite irrelevant to the truth or falsity of the doctrines summarised above. And that being so we have to say that Kant simply knows no way in which to exploit his thesis that algebra and arithmetic have recourse to the concrete in the interest of the positions he advances in the Aesthetic.

We are left, therefore, with the philosophy of geometry as Kant's last remaining hope. The main difficulty here is that Kant just assumes that Euclid's axioms, though not logically necessary, are true of space as experienced, true indeed in such a way that no exception to them is allowed as possible. The problem for him is, then, how they could possess these qualities, and he considers it a major merit in his own philosophy that it can offer an explanation as rival theories can not. If Kant were right other geometries, though not logically ruled out, would be essentially idle: their conclusions might follow from their premises, but would have no application to the world as it presents itself in experience. There would also be the difficulty that their exponents would have to find arguments which did not depend upon ecthesis, i.e. get on without resorting to the typical mathematical expedient of constructing concepts. Kant himself believed that these arguments showed that there was no serious alternative to Euclid. But the history of mathematics since his time has demonstrated that this is false. It is perfectly possible to work out geometries on a non-Euclidean basis, and even to find application for their results in parts of physical if not of perceptual space. As Bertrand Russell put the point (*A History of Western Philosophy*, p. 743):

'Geometry', as we now know, is a name covering two different studies. On the one hand, there is pure geometry, which deduces consequences from axioms, without inquiring whether the axioms are 'true'; this contains nothing that does not follow from logic, and is not 'synthetic', and has no need of figures such are used in geometrical text-books. On the other hand, there is geometry as a branch of physics, as it appears, for example, in the general theory of relativity; this is an empirical science, in which the axioms are inferred from measurements, and are found to differ from Euclid's. Thus of the two kinds of geometry one is *a priori*, but not synthetic, while the other is synthetic but not *a priori*.

Russell adds that 'this disposes of the transcendental argument'.

It certainly disposes of it in its strong form, leaving only the weak claim that we treat some propositions about space and time as being at once synthetic and necessary, e.g. that experienced space has three dimensions. And of this it might be said that the necessity in question is simply psychological: it is a case of something we can't help believing and nothing more. To establish his own position Kant would have to show that our conviction rests on insight, limited but nonetheless real, into the essential nature of space as experienced. I do not myself believe that he has any direct argument for this point. All that he has is the submission, correct but by no means decisive, that we treat the proposition that space has three dimensions with, as it were, more respect than, say, the proposition that ripe oranges are yellow. If the first turned out to be false we should be far more upset than we should by the falsity of the second. In practice we ascribe a higher degree of necessity to the spatial principle than we do to everyday empirical truths; it plays a more central part in our thinking, and to be forced to jettison it would cause us acute conceptual confusion. Its importance for us is by no means simply psychological. But though it thus possesses a relative necessity of its own that does not show that it must be known independently of experience.

To sum up: Kant has good grounds for claiming that, in his own terminology, the idea of space is not a concept but an intuition: as was said earlier, 'space' is the name of a unique individual, which has parts but not instances. He is also correct in arguing that the ideas of space and time are central in human perceptual experience, and are not picked up or come by in the same way as complex empirical ideas. His belief that we attach a special necessity to certain fundamental propositions having to do with space and time is not in principle mistaken. But his argument from geometry to the conclusion that the idea of space is a pure intuition has to be rejected: what he says about 'constructing' geometrical concepts can be accepted without our having to agree that they are constructed in pure intuition, while the suggestion that our knowledge of geometrical axioms rests on insight into the essential nature of space has become highly unplausible in the light of subsequent developments in geometry. And once he is deprived of his 'transcendental' arguments Kant's whole case in the Aesthetic is very much weakened. True, we are still confronted with the claim that awareness of space seems to be presupposed in any spatial description, with the corresponding claim about time; we also have the psychological fact to which Kant calls attention, that we can think space and time as empty of objects but not think them away. But even if these are allowed to stand it is not clear how much weight they will bear. That they will bear the amount of weight Kant needs to put on them seems very uncertain indeed.

§ 6 *Empirical Realism and Transcendental Idealism*

Despite this conclusion, we must proceed as if Kant had established his main points about the existence of pure intuitions, if only because he takes them for granted in the rest of the *Critique*. I believe myself that the arguments of the Transcendental Analytic can be presented independently of those of the Aesthetic, and deserve attention even if the latter are discounted. Historically, however, it is a fact that Kant wrote the Analytic on the assumption that he had proved his main contentions in the Aesthetic. We therefore need to examine the conclusions he drew from his treatment of the ideas of space and time, in particular the conclusion that the space-time world is a world of *phenomena* and not of *things in themselves*.

'What we have meant to say', wrote Kant in his 'General Observations on Transcendental Aesthetic' (B 59/ A 42),

> is that all our intuition is nothing but the representation of appearance; that the things which we intuit are not in themselves what we intuit them as being, nor their relations so constituted in themselves as they appear to us, and that if the subject, or even only the subjective constitution of the senses in general, be removed, the whole constitution and all the relations of objects in space and time, nay space and time themselves, would vanish.

As the point was put in an earlier passage, it is 'solely from the human standpoint that we can speak of space, of extended things, etc.' (B 42/ A 26). We do not know what objects may be in themselves, 'apart from all this receptivity of our sensibility' (B 59/ A 42); we know them only as they conform to our mode of perceiving, a mode which, as Kant is careful to point out, is not necessarily shared by all possible percipients, though it is by all human beings. The reason why we cannot get at things in themselves in perception is, put crudely, that space and time are the forms of all our intuition, and thus as it were stand as a barrier between us and independent reality. The detailed content of experience—what Kant calls its matter—is due to the particular vicissitudes of the senses; that *this* appears next to, or after, *that* is hence a contingent affair. But that the items concerned stand in spatial and temporal relations *of some sort* is not contingent: it depends on the constitution of the human sensibility, and above all on the fact that space and time are its universal forms. Accordingly we can refine or clarify our sense-experience as much as we please, without having any prospect of arriving thereby at knowledge of things as they are in themselves. We are doomed to perceive within a framework of space and time.

Perhaps not surprisingly, Kant shows himself sensitive to some possible criticisms of this position while remaining unaware of others. The criticism which most concerns him is that which takes him to identify the phenomenal with the illusory, and hence to maintain that the world of things in space and time is not really there. Against this he insists that he is not only a 'transcendental idealist', but also an 'empirical realist'; he also tries to say that the subjectivism he professes is general rather than particular, and acceptable just because of that. As will become apparent, the two points are closely connected.

Kant's thesis that transcendental idealism is compatible with empirical realism rests on a claim that we can speak of the reality of things at two quite distinct levels. First, we can speak at what may be called the level of common sense, a level at which we all move in our non-philosophical moments and which is also the level of scientific thought. Second, we can think and talk at the level of critical philosophy, which takes account of factors that common sense and science alike find irrelevant, and in turn is not impressed by distinctions they consider important. What makes Kant's view confusing is that he distinguishes reality and appearance at *both* levels. When he speaks from the non-philosophical point of view he invokes the classical contrast between primary and secondary qualities in bodies, and is apt to say that the first are real or objective while the second are merely apparent or subjective. The taste of a wine, he tells us, depends on 'the special constitution of sense in the subject that tastes it'; the colour of a body is not a property of that body, but only a modification of 'the sense of sight, which is affected in a certain manner by light' (A 28). Spatial and temporal characteristics, by contrast, are the same for all of us; they do not depend on the vagaries of individual perception. It follows that, from the first standpoint, we have to say that space and time and their contents—bodies spread out in space and enduring through time, bodies possessing primary but not secondary qualities—are as real as anything can be. To remain at this level and deny reality to the space-time world is absurd. But this need not prevent the critical philosopher from describing space-time objects as phenomenal when he speaks from his own point of view. For although those objects do not depend for their existence on *my* particular perceptions, as that of the colours I see depends on my particular perceptions, the fact remains that I experience the world as I do because my sensibility has a certain structure, a structure which I share with other men, but not necessarily with other percipients. Philosophical considerations, irrelevant at the common-sense level, force me to recognise that space and time and their contents are ultimately mind-dependent and hence, despite their empirical reality, transcendentally ideal. I must thus acknowledge that the objects of my perception are one and all phenomena. But in so doing I must take care to make clear that what for the philosopher is merely phenomenal remains fully real when looked at through the eyes of the non-philosopher.

Kant himself was troubled about one particular point in this account, as a result of objections made to him by his contemporaries J. H. Lambert and Moses Mendelssohn when he sketched the theory in the *Dissertation* (see Arnulf Zweig: *Kant's Philosophical Correspondence*, pp. 63, 69). Whatever might be the case with space, critics had said that time must be real not only from the empirical point of view but also absolutely, on the ground that (B 53/ A 37)

> Alterations are real, this being proved by change of our own representations—even if all outer appearances, together with their alterations, are denied. Now alterations are possible only in time, and time is therefore something real.

Kant's answer to the objection is in effect that the statement 'alterations really happen' is entirely true from the non-philosophical point of view; from that standpoint time is fully real. From the philosophical point of view, again, time may be described as 'the real form of inner intuition': it is not an illusion that I experience things under the form of time. But we need not conclude from this that time has 'absolute reality', i.e. that things would have temporal predicates even if they were not objects of human intuition. For reasons already given we have to say that time 'does not inhere in the objects, but merely in the subject which intuits them' (B 54/ A 37–8). The critics might reply, as Moore did to Bradley, that we cannot deny 'absolute' reality to time without also denying it empirical reality; Kant would insist on his distinction of levels as an answer to this. Alternatively and more pertinently, they could ask him what was the force of describing time as phenomenal when considered from the philosophical point of view. In what way or ways would the processes we now experience as temporal present themselves to an intelligence which grasped things as they really are?

Kant could answer only that the state of our cognitive powers is such as to preclude any knowledge of things as they are in themselves, with the result that no reply to the question is possible. But if it is not, what warrants him in using the distinction of real and phenomenal at this level?

I shall return to this problem (see section 29 below), but for the moment must direct attention to another. It is Kant's view that space and time and their contents are, when philosophically considered, properly described as 'appearances'. But what sort of appearances, or again appearances to whom or to what? What is their ontological status? In drawing his distinction between colours and tastes on the one hand and spatial and temporal objects on the other Kant suggests that, while the first are when properly considered only items in individual minds, the second are in some sense public to many minds. There is only one space and one time, with which all of us have perceptual contact. But how can this be, if we follow the general indications of the Aesthetic? The process of perception there described is said to begin with the occurrence in particular minds of what Kant calls 'representations' and what earlier philosophers had called 'ideas'. For Kant some representations are 'sensations', some 'intuitions', the difference being that the former are strictly only events in consciousness whilst the latter stand in immediate relation to an object (B 33/A 19). We have already seen that there are difficulties about the relation of intuition to objects, difficulties which can be brought out if we ask if the 'object' of an intuition is part of its content, or something wholly extra-mental. If we choose the first alternative every intuitional object will be private, and that will make the supposed public character of space and time quite gratuitous. But if we allow that intuition could have objects entirely outside itself we are faced with the question how we know that this is so, when it seems to be the case with colours and sounds but turns out in this instance to be false. In short, any attempt to proceed on these lines runs up against the difficulties which Berkeley found in Locke's discussion of primary and secondary qualities. And Kant in the Aesthetic shows no sign of having thought out a reliable way of escaping from these difficulties.

In order to make his general theory work Kant has to provide, at the transcendental or philosophical level, for two sorts of appearances: for those which belong to the experience of particular individuals, and for those which belong to the experience of men as such. As he interprets them, colours, tastes, sounds and smells are appearances of the first sort, space, time and spatio-temporal objects as understood by the scientist appearances of the second. Kant must make this distinction if he is to claim to be an empirical realist; if he does not he is open to the charge that his view is indistinguishable from Berkeley's. But how is he to make the distinction if he remains within the conceptual confines of the Aesthetic? He is committed to the view that there can be no perception without representations, and he holds that all representations occur in individual minds. Given this start, it looks as if he must say that all the immediate objects of our awareness are private: we sense only sense-data. But if that is so we are confronted at once with the problem of how we get from private data to consciousness of a public world, the public world which, in Kant's submission, exists in independence of particular percipients. It is not clear that, in the terms stated, we could even form the notion of such a public world. Nor is it obvious that distinguishing within the class of representations, a sub-class which is said to stand in immediate relation to an object, whatever that may mean, is going to help the situation in any serious way. Intuitions may in some sense point beyond themselves, but they remain private items in particular minds. Kant may have thought of them as somehow mirroring the public world, reflecting in their content what was happening there, but if he did that would not solve his problem. On these terms he would find himself not with one spatial system, but with as many spaces as there are perceivers. He could go on and say that these different private spaces would correspond one to another, as different tastes or colours might not. But if we asked him how he knew this, he would be hard pressed to produce any convincing reply.

I conclude that the thesis that space and time and what may be called their respectable contents are phenomenal is one which Kant fails to work out in the Aesthetic. However, we know that in the Aesthetic Kant professes to be isolating sensibility, 'taking away from it everything which the understanding thinks through its concepts', as he puts the point himself (B 36/A 22). As a result his failure to solve the problem here is not a final failure; he has an opportunity to tackle the problem again, and does so this time with altogether better prospects of success, in that he can now see it in the round, instead of from a one-sided point of view. In fact Kant produces two further attempted solutions, one of which proceeds broadly on the basis of the assumptions of the Aesthetic and attempts to get round their difficulties by invoking *a priori* concepts, the other of which is more radical and argues for a tie-up between the notions of objectivity or phenomenal reality (appearances in our second sense) and the activity of judgment, which is of its nature impersonal. I shall examine these theories at length in later sections (see below, especially section 17).

The Necessity of Categories

§7 *Transcendental Logic : Preliminary Considerations*

We come now to 'Transcendental Logic', which Kant explains
briefly before plunging into the details of his account of the powers
and the limitations of the human mind. Logic, he says enigmatically
(B 76/A 52), is 'the science of the rules of the understanding in
general', just as aesthetic was 'the science of the rules of sensibility
in general'. Logic divides into two parts, a general part which has to
do with the absolutely necessary rules of thought without whose
observance there can be no employment of the understanding, and
which hence does not vary as the objects of thought vary, and a
special part which 'contains the rules of correct thinking as regards
a certain kind of objects' (ibid.). Special logic seems to be what is
now called 'methodology', general logic is logic as it was traditionally
understood. Kant thought of it as having an applied division, concerned with the conditions in which people actually think, and
therefore spilling over into psychology. But he also insisted that pure
logic, logic considered simply as a 'canon of understanding and
reason, but only in respect of what is formal in their employment'
(B 77/A 53), has nothing to do with empirical principles. It is an *a
priori* science, dealing with 'nothing but the mere form of thought'
(B 78/A 54).

All this is quite unexceptionable; difficulty begins only when
Kant passes to the notion of Transcendental Logic. The Aesthetic
has shown, he claims, that there are pure as well as empirical
intuitions. Similarly a distinction might be drawn between the pure
and the empirical thought of an object, and if it were we should have
the possibility of a logic which, unlike pure general logic, did not
abstract from the whole content of our knowledge, but was rather

concerned with 'the rules of the pure thought of an object' (B 80/A 55). 'The pure thought of an object' is the thought of what general characteristics belong of necessity to an object of experience; the study concerned would thus have to specify the conditions which have to be satisfied by any thinking which claims to pronounce on what exists objectively. To describe such a study as a branch of logic sounds strange to modern ears: what Kant has in mind looks much more like a latter-day equivalent of traditional ontology, which purported to speak of the characteristics of *things* in general (cf. Wolff's definition: 'ontologia est scientia entis in genere, seu quatenus ens est', and for Kant's own recognition of the parallel B 303/A 247). That Kant despite this persisted in presenting his results as belonging to logic perhaps argues no more than that his idea of logic was idiosyncratic, just as his idea of aesthetic was. Anything which could claim to be a doctrine of concepts, or to deal with rules of thought, was entitled in his view to be called a form of logic.

Kant points to certain important differences between general and transcendental logic. The former has no concern with the origin of the concepts and propositions which come before it, but simply scrutinises their formal relations. The latter has to do essentially, not with concepts generally, but with a special class of concepts employed in a special way; it is therefore peculiarly sensitive to the distinction among concepts of those which are *a priori* and those which are empirical. Again, while general logic may be described as a logic of consistency, in so far as it lays down, or makes explicit, the rules which govern any thinking which is formally coherent, transcendental logic, or rather its first positive part (see below), is a 'logic of truth' (B 87/A 62). But this phrase should not be pressed too hard. Kant is not implying that transcendental logic will provide us with rules by which we can discover new truths; his logic of truth is not the useful logic Descartes and Mill hoped to produce. When he says that it is a logic of truth he means only that it does not abstract entirely from all the content of cognition, but pays attention to conditions which must be met if we are to arrive at truth about the world. It is clear, however, that these conditions are necessary and not sufficient: if we fail to observe them we cannot reach truth, if we do observe them we nevertheless may not. The laws of transcendental logic are thus *sine quibus non*, just as those of general logic are; in this respect the two disciplines run parallel rather than diverge. As for the general problem of truth, Kant's remarks about it are eminently sensible. Truth concerns the content of knowledge, not its form, and for that reason 'a sufficient and at the same time general criterion of truth cannot possibly be given' (B 83/A 59). Logic can produce a negative criterion of truth, having to do with the form of thought as opposed to its content, but cannot go further than that. And what holds for general logic here holds also for transcendental logic.

It turns out from this that transcendental logic is less of a monster than it sounds. But it must be admitted that Kant piles on the horrors, terminologically at least. General logic, he tells us, divides into two parts, Analytic and Dialectic. Analytic states the formal rules which govern correct thinking of any sort, and thus provides what Kant calls 'the negative touchstone of truth' (B 84/A 60). Dialectic is a perverse attempt to employ these rules as an *organon* or instrument for the production of what look like truths of a material kind. Kant gives no illustrations of this peculiar sort of misuse; presumably what he had in mind was sophistical attempts to 'make the worse appear the better cause', by simple logic-chopping. But in any case the division is more important for its consequences in transcendental logic than in itself. For in that study too it appears that we can draw a distinction between Analytic and Dialectic. 'Transcendental Analytic' is said to deal with 'the elements of the pure knowledge yielded by understanding, and the principles without which no object can be thought' (B 87/A 62); more simply, it lays down the rules without which objective, as opposed to formally correct, thinking is impossible, and indicates the proper sphere of application of those rules. It is properly seen as a 'canon for passing judgment on the empirical employment of the understanding' (B 88/A 63). It turns out, however, that we readily misuse the *a priori* principles provided by Transcendental Analytic, transferring them from the area to which they rightly belong, the sphere of possible experience, and using them, or attempting to use them, as a means of specifying the properties of things in general, without regard to whether or not they could fall within our experience. Given what he says about general logic, one might have expected Kant to apply the term 'Transcendental Dialectic' to this misuse, for here too a 'canon' is mistakenly converted into an 'organon'. In fact, however, he presents Dialectic, both in this preliminary passage and in the main body of the *Critique*, as a *critique* of such a procedure, an exposure of the 'jugglery' which is involved in this sort of dogmatic metaphysics. On this account transcendental logic as a whole becomes an account of the proper and improper uses of a series of *a priori* concepts. It holds that such concepts are necessary if there is to be objective knowledge of an empirical world, but are misapplied when the metaphysician appeals to them to establish e.g. that there must be a First Cause, or that reality must consist of one or more simple substances.

The defect of this initial discussion lies in its failure to make anything of Kant's own technical distinction between the faculties of understanding and reason, despite the frequent references to the two. It leads us to expect that Dialectic will be entirely negative, consisting in nothing but an uncovering of bad arguments and false metaphysical moves. In fact it contains a good deal more, in so far as Kant tries to make out that, over and above the pure concepts of the understanding, the faculty of reason has pure concepts of its own, and that these 'ideas', though misused in metaphysics, have a genuine role to play in the search for empirical knowledge. Ideas of reason give rise to principles which direct the operations of the understanding; without them knowledge would lack the systematic character which we regularly strive to confer on it. What can be made of this doctrine must be left until we examine it in detail (see section 41). But meantime it is important that it should get some mention, if only to guard against the false presumption that once Kant gets to the end of the Analytic he has no further positive theory to offer.

Many Kantian commentators condemn their author for being at the mercy of something they call his 'architectonic': they assume that distinctions such as those we have briefly explored were introduced for purely pedantic reasons and do not deserve serious attention. In contrast to many more recent philosophers Kant believed that philosophy must be numbered among the sciences, that its results must hence appear in scientific guise and that in consequence philosophical writing must be full of technical terms and precise distinctions. Kant himself was at once fertile in inventing such terms and making such distinctions and not always consistent in using them. Nevertheless, it is at the lowest estimate hazardous to neglect Kant's formal apparatus as unimportant. The vocabulary he uses is often difficult, but seldom totally baffling; some parts of it, as we have already seen in the case of the term 'transcendental', are more frightening in appearance than in reality. The faculty structure presupposed in the *Critique*, with distinctions such as those between sensation and imagination, understanding and reason, is sometimes difficult to defend, but equally is not adopted in a wholly arbitrary way, as I have tried to show earlier in discussing the fundamental contrast between sensing and thinking. The term 'faculty' has itself been too much abused, as if it stood for nothing when in fact it is only a short way of referring to a set of powers. As for 'architectonic', it may be true that some of Kant's later works proceed on a pre-arranged plan which sometimes distorts their subject-matter. But the same cannot be said of the *Critique of Pure Reason*, which introduces for the first time the divisions and distinctions pedantically reproduced in Kant's later works. There is no reason in principle why Kant's main divisions in the *Critique* should not mark real distinctions, and thus why discussion of them should not be profitable. I believe myself that they are never wholly negligible and often highly important, though I admit that there are places where reliance on out-of-date logic is carried too far (compare for instance the 'table of the division of the concept of nothing', B 348/A 292). It would be idle to deny that there are aspects of Kant's work which are pedantic and over-schematic. But we should not exaggerate their incidence. If Kant were as much in the grip of architectonic as his critics make out, he would not be the great philosopher that he is.

§ 8 *The Notion of a Category*

Transcendental Analytic is divided by Kant into two 'books', Analytic of Concepts and Analytic of Principles. The first explains the nature, function and necessity for human knowledge of the special class of concepts Kant calls 'pure concepts of the understanding' or 'categories'. The second examines and purports to validate a number of individual principles which rest on particular categories. The argument of the second thus to some extent duplicates that of the first; the difference is that in the Analytic of Concepts Kant offers a general argument, which claims to be true of whatever categories there are, whereas in the Analytic of Principles he is concerned with particular cases. He could in consequence be right in some of his contentions in the second book even if the main argument of the first were totally unacceptable.

I have described the Analytic of Concepts as offering a general argument, applicable to whatever categories there may be, when it is notorious that it opens with an attempt to produce a complete list of such concepts in the so-called Metaphysical Deduction. That it does so is among Kant's most serious mistakes of exposition. In order to get his theory under way he needs to make clear what it is he is talking about, and that means giving a preliminary account of what a category is and what it does. Instead of producing such an account Kant goes into a complicated disquisition about the logical operation of judging, constructs what he says is a complete list of all possible forms of judgment, and then declares, after a few baffling connecting sentences, that this can be used as a clue to the discovery of all pure concepts of the understanding. A table of categories, alleged to be complete, duly follows (B 106/A 80). Unfortunately the reader can have very little idea at this stage of the nature of the items it lists. Kant's only attempt to help him is to be found in a brief passage in section 3 (B 102/ A 76 ff.), which sketches the doctrine of synthesis developed in the later Transcendental Deduction and declares enigmatically that 'pure synthesis, represented in its most general aspect, gives us the pure concept of the understanding' (B 104/A 78). But this passage is virtually unintelligible as it stands; sense can be made of it, if at all, only in the light of discussions which come later.

I shall therefore relegate the Metaphysical Deduction to what I consider to be its rightful place in the argument, the end of the Analytic of Concepts (see section 12 below), and begin my own account by attempting what I say Kant should have offered, namely a preliminary sketch of the notion of a category. At the very beginning of Transcendental Logic (B 74–5/A 50–1) Kant draws an interesting parallel between pure intuitions and pure concepts. Pure intuition, he says, 'contains only the form under which something is intuited; the pure concept only the form of the thought of an object in general'. Pure intuition is, strictly, nothing in itself, but simply an empty form which lies ready in the mind awaiting empirical filling; the pure thought of an object turns out to be much the same, only this time at the level of universals rather than that of particulars. The pure thought of an object is the thought of the characters the object must have if it is to be an object at all. Since everything that is to be an object has to have these characters, to possess the concepts in question is not to have the idea of any particular kind of thing. It is rather to be master of the framework into which particular collocations of empirical characters must fit, to grasp the form of what can be objective in independence of its matter.

By 'objects' in this connection Kant means things that can be met with in experience: his whole account rests on the assumption that it is only of such things that we can speak with any knowledge. What things are like in themselves, considered apart from our experience of them, we do not and cannot know. But 'object' and 'thing' alike mislead us here if we take them as standing for substances or continuants. When Kant speaks of 'the thought of an object in general' he has in mind the thought of *an objective order* or *an objective world* rather than of the general form of experienced subjects of predicates. He is talking about existents in a loose sense of the word, one in which it can cover states of affairs as well as substances. His pure concepts relate to the characteristics which have to belong to things or situations if they are to count as part of an objective order, to be there regardless of our particular feelings or private experiences.

But why must these requirements be met? What reason have we for saying that nothing can count as objective unless it meets certain necessary conditions? An empiricist might argue that nothing could be objective unless it is given in experience or connects with what is given in experience. Kant starts from the same position, but elaborates it in an interesting way. He argues in the first place that being given in experience is not as simple a notion as some philosophers have supposed. For something to be given it is not enough that ideas of some kind should arise in consciousness, that a subject should have experience of sensory content of some kind or other. Ideas and experiences can be illusory, and we need to sort out the false from the true. To assert that something is a fact, that this or that is happening now, requires judgment as well as bare experience. Nothing can be a fact unless it is, at the lowest estimate, connectible with other facts and describable in the same general terms as they. And this brings us to his other major point. In empiricist analyses the realm of the objective extends beyond that which is given to its usual antecedents, attendants or successors, the argument being that we regularly find certain perceptions associated together, and therefore have reasonable grounds for postulating the second when the first turns up. It is insisted, however, that everything depends on experience here: if the association is not repeated, all warrant for the inference falls to the ground. Against this Kant wants to say, not that we can establish particular connections without regard to experience, but that we presume *a priori* that some such connections hold. We take it that the occurrence of this or that now implies that something else has happened or will happen; what that something else is, only experience can show, but that it is there we know, or think we know, independently of experience. It is this conviction which underlies our empirical investigations, and makes us persist with our enquiries however discouraging their results. We act as if the connection between one fact and another were not contingent, and in so doing subscribe to the view that the objective order has necessary characteristics over and above those which empiricism recognises.

It can of course be said in reply that if we do make such presumptions we have no right to them: inference in this area must be proportioned to experience, or lose all claim to authenticity. The question is, however, what 'experience' can mean in this connection. Do we mean by it anything which seems to be the case to any individual person, or has it a more restricted significance? There is a poem by Siegfried Sassoon, addressed to 'an Old Lady Dead', which contains the lines:

> These moments are 'experience' for me;
> But not for you; not for a mutual 'us'.

Kant's answer to the empiricists is that the 'experience' to which our inferences must be proportioned is experience for a 'mutual us', experience which is shared or shareable, rather than something which is essentially private. But experience of this kind is not so much given as agreed upon; it has to be made out on the basis of what goes on in individual minds. For this process to be carried out we need criteria of what is to count as experience proper, criteria which cannot be derived from fact since they determine what it is to be a fact. One way of putting Kant's case for pure concepts of the understanding is to present them as underlying such criteria.

A point which needs special emphasis here is that if there are such concepts as categories their role in the search for knowledge must necessarily be quite different from that of the ordinary run of concepts. They must not be taken as descriptive of features of the world, even its most general features. Categories are co-ordinating concepts, but not in the way in which some scientific concepts are. They do not serve directly to link phenomena, as for example the notion of a field of force does. Rather they operate on a higher logical level, licensing certain moves in the search for particular knowledge and precluding others. Indeed, it is because they have this formal character that they can form part of the subject matter of philosophy rather than belong to general science. Kant's own grasp of this point was perhaps less certain than it should have been. His account of the function of categories in the Transcendental Deduction is sound enough, but his association of them with 'pure physics' is far from happy, and the same must be said of his remark (A 127–8) that 'all empirical laws are only special determinations of the pure laws of understanding, under which, and according to the norm of which, they first become possible'. This sentence can be read innocuously, but it can also be taken to imply that 'pure laws of the understanding', the synthetic *a priori* principles of 'pure physics', are truths about the world mysteriously known without recourse to experience. Positivists who ridicule the notion of the synthetic *a priori* often pretend that those who accept it must believe in some non-empirical source of factual knowledge. Kant certainly believed in no such source, but was as insistent as any empiricist on the principle that factual truth can come only from experience. To guard against error here we have to recognise explicitly the logical peculiarity of the concepts in which he was interested and of the principles to which they give rise. Concepts of an object in general are presupposed in all enquiries into the character of particular objects, but are not found out as the latter are; they are accordingly not empirical. As for principles of the understanding, they are not, as Kant sometimes seems to suggest, the most general of all laws of nature, but are principles used in any search for laws of nature, principles which govern empirical enquiries and determine the general shape of the questions put and thus of the information sought. As Kant put the point in his second edition preface (B xiii):

> Reason, holding in one hand its principles, according to which alone concordant appearances can be admitted as equivalent to laws, and in the other hand the experiment which it has devised in conformity with these principles, must approach nature in order to be taught by it. It must not, however, do so in the character of a pupil who listens to everything that the teacher chooses to say, but of an appointed judge who compels the witnesses to answer questions which he has himself formulated.

Nature or experience has the last word, but the part played by Reason in supplying a framework for empirical enquiries is not to be overlooked.

Is there some simple test for detecting the presence of categories, or for deciding if a concept in fact has categorial status? This question can be answered more easily if we switch attention from categories proper to categorial principles, i.e. to the synthetic *a priori* propositions which the categories are alleged to ground, propositions such as 'There are no events without causes', 'All change is transformation', 'No quality is present except in a determinate degree'. In previous writings, and particularly in my paper on 'Categories' (*Kantstudien*, 1954), I argued that the special status of such propositions is shown up when we attempt to deny them: to do so seems peculiarly absurd. If someone says that failure to find a lost object may be due to its having gone clean out of existence, or that failure to find a cause may be explained by the fact that in this case there wasn't one, we think he is making a bad joke. Things don't go clean out of existence, or happen for no reason at all. The suggestion that they might, if made seriously, challenges some of our most fundamental assumptions. I am not saying that such assumptions can never properly be challenged, but only pointing out the status we assign to them. The fact that we can find such examples seems to me good empirical evidence that we do assign categorial status to some of our concepts, and thus to lend some plausibility to Kant's general position. But of course it does not amount to a full-scale defence of that position, nor was Kant himself under the impression that it did.

The various points made in this section have been sketchy at best: I have hinted at ways of thinking about categories rather than seriously explored them. I hope even so that enough has been said to make the main idea clear and even to give it some initial plausibility. I must now try to take the matter further by looking at Kant's own arguments in some detail, a process which will involve in the first place consideration of his celebrated 'Transcendental Deduction of the Categories'.

§ 9 *The Problem of the Transcendental Deduction*
'Deducing' the categories, for Kant, is offering a justification of them: 'deduction' is a legal term referring to the propriety of doing something or other, and to deduce a concept is to show that we are entitled to use it (see B 116–17/ A 84–5). Kant begins his discussion by mentioning a set of concepts which circulate without any challenge to their authority, namely 'many' empirical concepts; he says that we do not ask what justifies the use of these since they are obviously derived from experience. He then goes on to refer briefly to what he calls 'usurpatory' concepts such as 'fortune' or 'fate' which also circulate without challenge thanks to 'almost universal indulgence' on the part of the public; the implication here is that such ideas are not taken sufficiently seriously to be subjected to scrutiny about credentials, though they could be. Finally he passes to the concepts in which he is specially interested, those which are 'marked out for pure *a priori* employment' (B 117/A 85), and says that in their case we face the problem how they relate to an object of any sort. It is this problem which the Transcendental Deduction is designed to solve.

Kant's preoccupations here can best be clarified by a brief reference to the history of his own thinking. In the inaugural *Dissertation* of 1770 he outlined his theory of space and time as *a priori* intuitions and on its basis distinguished a sphere of phenomena or objects of the senses from one of noumena or objects of the intelligence. But though he conceded that we have no *intuition* of noumena, i.e no direct acquaintance with them, his view was that our intellect is furnished with certain pure concepts of its own and can use these to arrive at a 'symbolic cognition' of the intelligible world, that is at a description of its general character. That pure concepts thus relate to intelligible objects was simply assumed in the *Dissertation*. But less than two years after the publication of his essay Kant was expressing serious doubts about the propriety of that assumption. In his letter to Marcus Herz of 21 February 1772 he pointed out (see Zweig, pp. 71–2) that neither an ectypal nor an archetypal intellect would face a problem about the relation of its ideas to objects, the first because all its ideas would be empirically derived, the second because in its case ideas would create their own objects (they would be 'synthetic' universals in the terminology of the *Critique of Judgment*: see section 3 above). But the human intellect corresponds to neither type, for only some of its ideas come from experience and yet it is not, except in the special case of moral action, by the bare fact of having ideas the cause of the existence of anything. The question thus arises how those of its ideas which are not drawn from experience can be said to relate to an object of any sort. Might it not be the case that they have no such objective reference, and are therefore without significance? This question was the more serious for Kant in that he was persuaded that this was precisely the position with some metaphysical ideas, e.g. that of a Leibnizian monad. It is hardly surprising that ever after this the problem of the relation of pure concepts to objects played a prominent part in his philosophical thought.

In the *Critique* itself Kant tried to sharpen the issue by introducing a comparison and contrast on this head between categories and pure intuitions. The results were to say the least confusing. In one passage (B 119/A 87) he claimed that he had already undertaken a transcendental deduction of what he called the 'concepts' of space and time, only to add that there could be no serious problem about the objective reference of such ideas. The geometer can show that he is talking sense by simply constructing his concepts in pure intuition, and, in general, space and time must relate to objects, 'since only by means of such forms of sensibility can an object appear to us' (B 121/A 89). Pure concepts of the understanding, by contrast, in no sense belong to the given, nor have they anything to do with pure intuition; they cannot be constructed *a priori*, nor can we see without argument how they could determine an object. It follows that they are a proper target for suspicion: we find ourselves asking what objective validity they can lay claim to and what are the limitations on their use. So much so, if Kant is to be believed, that the suspicion spills over onto the ideas of space and time themselves, and we are led into undertaking a transcendental deduction of them too.

Generally, Kant is inclined to say that it is obvious that 'objects of sensible intuition' (B 122/A 90) must 'conform to the formal conditions of sensibility which lie *a priori* in the mind', not obvious that they must conform to the requirements of pure thinking. If something would not fit into the space/time framework it simply could not be an object of our intuition. But why should not the world be so constituted that, for example, the concept of cause and effect had nothing answering to it, and so was 'altogether empty, null and meaningless' (B 123/A 90)? After this formulation of the problem it is surprising to read Kant's provisional solution, which is that just as objects must conform to our *a priori* forms of sensibility because they could not otherwise be objects of intuition, so they must also conform to our *a priori* concepts because they could not otherwise be objects of experience (see B 125–6/A 93). Here he seems to be assimilating the two cases, instead of contrasting them as he had earlier.

To try to bring out the difficulties, it will be useful to distinguish two distinct theses with which Kant is concerned in this part of his work. First, that nothing could be an object if it were not intuited under the forms of space and time. Second, that nothing could be an object unless it were thought as conforming to the categories. Kant regards the first as obviously true, the second as less obvious but nonetheless provable. Regrettably, however, he fails to point out that the word 'object' must have a different sense in the two cases. An object as understood in the first thesis is essentially an item in private or personal experience, an object of intuition as Kant himself calls it. An object as understood in the second thesis is a public object, one which may not in fact be available to more than one percipient, but about whose existence and characteristics general agreement can be expected. The supposed parallel between the two cases is thus less impressive than may appear at first sight. There are other difficulties too. One is quite simply that, as has already been briefly argued, intuition strictly has no objects at all, if the indications of Kant's account of judgment are followed. Intuition involves the occurrence of sensory content, but cannot for Kant be a form of knowledge by acquaintance. The whole language of sections *13* and *14* of the *Analytic*, which constitute an introduction to the Deduction and sketch the lines on which Kant's solution will proceed, is misleading in so far as it uses terminology which Kant had outgrown; there are commentators (e.g. Robert Paul Wolff) who would dismiss the passage just on this account. My own view is that it is instructive despite its defects, but that does not mean that we should be blind to these. Another difficulty with the passage concerns the status Kant intends to assign to the two theses he puts before his reader. Is it the case that the first is meant to be analytic and the second synthetic? Are both thought of as analytic, the second being unobviously so, to use the terminology of Jonathan Bennett? Or could Kant be saying that both are synthetic? I regret that I have clear answers to none of these questions. The fact that Kant says (B 123/A 90) that 'appearances might very well be so constituted that the understanding should not find them to be in accordance with the conditions of its unity' would seem on the face of it to count strongly against the analyticity of the second, though it has to be admitted that 'appearances' has the same ambiguities as 'objects' (there are private and public 'appearances', and different things may well be true of them). Again, we know from other passages in the *Critique* (see especially B 145–6) that for Kant it is a contingent fact that we are endowed with just these and no other categories and forms of intuition, and even that we have a discursive intelligence. But it does not seem to be contingent that a discursive intelligence needs to correlate or synthesise its experiences in order to have objective knowledge, nor would Kant allow that it is accidental that our intelligence carries out its synthesis according to *a priori* rules. In general, he is disposed to say that the main conclusions of the *Critique*, and especially of the Deduction, take the form of necessary truths. But he does not ask how they can be such, nor examine closely the type of necessity involved. He explains the status of derived philosophical propositions such as 'Every event has a cause', but fails to discuss that of the more fundamental theses on which these derived propositions depend (see further section 42 below).

Kant's initial statement of his problem in the Deduction is thus far from satisfactory. We can see, perhaps, why he finds a general difficulty in the question how pure concepts might relate to objects. But his attempt to clarify the situation by comparing and contrasting this case with that of pure intuitions can only be pronounced a failure. Unless we are willing to go along with a crude account of perception, according to which intuition involves the grasp of a special (private) object of its own, we cannot acquiesce in the anti-thesis which Kant puts before us. But though this has to be said, the admission has no bearing on the nature and validity of Kant's solution. Whether he makes out his comparison with pure intuitions or not, it remains true that he has an independent case for saying that nothing could be an object of experience unless thought as 'an object in general' according to pure concepts of the understanding. His anwer to the question how categories relate to an object is that they are necessary if we are to have objective experience of any kind. We must now attempt to state and evaluate this argument at greater length.

§ 10 *The Central Arguments of the Transcendental Deduction*

The argument we are to examine appears rather differently in the two editions of the *Critique*, the Deduction chapter having been entirely recast for the second edition. In the first edition the main emphasis was on the need to hold together and connect diverse experiences if coherent consciousness is to be possible; synthesis of this sort, as Kant called it, had to proceed not merely at the empirical but also at the *a priori* level, thanks to the fact that the data encountered in experience include pure intuitions. As well as speaking of the activities of the understanding Kant in this version had much to say about those of 'the imagination' (see further below); indeed, the latter was presented as *the* synthesising faculty, though understanding was needed as well to 'bring the synthesis to concepts', i.e. to make it explicit and to label it as being of a certain kind. Kant did not fail to mention the relevance of the whole process, or set of processes, to the need to determine what shall count as an object, but this theme was less prominent than might have been expected. Similarly the categories were brought into the story in something of a backstairs way, on the strength of the unintelligible account already offered in the Metaphysical Deduction of their connection with logical forms of judgment. As far as the Transcendental Deduction itself was concerned they came in only because the argument showed, or purported to show, that there was a need for *a priori* concepts of some kind or other. Judgment had no real part in this version of the Deduction, and indeed the whole orientation of the passage, both in the 'preliminary' exposition Kant offered in A 98–114 and in the 'systematic' account which followed (A 115ff.), was psychological. On the face of things it looked as if Kant was describing activities which were not empirically accessible, but could all the same be reconstructed and assessed by a transcendental philosopher like himself.

In the second edition version of the Deduction many important changes were introduced. For one thing, Kant separated the question of the role of categories in discursive consciousness generally from that of their role in human consciousness, treating the first in the first part of his argument (B 129–143) and the second in later sections (B 150–65). This had the advantage of assigning intelligible but diverse roles to the faculties of understanding and imagination respectively, and of making clear that the importance of the categories was not exhausted by connecting them with the unifying of the pure intuitions of space and time. The change also had the advantage of pointing forward to the Schematism chapter, now prepared for in Kant's remarks about intellectual and figurative synthesis in B 151. As this reference shows, the general story about synthesis was retained, but the whole passage lost some of its psychological overtones thanks to the playing down of the activities of imagination and the playing up of the notion of judgment. Indeed, the respect in which the whole argument benefited most from the rewriting was in the prominence given to this notion and the emphasis put on its importance for objective knowledge. Judgment, Kant now argued, aimed at declaring what is the case, as opposed to what seems to be the case to some particular individual. It thus had an internal relation to the impersonal unity of apperception (see immediately below), whose activities were accordingly revealed as of logical rather than psychological interest. Kant still offered a rather poor account of the categories, bringing them in once again on the basis of his previous argument and not discussing whether judgment as treated by formal logic was identical with judgment as treated in his own philosophy. That judgment requires not merely the application of concepts (which is what it essentially is), but of concepts formed on the basis of *a priori* rules, was hinted at rather than spelled out. Despite this, the argument in its later form was altogether more impressive and persuasive than it had been in the earlier version.

I shall now attempt to summarise the argument as it appears in the second edition. Kant begins by contrasting the passivity of the senses with the activity of the understanding. The former provide us with a manifold or multiplicity of data for cognition, but cannot of themselves connect such data. Combination is the work of the understanding, and as such 'an act of the self-activity of the subject' (B 130). What subject? Kant answers by introducing his notion of 'the original synthetic unity of apperception'. The 'I think', he says mysteriously, must be capable of accompanying all my representations (all the items in my consciousness) if they are to belong to my consciousness at all, and this means that I have to have the power of connecting my diverse experiences. The 'I think', it should be made clear, is here seen as the vehicle of an impersonal consciousness, for 'I' come into the matter not as an individual but as what Kant sometimes calls 'consciousness in general'. This is why Kant draws a contrast in this connection between empirical and pure consciousness. The unity of my empirical consciousness is a contingent matter; it depends, as Kant makes clear, on 'circumstances or empirical conditions' (B 139). What connects with what, in my particular consciousness, is accidental. But the unity of pure apperception is not similarly contingent: on the contrary, it is presupposed as necessary. The subject of thinking must be one and the same in all its operations if it is to be a subject at all. And that means that the items which fall within its purview must one and all be connectible, standing in relations which hold for consciousness generally. Otherwise, as Kant says, 'something would be represented in me which could not be thought at all, and that is equivalent to saying that the representation would be impossible' (B 131–2).

Is Kant simply postulating a single continuing self, and thus solving the problem of self-identity by fiat? It might appear that he is, but the impression is mistaken. The 'unity of apperception' is not a concrete existent; it is 'pure' and therefore abstract. As I have tried to explain, the phrase refers not to any actual self but only to an ideal subject self, which is the same in all of us or would be if we were wholly rational. This is the self which operates in judgment rather than the self which interests the psychologist, something which it would be better to refer to as 'one' than as 'I'. That such a self must be thought of as unitary is not a piece of metaphysical speculation, but a mere tautology, as Kant keeps saying. Nevertheless it is a tautology which has consequences of major importance for our present topic. For if we can claim that all thinking presupposes a unitary subject of consciousness, what holds for that subject must similarly possess a formal unity: it must be possible to correlate one experienced item with another by bringing them under a unitary conceptual scheme and a single system of relations. This is not to say that the different things which fall within consciousness—the various events, for instance—must be internally or conceptually connected; the doctrine is neutral as regards what relations will hold, leaving it to experience to discover what these are. But the theory does claim that all such items will have some such relations, over and above that of being numerically different one from another. Anything which failed to meet this requirement could not fall within my consciousness; it would be, as Kant says, 'as good as nothing' (A 111), 'less even than a dream' (A 112).

The unity of apperception is described by Kant as 'original' because it is ultimate, and as 'synthetic' because of the implications about connectibility just set out. It is also 'objective' in a double sense. First, because it 'alone constitutes the relation of representations to an object', an object being 'that in the concept of which the manifold of a given intuition is united' (B 137). It is at least a minimum condition of whatever is to count as objective that it display order; the unity of apperception, as we have seen, is of its nature driven to postulate and seek out such order. The faculty of thought, to put the point in a somewhat unKantian way, must have as its correlate something which is properly thinkable; it cannot guarantee the existence of that something so far as its matter is concerned, but it can guarantee that, if data are forthcoming, they will have the appropriate form. When Kant says that unity of apperception *alone* constitutes the relation of representations to an object he clearly goes too far: thinkability is a necessary condition of objectivity, but not sufficient for it. Whatever is to count as objective fact must be thinkable, but it must also be given in experience or connect with what is so given. Kant would have made his view more palatable had he stressed this point, which he would have no difficulty in accepting. Secondly, the unity of apperception is objective as opposed to what Kant calls 'the subjective unity of consciousness, which is a determination of inner sense' (B 139), and which hence varies from individual to individual. The subjective unity of consciousness is simply the empirical unity of consciousness, the mass or congeries of perceptions which, as Hume said, a man finds when he looks within himself. That one thing makes me think of another depends on my personal circumstances; the connection between them may be no more than subjective association. By contrast, the unity of apperception or objective unity of consciousness is thought of as impersonal: what holds for it is 'necessarily and universally valid' (B 140).

How does the unity of apperception express itself? The answer is through the activity of judgment. Judgment, Kant says, must be distinguished sharply 'from the relation according to laws of reproductive imagination, which has only subjective validity' (B 141); judgment is one thing, the association of ideas quite another. Judgment 'is nothing but the manner in which given items of knowledge are brought to the objective unity of apperception' (ibid.). The presence in a judgment of the copula 'is' indicates that what is asserted is intended as holding without distinction of persons, in relation to 'original apperception and its necessary unity', as Kant puts it (B 142). This is true even when the content of the judgment is empirical and hence contingent, e.g. in the case of the judgment 'Bodies are heavy'. Kant explains himself clearly if somewhat clumsily in the next sentence:

> I do not here assert that these representations *necessarily* belong *to one another* in the empirical intuition, but that they belong to one another *in virtue of the necessary unit* of apperception in the synthesis of intuitions, that is, according to principles of the objective determination of all representations, in so far as knowledge can be acquired by means of these representations— principles which are all derived from the fundamental principle of the transcendental unity of apperception.

The main point here is precisely that made above, that the 'necessity' of the unity of apperception is less alarming than it may seem since it is essentially formal and hence need not go over into the content of what it connects. If something is judged to be the case, it relates of necessity to the unity of apperception, which in turn is a necessary unity. But this is to say nothing of the internal content of what is judged, which need possess no further necessity of its own. The objection that Kant's theory of judgment is inconsistent with his own distinction of necessary and contingent propositions thus falls to the ground.

Kant brings his whole argument together in a brief paragraph (section *20*) whose contentions I paraphrase as follows. Whatever falls within consciousness, and therefore the entire 'manifold given in a sensible intuition' (B 143), must if it is to be taken account of at all fall under the original synthetic unity of apperception. The act of understanding through which that unity operates is judgment: in bringing different items into relation with one another and connecting them in one consciousness I determine them 'in respect of one of the logical functions of judgment' (ibid.). But the categories are just these logical functions of judgment, considered as employed in determining what is the case. It follows that whatever falls within consciousness must, as related to the impersonal subject self, fall under the categories.

There are many difficulties here apart from the fundamental one of the connection of judgment and categories. But we must postpone discussion of them for the moment and return to Kant's text. Immediately after enunciating his conclusion Kant says that 'in the above proposition a beginning is made of a deduction of the pure concepts of understanding' (B 144). Why only a beginning? The answer is that so far Kant has carried on his argument at a deliberately abstract level: he has considered the issue without taking account of the special nature of human consciousness, the fact that the forms of its intuiting are space and time, and has concentrated instead on what he later describes as 'objects of intuition in general, whether that intuition be our own or any other, provided only it be sensible' (B 150). He has thus enquired into what must be true of the thinking of any discursive, as opposed to intuitive, intelligence, or again into what is required for objective knowledge of any sort. But we as human beings are aware of a world which is not thus abstractly objective, but takes the form of continuing objects set within a unitary spatio-temporal system. To complete his argument Kant therefore has to take the further step of showing the relevance of the categories to 'the manifold of sensible intuition' (B 151) as we know it, and this is the task which he undertakes in the later part of the Deduction, especially at the beginning of section *24* and the corresponding passage in section *26*.

Kant sets the stage for a new move by distinguishing two kinds, or two levels, of synthesis, one of which has to do with the 'mere' understanding and is purely *intellectual*, whilst the other belongs to imagination and is characterised as *figurative*. Every figurative synthesis, I take it, involves an intellectual synthesis as an abstract component. The reason Kant appeals to imagination here is that he sees that faculty as mediating between the senses and the understanding: as being like sense in so far as it involves or results in the envisaging of a particular state of affairs, as being like understanding in so far as it is 'an expression of spontaneity, which is determinative and not, like sense, determinable merely' (B 151); in other words, in so far as it is active. Because it has this twofold aspect imagination can operate directly on the human sensibility and so determine it *a priori*. But how exactly it does this is hard to gather from the text. The discussion in section *26* shows that the point on which Kant wants to focus attention is space and time considered not just as forms of intuition, but 'as themselves intuitions which contain a manifold' (B 160). We think of space and time as if they were objects or pseudo-objects, separately existing 'stretches' within which different things can endure, move or be located, and in so far as we do this are confronted with a problem about their unity. Kant appears to be suggesting, much as he had in the first edition, that over and above the general synthesis of which an account was provided in the first part of his argument, there has to be a further synthesis of the 'pure manifold' of space and time, one which will enable us to take cognisance of stretches of space and time as unitary. He says in a footnote (B 160–1) that his doctrine here is not inconsistent with that stated in the Aesthetic (it is a question of emphasis only), and implies that the synthesis is carried out by the imagination. He does not, however, succeed in this passage in clarifying what imagination possesses (and mere understanding lacks) which enables it to cope successfully with this task.

Later it emerges that it is the power to schematise. Kant's doctrine of Schematism will be discussed at length in a separate section (section 13); for the moment all that need be said is that schemata (more properly, transcendental schemata) are described as constituting 'the universal condition under which alone the category can be applied to any object' (B 179/A 140), and are thought of as being at once 'void of all empirical content' and yet in a certain way sensible. Schemata are not images and therefore not the product of ordinary 'reproductive' imagination; they are not concepts and so are not produced by the bare understanding. Their function, in essentials, is to do with the application of concepts: they provide palpable clues about how to apply ideas which are of a high degree of abstraction. Hence Kant's attempt to associate them with a special faculty, the 'productive' imagination, and to assign them a separate role in knowledge.

I shall argue in section 13 that the doctrine of schematism, despite certain obvious crudities, is of real philosophical interest. Yet it does little or nothing to help out Kant's final argument in the Deduction. The problem there was to explain the special relevance of the categories to the unification of space and time, and in particular to show why their application involved the faculty of imagination. The chapter on schematism has as its main object to discuss the application of pure concepts, and argues that this is possible only because of the existence of certain 'mediating' representations of which imagination is said to be the source. But it turns out that a transcendental schema is itself a 'determination of time' (B 177/A 138); it turns out further that it is supposed to bear on the application of categories generally, and not on their application exclusively to space and time. It looks from this as if Kant cannot invoke the Schematism chapter to eke out the insufficiencies of his argument at the end of the Deduction. There is certainly a connection between what he says there and what he has to say about schemata. But it is a connection of a general sort, and not one which throws direct light on the problem with which he is there concerned.

§11 *Some Basic Criticisms*

At this point I want to turn from exposition to assessment. I have tried already to show that there are certain criticisms against which Kant can defend himself, and have admitted that there is at least one point at which his argument is unsatisfactory because vague. I now want to consider criticism of a more fundamental kind.

Could it be claimed that Kant's whole argument in the Deduction begs the question? That it does was urged by some of his earliest critics. Kant, they said, purports to reveal the conditions which have to be fulfilled if experience is to be possible. But he understood the term 'experience' in a special way of his own: he took it to mean an orderly experience, in which everything is subject to law. What reason is there to think that all experience must be orderly in this way? Or to put the point in a form which relates more closely to the texts we have summarised, what reason is there to import into the analysis of human cognition the idea of an impersonal subject self which has to do with thinking as it should be, rather than thinking as it is? In his attack on the part of traditional metaphysics known as 'Rational Psychology' Kant wrote:

> We have here what professes to be a science built upon the single proposition 'I think' (B 400/A 342),

and went on to show that the basis was altogether too flimsy to bear the weight put upon it. Might one not argue that the positive doctrines of the *Critique* itself rest on the same basis and are open to doubt just because it is insecure? When Kant says that 'representations' which cannot be correlated with others and so related to the unity of apperception would be for us 'less even than a dream' he does not rule out their occurrence, nor could he if his theory were to retain any plausibility. What can fall within experience must be determined by what does fall within experience; we cannot legislate in advance and resolve that we shall experience only what is intelligible. If we cannot make sense of what turns up, that is a fact we must recognise. We cannot just dismiss it.

Perhaps the first thing to say in Kant's defence here is that he was himself aware of the gulf between theory and fact to which the critics draw attention. As we have seen, he drew a sharp distinction between empirical and pure consciousness, and stressed that connections in the former might well be arbitrary and merely personal. He would have found no difficulty in allowing that the different items in an individual consciousness could be united by similarity and contiguity as well as by causation. But against anyone who said that this was the end of the matter he would insist that coherent and continuing consciousness requires more than that each item should lead on 'naturally' to another. What is required is also that each such item be capable of recognition as belonging to a self-identical self, which means in turn that we have the ability to correlate it with other items and apply to it the same broad conceptual system which is applied to them. The application may fail on any particular occasion: try as we may we may not succeed in finding appropriate terms in which to characterise some individual item. But the lesson to draw from that, for Kant, would be not that after all the unintelligible can happen, but rather that intelligibility must not be measured by the actual conceptual systems at our disposal. The presumption that whatever turns up is intelligible in principle is not affected by the failure to find intelligibility in particular empirical circumstances. Hence what we have to do when the failure occurs is not to sit down in the acceptance of some ultimate mystery, but simply to try again. That this is what we do when these are the circumstances lends a certain empirical confirmation to Kant's theory.

But why should we take at all seriously the supposed self-identical self which represents 'consciousness in general'? Will not the bundle of perceptions, of which each of us from one point of view consists, do duty for purposes of self-identity provided that the conditions Hume specified are fulfilled, namely that there be certain continuities of content ('impressions' giving rise to their corresponding 'ideas', etc.) together with the constant operation of certain uniting principles (similarity and causation)? The first answer is that Kant is not concerned, as Hume evidently was, with empirical self-identity but with something more basic: the ability to say 'I' on different occasions and mean the same thing by it. If this ability were lost I should be without a self at all. Certainly it would not be enough in these circumstances for Hume's requirements to be satisfied, since what is needed is not just that related contents should *occur*, but that they should, or could, be *recognised* as content for the same subject. *I* have to acknowledge that the idea *I* now have is a copy of the impression *I* had yesterday; unless the same 'I' is involved the machinery will not work. It appears from this that Hume's theory presupposes Kant's rather than constitutes an alternative to it. And there is another reason why Kant's view is to be preferred. The unity of apperception, as I have tried to argue, expresses itself naturally in the activity of judgment; to take cognisance of different items as belonging together in a single experience is to see them for what they are and so, in the end, to declare what is going on in the world. To distinguish what is truly or objectively happening from what merely appears to be happening to a particular subject is a fundamental cognitive requirement. Kant accounts for the ability to fulfil this requirement in postulating a pure consciousness as an abstract aspect of every empirical consciousness; he recognises that the human mind, for all the diversity of its experiences, has a certain universal core which can be presumed to be the same in all of us. What the equivalent of this is in rival theories of the Humean type it is difficult to see. Hume allows that what *he* calls 'the imagination' is actuated by principles which are 'permanent, irresistible and universal' (*Treatise*, I iv 4, p. 225 ed. Selby-Bigge), and connects their operation with the ability to separate what is real from what is chimerical. But throughout his long discussion of belief he fails to lay stress on the most important aspect of that subject, namely the claim in belief to state what is true of the world. He thus tries to manage without judgment just as he tries to dispense with the unity of apperception or self-identical subject self. But in both cases it can be argued that he lets in by the back door what he had refused to admit by the front.

A second major objection which needs to be considered argues that Kant on his own terms has proved much less than he thinks. Let it be agreed that there can be no experience without a continuing self-identical subject; let it be allowed further that such a subject would need to take cognisance of its diverse experiences, to recognise them all as its own and in so doing to grasp them in the same conceptual net. If these things are true there is ground for saying that whatever comes up in experience will be thinkable or intelligible. But thinkable or intelligible to what extent? Kant wishes to show that all our intuitional data are necessarily subject to the categories, which are of course *a priori*. But it could well be said that the most he proves is that such data must be subject to concepts *of some sort or other*. To conform to Kant's requirements I certainly need a unified conceptual system. But what ground has he advanced for saying that that system must contain an *a priori* component? If the answer is that he has told a story about the unification of pure intuitions, the comment must be that the story is at once vague and unconvincing. And if he says that there is an internal connection between judgment and categories, we can observe only that the connection is difficult to make out. *Perhaps* it will emerge in the end that the argument of the Metaphysical Deduction is defensible, but in the meantime it would be safer to assume that it is not.

To put the point in a different way: Kant believes that it is necessary that whatever is experienced be conceptualisable. He produces arguments, which I myself find convincing, against those who say that it must be an open question, to be answered in the light of experience, whether it is conceptualisable or not. But though in so doing he proves an *a priori* proposition, it is not one which contains any reference to *a priori* concepts. It is one thing to claim that it is *a priori* certain that whatever occurs will be conceptualisable, another thing altogether to read this as saying that it is certain that whatever occurs will be conceptualisable in ways that can be specified *a priori*. The second of these propositions clearly goes a long way beyond the first. Does Kant anywhere in the Deduction show how to get from the first to the second?

One passage which looks at first sight as if Kant were addressing himself to the question is contained in the first edition. In A 111, at the point where he is giving a 'preliminary explanation of the possibility of categories, as knowledge *a priori*', Kant writes as follows:

> Unity of synthesis according to empirical concepts would be altogether accidental, if these latter were not based on a transcendental ground of unity. Otherwise it would be possible for appearances to crowd in upon the soul, and yet to be such as would never allow of experience. Since connection in accordance with universal and necessary laws would be lacking, all relation of knowledge to objects would fall away. The appearances might, indeed, constitute intuition without thought, but not knowledge; and consequently would be for us as good as nothing.

Closer attention shows, however, that what was troubling Kant was not our question of empirical versus *a priori* concepts, but rather the prior question of the applicability of a conceptual scheme of any sort. The reference to the possibility of wayward or disorderly experiences reveals that the opponent he has in mind is the man who says it is contingent that we can find order of any sort in experience; on these terms, Kant argues, objective knowledge would be impossible. This is simply to repeat the main contention of the Deduction. True, Kant adds that in the circumstances envisaged 'connection in accordance with universal and necessary laws would be lacking', and this looks like a reference to the categories and not just to the general apparatus of the understanding. But if it is meant as such, Kant offers no argument in its support. We have already quoted his own recognition of the fact that to be related to the necessary unity of apperception is not to possess some internal necessity. Kant sees a close connection between the ideas of objectivity and necessity, but justifies it only in the most general way in the passage we have been considering.

Could there be a better justification? It might be said that to operate with empirical concepts would not be enough to ensure objectivity, for what on these terms would prevent each thinker from having a conceptual system of his own? I might make sense of my experience in one set of terms, while you interpret yours in quite another. Each of us draws a distinction between the real and the illusory; each of us is convinced that sense will be found in whatever comes up. The only trouble is that we cannot communicate, and so have no possibility of agreeing on what really is the case. To avoid this difficulty it might be suggested that we must forego absolute liberty in framing conceptual schemes and agree to accept common criteria of what is to count as an admissible concept. Criteria of this kind must be brought to our cognitive activities rather than read out of them, and must hence be *a priori*. The argument would then be that objectivity can be achieved only if we operate with concepts selected according to *a priori* principles, these principles answering to the categories.

If this was Kant's argument in the Deduction, he has presented it very obscurely. But instead of asking if it was, we might ask if it could be. A lot depends here on what force we attach to the phrase 'criteria for admissible concepts'. There is a sense in which we all employ criteria for admissible concepts: we recognise, for instance, that a concept must retain the same, or roughly the same, content from one instance to another; and again that if it applies in this set of circumstances it must apply again in that, provided that we can discover no relevant difference between the two. But these are of course logical requirements; they have to do not with the content of concepts but with their form. They could be acknowledged and observed by different thinkers without that preventing them from developing quite diverse conceptual systems. The criteria we are considering must be far more powerful than that. They must shape our conceptualising activities not merely in a formal way, but in the sense of requiring them to proceed on certain predetermined lines. They must in effect provide a framework inside which we conduct our enquiries, and in so doing specify the general shape of the concepts we are to form. They will, for instance, require that in certain circumstances we always pose causal questions, and so form causal concepts. To describe principles which work like this as criteria for the choice of concepts may be formally correct, but is nonetheless misleading since it suggests something far less ambitious. Confronted with this account we naturally ask if we *have* to pose all our questions inside such a pre-existing framework. And we should not think it a sufficient answer if told a general story about the need for criteria for admissible concepts.

If Kant has a better answer to put forward, it is to be found in the argument already mentioned (see section 8 above) about the need for categories and categorial principles in the constituting of shared experience, experience for a 'mutual us'. There is no doubt that Kant was acutely aware, especially in writing the second edition of the *Critique*, of the distinction between something which is experience merely for me and something which belongs to experience generally, experience which is shared or shareable. It is also clear that the prominence he gave in the second edition to the notion of judgment connects in an important way with this preoccupation. When he talks of 'the possibility of experience', as of course he frequently does in both editions, and says that 'experience depends . . . upon *a priori* principles of its form, that is upon universal rules of unity in the synthesis of appearances' (B 196/A 156–7), the experience he has in mind is what I call shared experience. But if we ask for an *argument* to show that we could not have such experience without the categories, we have to turn to the discussion of individual categorial principles contained in the Analytic of Principles. In the three Analogies of Experience, for instance, Kant tries to show that, without the operation of this or that *a priori* concept, experience would lack features of central importance which we take it to possess, features without which it could hardy count as common experience at all. If he is correct here, a question to which we shall address ourselves in chapter IV, he will have made out an important part of his main contentions in the Analytic. But he will not have provided the general demonstration of the indispensability of categories which was promised in the Transcendental Deduction.

§ 12 *The Categories and Formal Logic*

I turn now to a topic which has been mentioned several times but whose discussion has so far been deliberately postponed: that of the relation between categories and judgment. In the passage entitled 'The Clue to the Discovery of all pure Concepts of the Understanding' and commonly known as the 'Metaphysical Deduction' (a phrase of Kant's own : B 159), Kant argued that formal logic could be used as a clue in the construction of a complete table of categories. Logicians were in possession of a complete list of all possible forms of judgment, and forms of judgment served to give unity at once to 'the various representations in a judgment' and to 'the mere synthesis of various representations in an intuition' (B 104–5/A 79). Hence (B 105/A 79)

> there arise precisely the same number of pure concepts of the understanding which apply *a priori* to objects of intuition in general, as . . . there have been found to be logical functions in all possible judgments. For these functions specify the understanding completely, and yield an exhaustive inventory of its powers.

The first problem here concerns Kant's claims about formal logic, a science which, he thought (A viii), had been brought to completion by Aristotle. I shall not discuss this view, but rather Kant's claim to be in possession of a complete list of forms of judgment. The list is set out in B 95/A 70, and is followed by a long disquisition on its construction. What makes this curious is that it emerges from the text that Kant was not simply reproducing logical doctrines, but tinkering with them for his own purposes. He announces, for example, that though logicians divide judgments under the head of Quantity into universal and particular, and under that of Quality into affirmative and negative, a third class can be distinguished in each case. Singular judgments deserve a separate place 'in a complete table of the moments of thought in general' (B 96/A 71), infinite judgments cannot be passed over in a 'transcendental table of all moments of thought in judgments' (B 98/A 73). If straightforward logical doctrines have to be doctored in this way to suit Kant's purposes one is left asking whether his Table of Judgments can be said to belong to formal logic at all.

Next we must enquire into the alleged parallel between giving unity to representations in a judgment and performing the same act on the synthesis of representations in an intuition. Both are to say the least obscure. Behind what Kant says here about judgment there lies a peculiar doctrine of concepts, according to which the forming of concepts results in, perhaps even consists in, the bringing of many otherwise diverse particulars together. Concepts, as Kant puts it in his opaque way, 'rest on functions' and 'by "function" I mean the unity of the act of bringing various representations under one common representation' (B 93/A 68). A concept on this account is something like a class of particulars. Further, the only thing we can do with concepts, if Kant is to be believed, is use them in judgment: concepts are essentially 'predicates of possible judgments' (B 94/A 69). When a concept is used in a judgment 'instead of an immediate representation, a higher representation, which comprises the immediate representation and various others, is used in knowing the object, and thereby much possible knowledge is collected into one' (B 94/A 69). Accordingly, 'all judgments are functions of unity among our representations', and to judge is essentially to unify.

But even if this is correct it is hard to see what it has to do with giving unity to the synthesis of representations in an intuition. We unify various items in an intuition in so far as we take cognisance of them and bring them under some connected description; the activity concerned results in a judgment. But the kind of unity here involved is surely quite different from that which Kant associates with forming and linking concepts. If I say 'Hymn books are black' I connect together one lot of diverse things under the heading of 'hymn book' and an even wider group under the heading of 'black', and I declare that whatever falls in the first group falls also in the second. And no doubt many peculiar connections are established in this way, representations of many diverse kinds being collected under the two heads. But the 'analytical unity' (B 105/A 79) which belongs to such representations is not at all like the 'synthetic unity' which is involved when we identify an object on the strength of its various appearances. If after deliberation on the available evidence I say 'It's a hymn book' or 'It's a fast car coming' I doubtless connect together a variety of different representations, of colour, shape, feel, smell, sound, among others. But I connect them not as identical instances of the same concept, but as different manifestations of the same continuing thing. The two operations are totally distinct, and to speak of the 'same function' (B 104/A 79) as being involved in both is quite mistaken.

Kant's attempt to enlist the aid of formal logic in order to give content to his own transcendental logic runs up against major difficulties of principle, as I argued in an earlier discussion (*Reason and Experience*, ch. VIII). Formal logic classifies forms of judgment, and judgment bulks large in transcendental logic. But Kant himself says (B 140–1) that there are defects in the account which logicians give of judgment, namely that it is the representation of a relation between two concepts, and proposes instead his own theory that a judgment is 'nothing but the manner in which given cognitions are brought to the objective unity of apperception' (B 141). Judgment is primarily and properly assertion or denial of what is the case. The question we have to ask at this point is whether formal logicians think of judgment in this manner, in so far as they think of judgment at all. And the answer would seem to be that, in the terminology of formal logic, a judgment is not so much an actual as a possible assertion; it is a proposition which can be asserted or denied, rather than an attempted declaration of what is the case. It is instructive in this connection to notice that some symbolic logicians have made use of a special sign for assertion, which they said should be prefixed to any formula that was to be taken as true (see Eaton, *General Logic*, p. 373). This would indicate that assertion is an activity performed on propositions, and not something which belongs intrinsically to propositions as such. But if this is correct no amount of scrutiny of the forms of propositions is going to throw light on what is involved in claims to objective truth. If this is agreed Kant's argument in the Metaphysical Deduction cannot of its nature succeed.

What is basically the same point can be put even more strongly. Formal logic may be said to concern itself with the broadest of all forms of possibility, namely logical possibility: it lays down rules to which any thought-content that is to be minimally coherent must conform. The thinking in which the transcendental logician is interested must of course abide by these rules. But its importance lies not in this but in its claim to fix the bounds of a different kind of possibility altogether, what Kant calls 'real' possibility. The latter is explained by Kant (B 265/A 218) as being agreement with the formal conditions of experience, i.e. with the *a priori* forms of intuition and the categories. Many things which are *logically* possible are not *really* possible because they are not in accord with these necessary conditions of experience; Kant mentions precognition and telepathy as instances (B 270/A 222), though he does not indicate how precisely they fail to conform (see further section 27 below). What is logically but not really possible is thinkable in the broadest sense of the term, but not thinkable as fact; possibilities of this kind could not belong to the structure of an objective world. Kant in fact may be said to distinguish three kinds of possibility: logical possibility, which is determined by the laws of formal logic; real possibility, which is determined by the results of transcendental philosophy; finally, empirical possibility, which is determined by the results of empirical science. Whatever is empirically possible must be both really and logically possible; whatever is really possible must be logically possible But the sphere of logical possibility is determined by formal logic alone; it is not restricted by considerations of what is found in fact, or even of what could be found in fact, logical coherence aside. It follows that the study of which it is the central notion cannot throw any light on thinking about matter of fact and existence. That there can be no inference from logic to fact is universally acknowledged. What needs to be added to this is that by the same token there can be no inference from logic to what might be called the form of facts. It is with the latter that Kant's philosophy is primarily concerned; from one point of view it could be characterised as an essay in real and unreal possibilities. But if this is the case any pretence that formal logic could offer a clue to transcendental logic must surely be mistaken.

Presented with this argument Kant might counter by asking where we can find a clue to the identity of the categories if we do not find it in logic. The categories as he sees them are pure intellectual concepts with nothing empirical about them; they spring from the nature of the intellect itself. And the fundamental operations of the intellect, those whose authenticity is least in doubt, are logical in the narrow sense of the term: the intellect is at the lowest estimate a logical instrument, concerned with the formation, classification and formal connecting of concepts and propositions. That pure intellectual concepts should be rooted in these operations sounds on the face of things not unreasonable. But how could they be so rooted if they are to perform the functions Kant proposes for them, namely to regulate thought about an objective world? Thought of this kind goes far beyond the bounds of the merely logically possible, and is significant just in so far as it does. Or if it is insisted that their roots must lie in logic, what importance if any attaches to that claim? It is interesting in this connection to observe that in practice Kant lays very little stress on what he regards as the purely logical component in the categories; it is the schema which at once 'restricts' and 'realises' them which attracts his main attention (see B 187/A 147 and section 13 below). That the category of cause is rooted in the logical notion of ground and consequent is less significant than that its schema is regular succession. One wonders, indeed, how much would be lost if all mention of the purely logical component were dropped, though this is a question which cannot be discussed now.

Kant several times complains that Aristotle, who invented the term 'category', made his list of categories in a wholly haphazard manner: he 'merely picked them up as they came his way' (B 107/A 81). Against this he wants to claim as a merit for his own list that it is constructed on a principle. His attitude here connects with the wider claim that transcendental philosophy is an *a priori* science and as such must be capable of being brought to completion at a stroke: it is not a study in which we can expect fresh discoveries as we can in the investigation of nature. But is transcendental philosophy an *a priori* science? If it is we must offer some account of its first principles, showing how reason can establish them on the basis of insight into its own nature. It cannot be said that Kant even begins to provide such an account. Indeed, as I shall argue later (section 42), it looks as if the only way to reconcile the existence of Kant's philosophy with the principles it propounds is to make out that its fundamental propositions are empirical. If this is so, the problem which exercised Kant himself, of finding a principle through which to constitute a complete list of the categories, may well turn out to be unreal. We can see why Kant in his own terms was obsessed with this problem, and struggled with such determination to solve it. But we need not go along with his solution, nor need abandoning it mean giving up anything of real importance in his philosophy. The value of the *Critique of Pure Reason* can after all lie in its detail rather than in the principles by which its detailed results are alleged to be reached.

To sum up the conclusions so far suggested about the argument of the Analytic: the case presented in the Transcendental Deduction, particularly in the second edition version, is strong in insisting on the general connection between having a coherent and continuing self and inhabiting an orderly world. The story about the unity of apperception, the activity of judgment and the imposition of concepts on the material of the senses is sound and well argued. The further suggestion that we could not make claims about what is objectively the case unless we employed not merely concepts, but also *a priori* concepts, is less well supported by argument on Kant's part. Some sort of ground in its favour may be found in the reflection that common or shared experience would not be possible unless there were agreed *a priori* criteria for choosing empirical concepts. But this idea is not worked out by Kant himself, nor is it clear that he had it in mind when he spoke of categories. He himself frequently connects the need for categories with the need to unify the pure manifolds of space and time, but it is difficult to make immediate sense of this doctrine. And though Kant is right to insist on the great importance of judgment for the matters of which he is treating, his pretence that there is a special connnection between forms of judgment and categories is entirely hollow. Even if we have to say that each category contains a purely logical component, that will not be the most important, and perhaps not even an important, thing about it.

§ 13 *The Categories and their Schemata*
Before going on to consider Kant's own conclusions from his arguments it will be convenient to investigate his doctrine of Schematism. The brief chapter on Schematism, one of the most difficult in the

whole *Critique*, is placed at the beginning of the Analytic of Principles and officially belongs to what Kant calls the 'Transcendental Doctrine of Judgment', the account of the application of the categories in the characterisation of human experience. The transcendental schema, as already briefly indicated, is a condition under which the pure category gets application; the effect of using it, as was mentioned in the previous section, is at once to restrict the significance of the category and at the same time to ensure that it is not an empty thought. The doctrine of Schematism is of immense importance for the development of the rest of the Analytic. But it also points back as well as forwards, carrying on naturally from the Transcendental Deduction, as I shall now try to show.

What problem, or problems, is Kant trying to solve in the Schematism chapter? His own initial statement on the subject presents it as a problem about the subsumption of cases or instances under concepts. In all such subsumptions, he says (B 170/A 137), a certain condition must be fulfilled: 'the representation of the object must be *homogeneous* with the concept; in other words, the concept must contain something which is represented in the object that is to be subsumed under it'. The homogeneity here demanded is between what is thought in the concept on the one hand and intuited in the instance on the other: for successful subsumption to take place we have to see a correspondence between the one and the other. Kant supposes that there is no difficulty in meeting this condition in the case of empirical concepts and intuitions (he should clearly have thought more about scientific concepts in this connection); for him trouble arises only when we move to pure concepts of the understanding. The latter, as we have just seen, are of their nature entirely distinct from the data of the senses; they are not abstracted from the given, but on the contrary spring from the inner resources of the intellect itself. This being so, a question arises about how any intuitions can be properly subsumed under them. How can concepts which answer this description ever gain application, seeing that what they apply to comes from a wholly heterogeneous source? May it not be, indeed, that they apply to nothing, and are thus essentially without significance?

Kant's answer to his own question is that the categories, in contradistinction to certain other kinds of *a priori* concepts (the concept of a monad, for instance), can gain application in experience thanks to the existence of a 'third thing', the transcendental schema, which is at once intellectual and sensible and acts as a 'mediating representation' linking what at first appeared to be totally distinct spheres. To put the point crudely, the schema is a counterpart of the pure category, like the latter in being universal but unlike it in being capable of presentation in intuition. We can *perceive* what is meant by the schema, and since the schema represents the pure category, that means that we can understand what is intended by the category and so find application for it. The pure categories are not, as seemed possible, mere *entia rationis*, but have a function in genuine enquiry. But to show how they have this function is also to show the limits of their effective use. It is only when used in conjunction with schemata that they have any proper application.

The terms in which Kant presents his problem indicate clearly its relationship to analogous questions asked by other philosophers before and since his time. The word 'schematism' is peculiar to Kant, but the general idea that *a priori* concepts must show their credentials or be dismissed as insignificant is shared by most if not all empiricists. When Hume asked his key question, 'From what impression was that idea derived?' he took for granted that an idea which has no empirical counterpart is one which need not be taken seriously. Thus the idea of substance was an 'unintelligible chimera' (*Treatise*, I iv 3, p. 222 SB) because those who used it could not point to anything in the world which just was substance as, Hume thought, those who used the idea of blue could point to something that just was blue. As Locke had said, 'substance' stands for 'the supposed, but unknown, support of those qualities we find existing'; when we ask ourselves precisely what this is we find ourselves murmuring that it is something we know not what (Locke, *Essay* II xxiii 2). Kant is less absolute in his demands than Hume or Locke; he is prepared to allow that an *a priori* concept can have a meaningful use despite being wholly heterogeneous with the intuitions on which it is brought to bear. But he nevertheless insists in true empiricist fashion that concept and instance must have something in common if the concept is to be regarded as respectable. So much so, indeed, that a modern philosopher might suggest that problem and solution alike are unacceptable just because Kant, like Hume, misconceives the nature of concepts, assimilating them too closely to images and failing in consequence to see that, even when they are empirical, they and their instances cannot literally have anything in common.

I have some sympathy with this criticism, but not enough to take it as ruling out of court Kant's whole enterprise in the Schematism chapter. To possess a concept is to possess a capacity rather than contemplate an entity; questions which presuppose that instances can resemble concepts are accordingly absurd. But it is not absurd to ask what circumstances have to obtain if a concept is to get application; it is not absurd again to suppose that the content of the concept must determine what these circumstances are. If the concept is such that its content has nothing to do with the empirically given, there will be a real question about how anything in the given can demand its application. We shall be faced, in fact, with Kant's old problem about the objective reference of *a priori* ideas. This is the problem that Kant is struggling with in the pages under consideration, as it was in the Transcendental Deduction. Indeed, this is what explains the evident continuity of the two sections, despite the formal separation between them (their inclusion in separate 'books') in Kant's text.

Kant's problem, I shall hence assume, is at least philosophically respectable. What about his solution? He says (B 184/A 145) that 'the schema of each category contains and makes capable of representation only a determination of time', and again (same reference) that schemata are 'nothing but *a priori* determinations of time in accordance with rules'. That they have to do with time is very important for Kant, since time is at once the *a priori* form of inner sense and therefore of all experience and, as an intuition, something which of its nature belongs to sensibility. Time can be said to mediate between pure concepts on the one hand and the empirically given on the other. As for 'determinations of time', we can to some extent gather what Kant meant by that obscure expression if we concentrate on what he says about particular categories. The schema of cause is described (B 183/A 144) as 'the real, upon which, whenever posited, something else always follows', in plainer words invariable succession. The schema of substance is said to be 'permanence of the real in time' (B 183/A 143). The schema of necessity is given as 'existence of an object at all times' (B 184/A 145). The schema of quantity is said to be number, a concept which Kant connected with numbering and therefore with 'the generation (synthesis) of time itself in the successive apprehension of an object' (B 182/A 142, B 184/A 145).

It appears from this as if a 'determination of time' is a condition or state of affairs, or perhaps a feature of things, which is characterisable in temporal terms, and whose presence is readily detectable by empirical means. Because it has this palpable quality, and because its own occurrence is alleged to be determined by a rule, it can both represent the pure concept, giving it empirical embodiment, and facilitate its application in the concrete. Without the schema we may possess the pure concept, but simply not know what to do with it.

With the schema, or rather with its occurrence in the concrete, we have what may be described as a sure sign of the concept's being applicable. Schemata thus serve to bring down to earth concepts which in themselves are wholly remote from sense and to give them real employment, though in so doing they also restrict the range of their application. Thus the pure concept of ground and consequent, whose content is narrowly logical, is transformed into the useful concept of cause, thanks to its association with the schema *invariable succession*. Similarly the pure concept of Inherence and Subsistence becomes the empirically usable concept of substance because of its connection with the schema *permanence of the real in time*. We know how to apply the categories in their schematised form, or when taken along with their schemata. But the pure categories are such that we can make no determinate use of them.

The main internal difficulty in this ingenious theory lies in the nature of the relationship supposed to hold between pure category and schema. I have spoken of the schema as embodying the category in what may be described as phenomenal form, as representing it, as associated with it and as serving as a sign of its applicability. It hardly seems likely on the face of things that these descriptions are all compatible, yet there is warrant for each of them in Kant's text. Mostly he speaks as if category and schema were sharply separate, if only because the first is an object of thought and the second an object of intuition, a particular or particular state of affairs. But he says in the final paragraph of the Schematism chapter (B 186/A 146) that 'the schema is, properly, only the phenomenon, or sensible concept, of an object in agreement with the category', and adds some words in Latin which claim that *number* is phenomenal quantity, *sensation* phenomenal reality, *the permanent* phenomenal substance, *eternity* phenomenal necessity. The implication here would seem to be that the schema is itself a concept, one in fact which can be *substituted* for the pure category or at least can be taken as its embodiment or partial embodiment. Whether we interpret the schema in this way or not, Kant must show that it has some internal connection with the category with which it is associated; it cannot be just a brute fact that invariable succession is the schema of ground and consequent, that permanence of the real in time is the schema of Inherence and Subsistence, and so on. But he makes little or no attempt to show how the connection works out. All too often he forgets in practice about the pure category and works with what commentators call the 'schematised category', a term not found in Kant himself but which seems to denote the category understood in terms of the schema. He retains the idea of the pure category for theoretical purposes (he needs it in connection with his unsatisfactory doctrine of the 'thinking' of things in themselves; see section 15 below), but it plays no real part in his account of human cognition.

Kant's failure to produce a defensible view of the relationship of category and schema mars his theory but does not destroy it altogether. He deserves credit at least for seeing that someone who believes in pure intellectual concepts must show how they get application; in this respect what he says constitutes a substantial advance over all previous writers. The doctrine of schematism played an important part both in giving body to 'metaphysics in its first part', the metaphysics of experience in which Kant himself believed, and in discrediting the claims to knowledge of God, the soul, and the world as a whole, made by traditional metaphysicians. It achieved the first result by demonstrating that *a priori* concepts can, despite first appearances, be brought to bear on the data of the senses, provided that a certain condition is fulfilled; it achieved the second by pointing out that nothing comparable could be found when we moved to the supposed metaphysical sciences of Rational Psychology, Rational Cosmology and Natural Theology. The ideas handled by those disciplines were ideas of reason, and ideas of reason were of their nature incapable of schematisation. True, we could provide even in their case something which Kant called (B 693/A 665) 'an analogon of a schema of sensibility': we could find empirically intuitable situations which could serve as models by reference to which the ideas in question became comprehensible, and so 'present' such concepts in symbolic form (see particularly *Critique of Judgment*, section 59). Thus the idea of God is strictly incapable of being schematised, but we can nevertheless make partial sense of it for certain purposes by making a father's relationship to his children the symbol of God's relationship to the world. The qualification 'for certain purposes' is, however, all-important here. The purposes which Kant had in mind in putting his doctrine forward were primarily practical; the idea of God, as he saw it, belonged properly not to physics, or even metaphysics, but to ethics (*Critique of Practical Reason*, Berlin edition, V 138). In moral contexts the idea of God could come alive by being interpreted as that of a loving father, a just judge or a wise lawgiver. But to make it practically real in this fashion is not to provide knowledge of God in the strict sense of the term (see further sections 39–40 below).

We must also recognise the insight as well as the ingenuity Kant shows in assigning schemata to particular categories. His explication

of the concept of substance in terms of the permanent which underlies change is especially noteworthy, for here Kant fixes on a concept
which undoubtedly plays, or has played, a major role in everyday
and scientific thought, and which also figured prominently in crucial
metaphysical discussions, e.g. those of the pre-Socratics. Kant could
hardly pretend that the whole force of the metaphysical concept of
substance was carried over into its schema, but he could say that
whatever sense there was in the former was represented in the
latter. Similarly he might claim, in his account of the schema of
cause, to have done justice to Hume without going the whole way
with him. We shall have to examine later how far these claims are
justified (below, sections 24.–5). But the very fact that the claims
are worth discussing shows that the theory of schematism was not,
as some critics pretend, a production of pure pedantry, but a serious
attempt to solve a serious philosophical problem.

Was Kant wise to argue that schemata are transcendental
determinations of *time*? He did so because of a circumstance which
has so far been passed over in silence, that time differs from space in
being the universal form of human intuition. Whatever falls within
sense-experience must, as it were, wear the form of time, whereas
only the data of the external senses wear the form of space. To have
connected schemata with space would thus have had the undesirable
consequence of making the categories inapplicable in circumstances
where we might wish to apply them, e.g. to the phenomena of the
self. But though this explains why Kant argued as he did, it does not
fully justify his procedure, if only because of doubts he developed
about separating the perception of time from the perception of space.
In the Aesthetic he spoke, in what may be described as the orthodox
philosophical way, of the mind being presented with two distinct
manifolds of sense, one that of the external senses, the other that of
'inner sense'. Everything which fell within outer sense fell also
within inner sense, but the reverse was by no means true. The
difficulty here was to know what was left over when the data of the
external senses were abstracted from inner sense, and it was a
difficulty which Kant found harder to deal with the more he thought
about it. He was clear that thoughts, feelings and desires are not
spatially located, and yet realised that when we think of them as
occurring in succession or as simultaneous we make use of a spatial
analogy to give body to our concept of time. In arguing against
vulgar idealism he insisted that we can make sense of mental
happenings only against a background which is physical and therefore spatial. And in discussing the principles of substance and

reciprocity he talked ostensibly about modes of time, but in practice about spatial conditions as well.

In a passage added in the second edition of the *Critique* (B 291) Kant said that to demonstrate the objective reality of the categories 'we need, not merely intuitions, but intuitions that are in all cases outer intuitions'. He went on to explain how this worked out in the case of the categories of relation, substance, cause and reciprocity. The permanence associated with substance is permanence of matter. Causality involves alteration, a 'combination of contradictorily opposed determinations in the existence of one and the same thing' (B 291), which is incomprehensible without intuition. The intuition required is that of 'the movement of a point in space'. Inner alterations become intelligible only when we represent time as a line. Lastly, reciprocity can be understood only if we think of it as involving bodies interacting in space. One reason why Kant dismissed telepathy as not really possible was because it went counter to spatial requirements, ignoring for example the principle that the further two bodies were from each other the less mutual influence they could exert.

These passages suggest that Kant might have recast the doctrine of schematism to make schemata determinations (aspects, conditions) of space instead of, or perhaps as well as, time. But if he ever had this idea he did not carry it out. Officially he connects schemata with time and not at all with space, and we must make what we can of his views on this basis (see further section 28).

§ 14 *Schematism and the Imagination*

What has schematism to do with 'the imagination'? To answer this question we have to consider bits of the doctrine which have so far been left out of account. Up to this point I have proceeded as Kant does at the beginning of the Schematism chapter, where he writes as if the problem which bothers him arises only for *a priori* concepts. It is pure concepts of the understanding that need to be schematised if they are to possess sense and significance. But it turns out as Kant goes on that schemata are involved in the use of other concepts as well. It also turns out that, in relation to these concepts at least, a schema is not so much an entity as a procedure, a procedure which has to do with the production of images and therefore belongs to the imagination.

Let me try to indicate how this works out in the cases of empirical concepts and 'pure sensible', i.e. mathematical, concepts. Kant distinguishes three things in each case: the concept proper, the image and the schema. His remarks about the three are maddeningly imprecise, but the main thought which underlies them is not in doubt. If I possess the bare concept of 'dog' or 'triangle' (Kant's own examples) I can frame intelligible sentences containing the corresponding words, offer explanations of the meaning of the terms ('A dog is a four-footed animal') and perhaps even define them formally. But I may be able to do all this without being able to recognise a dog or a triangle, like an examination candidate who knows what inflation is but cannot tell if inflation is now raging in Bulgaria. Similarly if I have in my mind an image of a dog or a triangle my mastery of the relevant idea is far from complete. I know that anything that looks like this is a dog, and that anything that looks like that is a triangle, but I know nothing about the range of cases to which these concepts apply. The dog in my mind's eye is a dachshund; how on the strength of this am I to know that my neighbour's golden retriever is also a dog? To be able to wield the concept with full force I need (a) the verbal skills of the man who possesses the bare concept, and (b) the power to envisage a repre- sentative range of circumstances in which the concept applies. I must know what it would be like for the concept to have instances, and in this connection it will not do if I can picture to myself a single instance only. In Kant's language I need the schema as well as the image.

Kant describes this 'schematism of our understanding' as 'an art concealed in the depths of the human soul' (B 180/A 141). It is certainly a fundamental human ability, without which thought would be useless, or at least have no grip on the world. Was Kant right to ascribe it to imagination? Not in so far as he thought the envisaging concerned must result in the occurrence of images. When I ask myself if I know what a porcupine is I try to form a picture in my mind's eye, that is, to call up an image. But I might equally well, if I had the necessary skill, try to draw one or produce a model in plasticine. As Wittgenstein pointed out, images are only one kind of thing which can serve as an instance. The important point in Kant's theory, however, is not his connection of schemata with images, but his insistence on ability to envisage a range of cases. Envisaging here is simply thinking what it would be like, and that might be done without any use of images. What is less clear is whether it could be done without any appeal to the senses. My inclination is to say that it could not, since that would involve pro- ceeding in terms of pure universals, and to that extent to uphold Kant's claim that this important aspect of human thinking involves something more than the bare intellect.

Kant's general theory of schemata, as just explained, seems to me not only highly ingenious but also substantially correct. Its philosophical importance is shown by its obvious relevance to traditional discussions about abstract ideas. The question is, however, how it relates to what he says about transcendental schemata. After explaining that

> the schema of sensible concepts, such as of figures in space, is a product and, as it were, a monogram, of pure *a priori* imagination, through which, and in accordance with which, images themselves first become possible

Kant adds the words

> On the other hand, the schema of a pure concept of the understanding can never be brought into any image whatsoever (B 181/A 141–2).

I take this to imply that we cannot literally envisage the circumstances in which such a concept would apply, and so cannot have in mind a range of possible instances of the concept. Instead, what Kant offers us is the transcendental schema, a condition or state of affairs which is invariant whenever the concept is used. The transcendental schema can perform its task thanks to the fact that it is palpable: there is a sense in which we can *see* regular succession as we could never see ground and consequent. This means that this type of schema too must be the product of a faculty other than the intellect. But the case for connecting it with the imagination, and particularly with what Kant calls the 'productive' as opposed to the 'reproductive' imagination, is really very weak.

What Kant shows in this part of his work is, first, that you cannot be said to possess a concept in the full sense of the term unless, in addition to being able to account for it in terms of other concepts, you know how and in what circumstances to apply it, a process which involves having the power to envisage a range of possible instances. This doctrine is quite general, and could stand in independence of the rest of Kant's philosophy. Secondly, Kant shows how this general feature of the human mastery of concepts presents a special problem in the case of pure concepts of the understanding, which are supposed to originate in the intellect and whose application to the material of experience is accordingly dubious from the first. Kant proposes to solve this problem by arguing that such concepts can get application thanks to their association with a special 'restricting condition' (B 186/A 146), the transcendental schema, which 'realises' them but at the same time limits them 'to conditions which . . . are due to sensibility' (ibid.). Because of the way in which he first set up his problem, with its strong reliance on faculty psychology and artificial talk about the heterogeneity of pure concepts and intuitions, Kant presents the transcendental schema as a 'mediating representation' and argues that it is the product of imagination, the faculty which bridges the gap between sense and understanding. We can perhaps just stomach the description of the schema as a 'mediating representation', though it is by no means easy to square it with everything Kant says on the subject (e.g. 'It is simply the pure synthesis . . . to which the category gives expression': B 181/A 142). But there is no serious reason for connecting schemata of this sort with the imagination. They would be unintelligible to a pure intellect, but that is only to say that they have something to do with sensibility, or belong to a mind whose intuitions are sense-intuitions.

Could Kant have written the Analytic without invoking the imagination, or without invoking it in any serious way? It would certainly be necessary to rewrite the entire *Critique* if the present references to imagination were to be excised. The trichotomy *understanding, imagination, sense* is one which fits very nicely some of Kant's basic assumptions: his belief in the fundamental distinctness of thoughts and intuitions as regards their origins; his conviction that in the human case thoughts without intuitions are empty and intuitions without concepts blind; his inclination despite this to take the pretensions of metaphysicians with total seriousness, as if it were only by accident that we could not have intellectual apprehension of true reality. By distinguishing understanding from imagination Kant was able to suggest that the intellect has two sides, one where it co-operates with the senses, the other where it tries to proceed on its own. In general, it is the first of these that he emphasises: the understanding as it actually operates in human consciousness goes hand in hand with the imagination and is powerless without it. As Kant put it in the first edition Deduction (A 119), the understanding so considered *is* 'the unity of apperception in relation to the synthesis of the imagination'. But Kant was unwilling to sink the understanding in the imagination as Hume had done, partly because he thought that imagination, though 'indispensable', was also 'blind' (B 103/A 78)— it needed rules to guide it, and not just Humean 'habits'—, partly because he believed it necessary to reserve to the intellect powers which it might exercise in independence of the senses. Although intellectual intuition was ruled out for human beings and with it knowledge of anything that lay beyond possible experience, it was nevertheless within their power to form the idea of purely intelligible objects, thanks to their possession of pure concepts of understanding. And though this ability was of no account when knowledge was in question, it could be and was of importance in connection with men's practical activities.

Readers who do not share Kant's wider philosophical preoccupations are not likely to feel much sympathy with this overall set-up: they will see the Kantian faculty of imagination as an intellectual odd-job man, whose functions can and should be assigned to members of the permanent staff. Instead of dissolving understanding in imagination, we should get rid of the latter (except as the faculty of reproduction) by dividing its powers between the senses and the intellect. Could we do this without remainder? To answer this question we should consider what would be the situation of a being which possessed senses, memory and intellect, but was without imagination. Presumably such a being would not be able to form any images other than memory images; its visualising powers would be severely limited. A defect of that kind might seem comparatively trivial, seeing that there are many able people who are poor visualisers. But a being so described would suffer from a further, more serious, disadvantage: it would not be able to 'think in absence'. It could certainly work out the consequences of any ideas it took into consideration or of any premises it accepted; it might (though this is more controversial) be able to characterise any thing or situation of which it was immediately aware through the senses. But could it plan a course of action, or take avoiding action when in danger? For both of these it would have to ask itself what would be the case if such-and-such a state of affairs were to obtain, and this process would involve envisaging, though not necessarily visualising, particular situations. A being deprived of imagination could not envisage anything, and that being so imagination is an indispensable and irreducible factor in human thinking.

This demonstration, if demonstration it is, will not give Kant all he wants to claim for imagination in this part of his work. It will lend support to, and indeed underwrite, his general theory of schematism, but it will not in itself be enough to give respectability to the story about transcendental schemata, still less to the account of the imagination's synthetic activities. The idea of a triple synthesis, laboriously worked out by Kant in the 'provisional exposition' of the first edition and drawn on lovingly in the 'systematic' account which follows, cannot be authenticated by showing that, in some sense, imagination is a respectable faculty and not a monster of Kant's private devising. The suspicion which we feel when we read these pages, a suspicion generated by the thought that Kant must see himself here as opening to view the innermost recesses of the mind, which are not accessible to the mere empirical enquirer, is not in the least dissipated by the considerations advanced in the last paragraph. But they do at any rate show that talk about the imagination in an epistemological context is not all necessarily idle.

§ 15 *Categories and the Thought of the Supersensible*

We must now consider some consequences which Kant draws from the Deduction and the Schematism chapter. One such consequence is brought out clearly at the very end of the latter passage, where Kant reiterates his view that the only objects categories can determine are objects of possible experience. We might suppose, he says (B 186/A 146–7), that if we dispense with the restricting condition represented by the schema, the scope of the concept concerned would be extended.

> Arguing from this assumed fact, we conclude that the categories in their pure significance, apart from all conditions of sensibility, ought to apply to things in general, *as they are*, and not, like the schemata, represent them only *as they appear*.

But the assumption is not warranted and the conclusion groundless. The pure concepts of the understanding, considered apart from their schemata, have only a 'logical' meaning; they are, as it were, bare forms awaiting application to given data, yet such as to contain no indication of how or to what they are to be applied. As Kant explains over a particular instance (B 186–7/A 147):

> Substance . . . when the sensible determination of permanence is omitted, would mean simply a something which can be thought only as subject, never as a predicate of something else. Such a representation I can put to no use, for it tells me nothing as to the nature of that which is thus to be viewed as a primary subject.

The categories in their pure (unschematised) form are thus 'merely functions of the understanding for concepts'; they convey no knowledge, or even any determinate thought. They are empty abstractions rather than meaningful ideas, and as such must be taken as wholly lacking in cognitive significance.

Behind these and similar remarks (compare in particular sections *22* and *23* of the second edition Deduction) lies Kant's ongoing polemic against speculative metaphysics. Metaphysicians as Kant saw them sought to arrive at indisputable knowledge of the essential nature of things, using methods which were purely intellectual. They claimed ability to pronounce on the properties of things in general, and what gave substance to their claim was the fact that the human intellect was undoubtedly equipped with concepts of its own, concepts which were in no wise derived from experience. But though it was true to say that such concepts did indeed spring from a source which was purely intellectual, the construction put upon them by metaphysicians was radically mistaken. It was only when taken along with their schemata that concepts of this kind could claim to be fully meaningful, or be brought in relation to real objects. The pronouncements of metaphysicians (or at least of this type of metaphysician) thus turned out to be essentially empty: they failed to say anything determinate. Knowledge of things in general, of the kind promised in traditional metaphysics, was an impossibility. The only knowledge we could hope for was knowledge of objects of experience, that is of things as they appear.

Let us take this case a little further. In section *23* of the second edition Deduction Kant says that pure concepts of the understanding, unlike space and time, 'extend to objects of intuition in general, be the intuition like or unlike ours, if only it be sensible and not intellectual' (B 148). They belong in other words to discursive consciousness as such, not just to human consciousness. But this circumstance does not open up to us prospects of wider knowledge. Taken apart from any determinate form of intuition, concepts of this nature are nothing but empty forms of thought, without objective reality. To get 'body and meaning' (B 149) they have to be brought to bear on intuitions, and the only type of intuition on which we know they can be brought to bear is '*our* sensible and empirical intuition' (ibid.).

Kant then considers the possibility that they might apply to the objects of a non-sensible intuition. About such supposed objects we could make certain negative pronouncements: that they do not occupy space nor endure through time, that change in the form of succession of diverse states is not found in them, and so on. But here all we are doing is making explicit what is involved in the notion of an object of non-sensible intuition; we are not even showing that such objects are real possibilities. In what terms should we think of them if they were? One thing is clear, and that is that 'to such a something not a single one of the categories could be applied' (B 149). The reason is once more that, when taken apart from its corresponding schema, the category is too general in its content and too uncertain in its application to function as a specific idea. Given only the pure categories we could say nothing definite about the objects we were seeking to characterise.

After all this it is surprising, to say the least, to find Kant maintaining that though the pure categories are useless for *knowledge* of things in themselves, they can nevertheless be used to '*think*' them. This doctrine is made explicit in the second edition of the *Critique*, apparently because of the positivist interpretation put by some readers on the conclusions of the first edition (see B 166 note). What lies beyond possible experience—in fact, God and the soul—also lies beyond human knowledge. But that does not mean that it is wholly without significance. The concept of a reality of this sort is a perfectly coherent one; it could very well have value, though not necessarily cognitive value. In the second edition preface (B xxvi and note) Kant seems to be claiming that it is indispensable even from the cognitive point of view: in order to characterise the things we know as 'appearances' we have to have the concept of that which is not appearance. Elsewhere he argues that the point of forming the concept is practical: reason can be used not only to determine objects, with a view to knowledge, but also to determine the will, with a view to action (B 166 note). There are, however, grave difficulties in both versions of the theory.

The problems of the first are recognised by Kant himself in a candid passage added in the second edition to the chapter on Phenomena and Noumena. The understanding, we read there (B 306–7),

> when it entitles an object in a ((certain)) relation mere phenomenon, at the same time forms, apart from that relation, a representation of an *object in itself*, and so comes to represent itself as also being able to form *concepts* of such objects. And since the understanding yields no concepts additional to the categories, it also supposes that the object in itself must at least be *thought* through these pure concepts, and so is misled into treating the entirely *indeterminate* concept of an intelligible entity, namely of a something in general outside our sensibility, as being a *determinate* concept of an entity that allows of being known in a certain manner by means of the understanding.

He goes on to say that 'the doctrine of sensibility', i.e. the theory of the Aesthetic and Analytic, involves the thought of 'a thing so far as it is not an object of our sensible intuition', the concept of a noumenon in the negative sense of the term. This concept serves only as a 'limiting' concept, 'to curb the pretensions of sensibility' (B 310–11/A 255). One wonders even so what content it can have, more particularly since Kant emphasises that we cannot use the categories, which 'have meaning only in relation to the unity of intuition in space and time' (B 308), in order to give body to it. Presumably what he has in mind here are the schematised categories; the pure categories have no such relationship to space and time. But even if the pure categories are available, how will they help? Suppose that we try to fill out the statement that *there might be something outside our sensible intuition* by employing the pure category of existence. We can say that this something might exist, but not as physical objects or minds or even numbers exist; it might exist in the minimal sense represented by the logical symbol 'Ex'. But what have we said when we have said this? The answer must surely be nothing determinate at all. And the same is true when we try to use the other pure categories. Our something can be a substance, but not one which persists through time, a cause, but not one which precedes its effects, and so on. In fact we have to say in the end that in these terms our something is a something we know not what. How then it could count as a coherent idea, let alone one to which something real might correspond, is not apparent.

That Kant himself failed to draw this conclusion, and continued throughout the period of the *Critiques* to speak as if the concept of the thing in itself were entirely intelligible, can hardly count against it. Nor can the supposed necessity of the doctrine for moral purposes. Certainly it is important to recognise, as was pointed out at the beginning of this book, that the implications of the Critical Philosophy are not all intended to be negative. As well as denying knowledge, Kant is anxious to make room for belief or conviction, and this of course involves forming an idea of that which is believed in. But when we turn to the details of the doctrine of moral belief as expounded in the *Critique of Practical Reason*, it emerges that the conception of God which actually functions in the thinking of the moral agent and exercises a real influence on his actions is not the metaphysical concept of an Original Being or First Cause, but one which has its root in moral practice itself. God is thought of as having certain 'metaphysical perfections'—omnipotence, omniscience, perfect goodness—but these are consequent on more fundamental properties which are all moral, and according to which he is seen as the holy lawgiver, the beneficent ruler and the just judge (see *Critique of Practical Reason*, Berlin edition V 130 note, and section 40 below). The effective conception of God is thus quite simply anthropomorphic, a circumstance which causes Kant no qualms in view of his belief that we have here to do with matters on which the learned have no advantage over the plainest of plain men. No doubt he would himself add that underlying this popular concept there lies the philosophical concept of the noumenon, itself to be understood in terms of pure categories. But it is hard to see what positive work this concept performs, or what is lacking in the thought of the moral agent who is ignorant of it.

I shall be returning to the notion of moral belief, and again to that of the thing in itself, later in the book (sections 40, 29). I hope, however, that enough has been said to show that the idea that pure categories are available for 'thinking' supersensible objects leads to many difficulties, and should if possible be abandoned. If I am right, it is not necessary for the wider purposes of Kant's philosophy, nor sufficient to give body to his own internal concept of that which is not appearance. Nor of course is it central to his polemic against the possibility of speculative metaphysics, but rather weakens the latter by suggesting that pure concepts of the understanding are not the empty shells Kant so often says they are. To dispense with this doctrine would at least have the effect of tidying up Kant's theory, though whether it would be defensible in its tidied-up form remains to be seen.

§ 16 *Is Kant fair to Metaphysicians?*

Returning to the more general question of the bearing of the categories on metaphysics, I now want to ask if Kant's overall procedure in the Deduction is fair to his opponents. He begins as we have already seen by admitting something which the transcendent metaphysician claims but which would not be allowed by the latter's empiricist critics, that the human mind is in possession of pure concepts of its own. Kant's allegiance to Leibniz, despite his life-long struggle to shake himself free of Leibnizian ideas, comes out nowhere more clearly than in this remnant of traditional rationalism. But whereas Leibniz, like Descartes before him, took the existence of innate ideas as pointing unmistakably to the possibility of knowledge of the supersensible, Kant argued that no such conclusion was warranted in the case of his pure intellectual concepts. It could not just be assumed that the presence in men of such concepts afforded a point of contact with things intelligible, as Kant himself had in the *Dissertation*. The critical philosopher must on the contrary enquire into the circumstances, if any, in which concepts of this kind might be said to determine an object, and specify what that object is. Hence the complicated story about categories, schemata and intuitions with which we have been concerned.

It might be suggested that Kant approaches this enquiry in a way which begs the question: he takes it for granted that the only thing we could do with a concept is bring it to bear on a manifold of intuition, and maintains without examination that the only such manifold available to us is one provided by the senses. Given these assumptions, schematisation may well be a necessity for anyone who hopes to hang on to a theory of *a priori* concepts, and even a limited insight into an intelligible world is ruled out. But do we have to accept the assumptions? It depends on what the alternatives are, and indeed on whether there are any alternatives.

One thing which is clear in this connection is that you cannot defend a metaphysics of the supersensible so long as you agree to the sharp Kantian dichotomy of concepts and intuitions. The idea that the senses, or at any rate some non-intellectual faculty, supply data which the intellect subsequently conceptualises, has got to go if the metaphysical case is to stand a chance. In its place prime emphasis will need to be laid on judgment, which must be interpreted as involving apprehension and conceptualisation in a single act. Further, it has to be argued that judgment is not something which takes place in isolation, that is to say without regard to the other aspirations, interests and achievements of the person concerned, but is rather to be seen as part of an ongoing and, in general, successful search for knowledge. The subject of judgment on this view is never in a position where his experience baffles him completely; he never confronts raw and totally uninterpreted data, but is invariably able to make something of what comes before him, even if it is often less than he could have wished. Equally, it is false to say that he possesses a store of concepts whose credentials must remain in doubt until authenticated in successful use. Concepts are properly at home in judgments, which means that they must be presumed to have authenticity from the first; seen apart from judgment they are not so much tools awaiting testing as misleading abstractions. We can and do improve on our available conceptual apparatus, but we do it by making tentative new judgments rather than by thinking up new ideas with no regard to their application. There are situations in which someone comes forward with a new idea whose value has to be decided. But we decide it by seeing how far it can be made to fit in with the large body of ideas to which we are already committed, not by seeing if we can establish a relationship between it and separately existing intuitions.

How if at all could these views be appealed to in support of traditional metaphysics? First, by reversing the ordinary assumptions in this area according to which every intellectual activity must be treated with suspicion until it has shown itself to be innocent.

The occurrence of an idea will now constitute a presumption that the idea has a use, rather than leave it an open question. Secondly, through the suggestion that the proper way to arrive at truth about the world is to think and judge: ultimate truth, on this view, will be found when we attain to a system of judgments which is at once wholly comprehensive and wholly coherent. But to put the matter in these terms may well be misleading, for it is not a question here of abstract but of concrete thinking. The judgments we are examining are one and all made in contexts where the judging subject is in the world and able to grasp the world; his judgments accordingly have a material content and are not merely formal. To represent truth as consisting in what we are driven to think when we think as long and hard as we can is thus not so paradoxical as it sounds, for we think in concrete situations and our thinking in consequence has a hold on fact as it evidently has not on the alternative view of the cognitive position.

The theory just sketched takes the difference between reality and appearance to depend on a difference between using well-founded ideas on the one hand and ill-founded ideas on the other. All our cognising is aimed at a systematic account of experience; we seek always to make continuous sense of whatever we encounter. But the basis on which we construct such systematic accounts can vary enormously. Sometimes the ideas we employ are properly at home only in highly restricted areas; to attempt to take them beyond can lead to difficulties both in the internal formulation of judgments and in reconciling what we would like to think with other positions to which we are already committed. On other occasions, where different ideas are in question, the problems we face are less troublesome, and that gives us hope of having got hold of reality, as opposed to mere appearance. To claim final truth in these conditions would doubtless be the height of presumption. But just as truth in general is not beyond human competence, as the general story about concepts and judgments makes clear, so metaphysical truth—grasp of reality as such—is open to us in principle. We may not reach it in practice, but we have no reason to think of it as wholly beyond our ken, as Kant tried to say that it was.

Strictly speaking, the theory we are concerned with has no room for *a priori* concepts proper, that is to say for concepts which spring exclusively from the faculty of conceiving. The faculty of conceiving is itself no more than an abstraction, and every concept has some empirical connections (it is, as it were, born in the context of judgment, and the judging subject is in the world from the first). But though this makes 'pure thinking' impossible, it does not discredit the special class of concepts which Kant marked out under the title of categories. That the search for knowledge is directed and presided over by concepts of a high degree of generality and possessing a special sort of necessity can be accepted on this view as easily as on Kant's. Where the two theories differ is on the following points. First, Kant believes that there is an important sphere, that of things lying beyond possible experience, to which the categories do not apply; his rivals think this sphere a myth. Secondly, Kant holds in consequence that the only metaphysical system which can be defined by the categories is an account of the necessary form of experience, i.e. of the form of the phenomenal world; on the alternative view it is accepted that metaphysics cannot go beyond the empirical, but denied that the experienced world has to be phenomenal. Whether it is phenomenal or not depends on the terms in which we seek to construe it. And that brings us to a third and very important difference, that Kant thinks that *all* his categories are required in order to specify the necessary form of the experienced world, whilst his critics argue that concepts of this kind differ in respect of truth and adequacy, and accordingly must be thought of as rivalling rather than complementing one another. In their view there is not just one possible account of the world, but many, and to arrive at it we have to weigh up the merits of different categories or sets of categories.

I turn now to comment, which should begin by underlining the fact that Kant himself moved at least some way in the direction of the critics in what he had to say about judgment. In the first edition of the *Critique* he described concepts as 'predicates of possible judgments' (B 94/A 69), and in the second edition Deduction he emphasised the importance of the activity of judgment as central in the whole of human thinking. The account he gives here sharply contradicts the implications of the Aesthetic, according to which the senses present us with intuitions, complete if not quite describable as they stand, which the intellect subsequently conceptualises. If the argument were put forward that both concepts and intuitions exist only in abstraction from the concrete activity of judgment, Kant in his better moments at least would be inclined to agree. But he would deny that this committed him to going further along the road with the critics. Had he good reasons for taking this view?

One can imagine him making a case along the following lines. Although it is true that judging is the fundamental intellectual activity, and that concepts and intuitions alike would have no existence if no judging occurred, this does not mean that we can never legitimately think of concepts or intuitions on their own. Concepts normally function in judgment, which means that there is no problem about the authenticity either of concepts in general or of most individual concepts. But this could be true without entailing the conclusion that we can never question the objective reference of any particular concept or set of concepts. That we should thus be sceptical in some cases scarcely needs arguing: we have only to think of the 'usurpatory' concepts (*fate* and *fortune*) to which Kant refers at the beginning of the Deduction. But there are more serious examples. Mathematical ideas, which as Kant insisted have about them an element of the artificial, constitute an obvious instance: we quite readily and quite properly find ourselves asking whether mathematicians are engaged in an idle play with symbols, and if not what gives the concepts concerned real significance. That Kant's own answer to the latter question finds few supporters today does not mean that he was wrong to pose the problem. Nor was he wrong to raise questions about another case in which the credentials of a set of concepts have frequently been viewed with suspicion: that of traditional metaphysical concepts. Notions like that of a Form in Plato, of God in medieval metaphysics, of the monad in Leibniz and of the Absolute in Hegel were doubtless introduced in a context of concrete thinking, by authors who had solved some problems and were hoping by means of them to solve others. But that in itself is not enough to authenticate them. The least we can ask of those who accept them is that they show us their significance, by clarifying the role they play in the system of thought to which they belong and by bringing out the merits of that system. And if it is reasonable to follow this procedure in that sort of case, it will equally be reasonable to follow it in the case of the categories.

But what about the tests to which such concepts are to be subjected? I have spoken vaguely of clarifying the role they play in their own system of thought and of bringing out the merits of the system itself. What Kant does, however, is to insist that the concepts he examines can pass muster only if they can be shown to have a certain bearing on sense-intuitions. Categories are significant because they have an essential relation to schemata, and schemata are temporal conditions whose presence in the world is directly detectable. By contrast, concepts such as that of a Leibnizian monad remain in an intellectual heaven, and consequently lack any serious significance. Kant has to admit, as we shall see when we come to the Dialectic, that there are authentic *a priori* concepts whose connection with sense-experience is more remote than that of the categories, but he nevertheless insists that there be some such link even in their case. But in so doing does he not reveal quite unwarranted philosophical prejudices, including an unthought-out and indeed indefensible commitment to a form of verificationism? And if this is so will not his demonstration of the impossibility of traditional metaphysics fall to the ground?

That Kant was not an out-and-out verificationist is clear from his writings on ethics. Moral concepts get their significance as far as he is concerned from the part they play in a context where there is something to be done rather than something to be found out; Kant's efforts to establish their authenticity proceed very much along the lines sketched above. Moreover, to show the respectability of moral ideas in this way is for Kant also to authenticate at least some of the ideas of law and religion, indeed of practical life generally. The final justification of the concept of God, for instance, is that this idea is needed to sustain moral effort: without the conviction that the world is ordered by a just God the moral agent might wilt in the face of continuing adversity. There is no trace here of a too pervasive empiricism: on the contrary, Kant protests repeatedly that moral notions cannot be discredited by showing that they are not in practice acted on. But his attitude changes when he moves from ethics to metaphysics. The whole object of this discipline, as he sees it, is to arrive at knowledge of the true nature of things; metaphysics, if it is to be respectable at all, must make good its claim to be a species of science. That being so, defenders of metaphysics must meet the requirements set for less controversial sciences such as mathematics and physics: they must explain how metaphysical knowledge is possible, by explaining how metaphysical concepts get their meaning and how inference in metaphysics is possible. Traditionally, confidence in metaphysics was sustained by the successes of pure mathematicians in arriving at synthetic *a priori* truths on the basis of pure thinking; in his philosophy of mathematics Kant strove to prove that such confidence was misplaced, since mathematics depended on the construction of its concepts in pure intuition. And since he was convinced that intellectual intuition was not a possibility for human beings, that left him with no test for metaphysical concepts other than that of asking after their empirical bearings. *A priori* concepts, unless they were mathematical, must be seen to be relevant to experience, or involved in empirical enquiries, if they were to be retained. Hence the procedures followed in the central chapters of the Analytic.

Should Kant have argued on these lines? As long as it was insisted that metaphysics is a branch of knowledge he had good reason to do so. His attitude to individual metaphysicians is often somewhat unsympathetic: despite his continuing preoccupation with metaphysics he does not stir himself unduly to find empirical connections for actual metaphysical concepts. Like the man of the Enlightenment that he is, he comes on the scene in the character of a critic, indeed of an accuser; he hopes to put paid to the pretensions of pure speculation once and for all. But though his patience here is somewhat less than it should be, that in itself will not discredit the general policy he adopts. For that it would be necessary to demonstrate that Kant, in suggesting that the metaphysician aims at knowledge, has misconceived the whole nature of the metaphysical enterprise. The alternative here would be to connect metaphysics with certain of men's practical aims: to argue that the stories the metaphysician tells are not to be taken as literally true, or as parts of explanations in the ordinary sense of the term, but must rather be seen as ways of speaking which are internal to something that lies beyond them, the advancing of some moral cause, for instance, or even the provision of consolation in a harsh and unpleasant world. Metaphysics on this view is not a pseudo-science, since it is not a branch of learning of any sort. But it is, or at any rate can be, a branch of rational activity, and its concepts may therefore have a justification even though they lack the empirical bearing which Kant demands of them.

Kant most certainly did not conceive of metaphysics in this way, and in so far as he failed to consider the idea his criticism of metaphysics must be described as incomplete. What makes this omission more remarkable is that some commentators attribute to Kant himself what they call a 'practical-dogmatic metaphysics', a set of ultimate convictions grounded in moral activity rather than in any form of sense-experience. I have already (see section 1 above) expressed doubts about the propriety of describing such a set of convictions as a metaphysics, in view of the strong connection Kant sees between metaphysics and claims to knowledge. But even if these doubts are set aside and it is maintained that Kant recognised a different form of metaphysics in practice, the fact remains that he never formulated the difference. Nor is it clear that his attitude to traditional metaphysicians would have softened had he done so. It is interesting in this connection to observe that, though Kant praises Plato for the lofty character of his moral ideas, he nevertheless remains sharply critical of his speculative pretensions, claiming in effect that Plato has the illusion of making progress only because he moves in a total void. Platonic metaphysics might just be presented as a fairy story intended to support moral aspirations; Kant shows no inclination to read Plato in this way. Other metaphysical writers, such as Leibniz, are much more difficult to deal with from the new point of view, and Kant takes them very much *au pied de la lettre*, as offering what purports to be knowledge of an intelligible world. There is every reason to think that this is how Leibniz himself meant his works to be taken. If so, Kant's method of challenging his claims is, in principle, quite legitimate.

I conclude that the criticism of speculative metaphysics Kant advances on the strength of his account of the function of categories is, in general, just. More needed to be said about the nature of metaphysics itself than Kant contrives to say, and individual metaphysicians should have been treated with greater charity and patience than are apparent in these pages. The question whether alternative sets of categories, and therefore alternative versions of the necessary conditions of experience, are conceivable is one which arises naturally out of Kant's enquiries, but is not pursued by him directly, except perhaps in the debate about mechanism and teleology in the *Critique of Judgment*. Kant was at fault in not seeing this difficulty, as he was at fault in failing to realise the tremendous problems created by his concept of the unknowable thing in itself. We shall need to return to these topics at a later stage. But meantime I shall leave the question of metaphysics, and turn to a different consequence of Kant's argument in the Deduction.

§ 17 *The Mind as 'making Nature'*

In a passage near the end of the first edition Deduction Kant writes (A 125–6):

> Thus the order and regularity in the appearances, which we entitle *nature*, we ourselves introduce. We could never find them in appearances, had we not ourselves, or the nature of our mind, originally set them there. For this unity of nature has to be a necessary one, that is, has to be an *a priori* certain unity of the connection of appearances; and such synthetic unity could not be established *a priori* if there were not subjective grounds of such unity contained *a priori* in the original cognitive powers of our mind, and if these subjective conditions, inasmuch as they are the grounds of the possibility of knowing any object whatsoever in experience, were not at the same time objectively valid.

The understanding, he goes on to explain, is itself the 'lawgiver of nature'; it imposes rules on appearances, which 'exist only in our sensibility' (A 127), and in so doing creates nature in one sense of the term. It creates nature considered as a formal system, as 'the totality of rules under which all appearances must stand if they are to be thought as connected in an experience', as the point was put in the *Prolegomena* (section *36*). However, a set of rules of this kind would be empty unless there were material for them to apply to. According to Kant, the understanding has nothing to do with the provision of material in the case we are considering; such material is supplied by sensibility. In one sense, then, it can be said that the mind makes nature, in another sense it can not.

The doctrine that the mind makes nature raises difficulties in whatever form it appears. One such difficulty turns on the problem of what mind is in question: is it this or that particular mind, or is it mind in some more general sense? That Kant intended the latter answer should be clear from our whole account of the Deduction. 'Nature', he writes in one of the passages under consideration (A 127), 'is only possible in the unity of apperception', and the unity of apperception, whatever else it is, is something impersonal. In so far as the unity of apperception operates in my consciousness I think as a rational being and not as a particular individual. I function as a logical subject rather than in a genuinely personal capacity. Hence it is mind as such, or *the* understanding, which is 'the source of the laws of nature' (A 127), not my individual mind or yours.

But what of nature itself? Is that also to be thought of as something common to many minds? The difficulty here is the one we discussed earlier when commenting on the conclusions of the Aesthetic, that Kant normally thinks of the process of perception as beginning with the occurrence of 'representations' (*Vorstellungen*) in individual minds. If we accept that this is so, and follow Kant in identifying such representations with appearances in the broadest sense of that term, 'nature' will turn out to signify a certain set of each experient's particular perceptions, namely those that can be connected together under universal and necessary laws. What I take to be part of nature will correspond to, or complement, what you take to be part of nature, but the two will not and indeed cannot be literally identical, since you cannot have my perceptions nor I yours. Kant says in a passage (A 127) already quoted in part that 'appearances, as such, cannot exist outside us—they exist only in our sensibility'. But the use of a plural personal pronoun and a plural possessive adjective here are highly misleading, since the term 'appearance' in this context is plainly taken to mean private sense-contents. The appearances which, as Kant says (A 128), 'take on an orderly character' when brought in relation to the unity of apperception, must be something before the process begins; most commonly, Kant thinks of them as the contents of this sensibility or that. There are contexts in the *Critique* where the term 'appearance' has a different significance and means what forms part of the common experience, but this is not the sense here in question.

In the first edition of the *Critique* the account of nature Kant offered ran mainly, if not exclusively, along the lines just sketched. What was objectively there, as opposed to what fell within this consciousness or that, was a resultant of the imposition on essentially private data of a structure of universal laws. Perceptions were connected in two wholly heterogeneous ways, by laws of association which held only for particular individuals, and by laws of nature which were the same for all men. Perceptions of the first kind were of merely psychological, or personal, interest; perceptions of the second were far more important, since attention to them would enable their owners to anticipate the future, communicate with their fellows, and so on. Kant tried to go further and show that, unless it were possible to make connections between perceptions according to universal laws, the private association of ideas would not itself be possible; this is the point of the passages in the first edition Deduction (see especially A 112–14, 121–3) in which he maintains that association presupposes what he calls 'affinity', something which itself depends on the synthetic activities of the imagination and the understanding. These passages are, of course, intended as a refutation of Hume's view that the operation of the law of causality itself is simply the result of the working of custom and habit. But though Kant's overall position thus diverges sharply from Hume's, in other respects the two come relatively close together. Hume singles out causality as a particularly privileged principle of the imagination; Kant, as here presented, goes along with Hume in making the having of perceptions fundamental to the whole cognitive situation. On these terms neither can believe in a nature which is literally the same for all of us, and both confront the objection how in such circumstances different individuals can be said to inhabit a common world.

Kant's theory is open to the further objection that, if the position is as stated, the data which are to be connected under universal and necessary laws to form an order of nature may prove recalcitrant, unamenable to the demands of the understanding. Possessing as they would an existence of their own, representations could well turn out to be such that they were simply not connectible, with the result that no order of nature could emerge. Kant himself tries to rule out this possibility by arguing that on these terms not only would nature be lost, but also any kind of coherent consciousness: unless different items could be united in a common experience, there would be no unitary continuing self. There might, however, be a continuing self of a sort, a bundle of perceptions which successively introduce one another, to use Humean language. The experiences of such a self would admittedly be fragmentary and disconnected, and, to the extent that they were, the continuity of its consciousness would be more like that of a person deeply disturbed mentally than of a normal human being. But it would not be true to say that in these circumstances experience of any sort would be impossible. The very fact that representations were supposed to occur would be enough to make that false.

Apart from this, the whole first edition story about the need for synthesis, especially transcendental synthesis, has a highly un-satisfactory air: one finds oneself asking when and where these synthetic processes are supposed to be taking place, what is involved in them and whether they have the ubiquity Kant assigns to them. The difficulty about the first points is that these supposed adventures of the mind do not seem to be chronicled by psychologists, the difficulty about the last that, though it is true that we do sometimes decide what is going on by piecing together fragments of experience —shapes or colours seen, sounds heard and so on—it is by no means obvious that we are always engaged in such activities. If Kant were correct we should constantly be synthesising pre-existing data; unless we did so knowledge of objects would be an impossibility. In this respect, again, Kant comes close to his empiricist predecessors, who also present 'things' as 'collections of ideas' (e.g. Berkeley, *Third Dialogue*, pp. 282–3 in the Everyman edition). Kant himself would claim, rightly, to have introduced a very important amendment into the theory by insisting that the collecting be governed by *a priori* rules. But on the evidence considered so far he could not be said to have made a decisive break with the empiricist point of view.

In the second edition of the *Critique*, however, and to some extent in the *Prolegomena* of 1783, Kant did make such a break. The important point here was the stress laid on judgment, which in effect took the place of synthesis in the story Kant had to tell. The main advantage of judgment is that it can be intelligibly presented as an activity which is not only impersonal and hence intersubjective in itself, but also results in the constitution of an intersubjective world. The essential purpose of judgment is to affirm how things are, or what is the case; the person who makes a judgment says what he takes the facts to be. If then there is, as Kant tried to argue in detail, an internal tie-up between judgement and awareness of an objective order, the latter must be seen not so much as a world of things as a world of facts. And this has consequences of the greatest importance for the concept of nature. If my exegesis of the first edition argument is correct Kant at that time was committed to the view that 'nature' is properly the name of an abstraction. There is no single thing which constitutes nature, only a plurality of sets of subjective representations organised on identical principles. On this view we all inhabit private worlds of our own, though it is possible to discern in each of our private worlds an objective core which is formally though not materially identical. But if we shift to the position of the second edition we have no need to accept such extravagances. For what we can say now is that nature is not a set of things, public or private; it is a set of facts about which we can all be got to agree. Facts are not entities of any sort, though of course entities of many different kinds figure among their constituents. It is, however, part of the grammar of the word 'fact' that, if something is a fact for me, it is also a fact for you, and conversely that if it is not a fact for you, it cannot be a fact for me either. There may well be facts which are known to only one person, but there are no merely personal facts. Hence to inhabit the world of facts which is constituted or discerned in judgment is to inhabit a common world.

There are two particular difficulties in this theory as stated by Kant. The first arises from an aberration of Kant's own, an aberration which is, however, confined to the *Prolegomena*. In the course of an interesting but nevertheless confused attempt to provide a new argument for the necessity of categories Kant in that work made a distinction between two sorts of judgment, judgments of perception and judgments of experience, and claimed that categories were needed for the second though not for the first. We can ignore the wider bearing of the argument here and simply concentrate on the distinction. 'That the room is warm, sugar is sweet, wormwood is nasty', Kant wrote (*Prolegomena*, section *19*),

> are merely subjectively valid judgments. I do not demand that I shall find it so at all times, or every other person the same as I. They only express a reference of two sensations to the same subject, namely myself, and this only in my present state of

perception, and hence are not intended to be valid of the object; such judgments I call judgments of perception.

Judgments of experience are a very different matter, for 'what experience teaches me under certain circumstances, experience must teach me and everybody always, and its validity is not limited to a particular subject or to its state at a particular time' (ibid.). In the case of the first class of judgments I simply connect two perceptions in myself, or as Kant says 'conjoin them in a consciousness of my state' (section *20*). In the case of the second 'I require that I and everybody must always necessarily conjoin the same perceptions under the same circumstances' (section *19*); I 'conjoin them in a consciousness in general'.

What Kant is saying here is that there are judgments which have merely personal validity, contrary to what was claimed above and explicitly set out in the general account of judgment given in the second edition Deduction (B 142). What is worse, Kant declares in the *Prolegomena* (section *18*) that

> All our judgments are at first mere judgments of perception, they are valid only for us, i.e. for our subject, and only afterwards do we give them a new reference, namely to an object, and want the judgment to be valid for us at all times and equally for everybody.

This last contention is surely quite absurd. Judgment may be grounded in something that happens in the subject alone, to wit sensation (I shall be discussing this shortly), but that does not mean that one form of judgment is grounded in another. If the expression 'judgment of perception' is in order at all, judgments of perception depend on judgments of experience rather than *vice versa*. Judgments of perception purport to state how things seem to me, judgments of experience how things are, and what seems to be the case is parasitic on what is the case (the apparent diverges from the real). The fact that Kant's examples of judgments of perception contain references to public objects such as the room, sugar and wormwood can be taken to support this point. But in any case there is grave doubt whether Kant's judgments of perception are properly named. There is indeed a class of utterances which corresponds to what he has in mind, a class of utterances in which a subject expresses his feelings or declares simply how things are in himself. Such utterances have the peculiarity that the person who makes them cannot be wrong on the matter, since in each case he is the last authority on it. He can of course abuse his authority and mislead others about his private thoughts and feelings, but provided he is sincere it makes no sense to think of contradicting him. There is no room here for the distinction between the real and the apparent: what seems so to the subject concerned is so. But should we conclude from this that we are dealing here with a special class of judgment which has only subjective validity?

The answer to this question seems to me plainly negative. What Kant calls 'judgments of perception' are one of two things: either personal avowals, mere declarations of feelings, which are not judgments at all, or else intended statements of fact which are such that only one person can make them, but which for all that claim general validity. The last phrase should not be misunderstood. 'I feel cold' can be a true statement of how things are with me without its following that I should always feel cold in similar circumstances or that anyone else would feel cold if in my situation. A statement of that kind has an essential personal *reference*, since it is about what is going on in a particular person. But it is false to say that it has merely personal *validity*. For after all it is, I take it, a fact that I feel cold, and every fact is a common fact. If I were making a list of everything that is true of the world, I should have to include the truth that I feel cold.

'Judgments of perception', though philosophically interesting, are thus seriously misrepresented by Kant. But it may be said at this point that the general account of judgment given above, according to which it is an intersubjective or impersonal activity, resulting in the construction of a common world, breaks down over a fact which we passed over in silence, the fact that judgment is made on the basis of data which are necessarily private. Judgment is an attempt to specify what there is or what is happening in the world, and our immediate access to the world is through sensation. But sensation takes place in individuals, and a man's sensations are very much his own. The sensory content in my mind may well correspond to or resemble the sensory content in yours, but the two cannot be literally identical. But if, as seems reasonable to hold, judgment gets its basic material from sensation, will not that mean that judgment too has a purely personal side? Will it not turn out, in fact, that Kant's supposed later position is substantially the same as the view he held at first, according to which knowledge begins with the contemplation of something which is private and advances from that to the grasp of an objective world?

The answer here depends on what we make of Kant's account of sensation, understanding by that his general view of sensing, not just what he says about *Empfindung*. I suggest that he hesitated between two quite different positions here. One was the standard empiricist view according to which sensation consists in the having of ideas, the being acquainted with this or that sensory content, colours, shapes, smells and the like. Sensation is here a species of knowledge, though it is knowledge which cannot be made articulate at the barely sensory level. Kant produced what looks very much like a version of this view in the Aesthetic, with special variations of his own intended to take care of the distinction between immediate awareness of primary qualities on the one hand and secondary qualities on the other. He persisted with the same general account in much of the Analytic, particularly in the first edition version of the Deduction. But it was clear even then that the main theory of knowledge advocated in the *Critique,* according to which knowledge demands both a sensory and an intellectual component, must rule out any doctrine of immediate knowledge whether sensory or intellectual, and so would exclude thinking of sensation as a form of knowledge by acquaintance. To fit in with the rest of the *Critique,* sensation must be conceived of as a form of experience which is *sui generis.* There can be no knowledge (or at least no basic knowledge) without sensory input, but sensation is an experience to be enjoyed rather than a matter of contemplating objects: bare sensing conveys no knowledge, but simply qualifies the subject. What is present in sensation is made articulate in judgment, but this does not mean that we attach a label to something of which we were fully aware in the pre-judgmental state. Sensation without judgment is not a form of awareness. *A fortiori,* it does not involve awareness of an object which is essentially private, and does not give rise to the philosophical problem of how we are to escape from ourselves and get into a wider world. Sensation occurs in individuals, but the sensory component in knowledge is not a purely private datum.

Did Kant actually hold this second theory? I cannot point to a passage in which he states it explicitly, and may even be over-charitable in suggesting that he toyed with it. But it is, as I have tried to show, the view of sensation which is demanded by his general account of knowledge, and above all by the theory of judgment which came to the fore in the second edition of the *Critique.* I see no reason why Kant should not have accepted this revised account of sensation, and many reasons for thinking that he should have accepted it. To have done so would certainly have rendered his whole account of nature as an objective order more credible, by removing the paradoxical thesis that nature is only a construction out of individually owned representations, a construction governed by necessary principles, but having all the same something artificial about it. That nature is no more than that is at the lowest estimate hard to believe. But given the second account of sensation we do not have to believe it at all.

The Application of Categories

§ 18 *The Analytic of Principles : Preliminaries*

At this point I pass from Kant's doctrine of the pure concepts of the understanding to his discussion of the detailed synthetic *a priori* principles he says are based on these concepts. I do not of course wish to imply that no problems of importance, other than those touched on above, are involved in the Kantian theory of categories. To mention two only: we have not yet asked whether Kant had good reasons for describing the world constituted in judgment as a *phenomenal* world, and we have said nothing about his paradoxical claim that we know ourselves, not as we are, but only as we appear to ourselves. These topics, however, are best treated in connection with later passages in the *Critique* (see below, sections 29, 52). For the moment we must address ourselves to chapter II of the Analytic of Principles, chapter I having been devoted to Schematism.

In this section of his work Kant does two things. First, he discourses briefly and unsatisfactorily on the notion of a principle of the understanding and on what is required if such principles are to be proved. Fortunately it is possible to fill out his remarks by referring to other passages in the *Critique*, including some in later sections of the Analytic of Principles. Secondly, he produces what he says is a complete list of all the principles of the understanding which operate in human thought, together with what purport to be proofs of the individual principles concerned. The proofs are each supposed to show that the principle must be applied without exception if experience as we have it is to be possible. Since, in the clearest cases at least, Kant succeeds in relating the principle to some definite and pervasive feature of human experience, what he has to say on the subject should interest even those who find the general argument about categories hard or impossible to accept. It could be, as was remarked before, that Kant was right in some of his detailed contentions, about cause or substance, for instance, but failed to construct a convincing general defence of the need for categories.

Before going further it is necessary to deal briefly with one or two scholastic points. Kant writes (B 200/A 161):

> The table of categories is quite naturally our guide in the construction of the table of principles. For the latter are simply rules for the objective employment of the former.

He then goes on to produce four sets of principles, Axioms of Intuition, Anticipations of Sense-Perception, Analogies of Experience and Postulates of Empirical Thought, corresponding to the four main groupings of categories under the headings Quantity, Quality, Relation and Modality. At this point, however, the parallel between categories and principles breaks down without any explanation being offered. There is one principle of the understanding in the cases of the Axioms and Anticipations, but when we come to the Analogies we find a general principle together with three detailed ones. The Postulates of Empirical Thought are also three in number, though as we shall see they do not appear to be principles of the same kind as the others. In general, Kant works out his theory only in the case of the Analogies; commentators have rightly tended to decide whether the whole Analytic of Principles succeeds or fails predominantly by reference to this section.

Kant entitles the Axioms and Anticipations 'mathematical' principles and calls the principles dealt with under the other two headings 'dynamical'. This is a distinction to which he became attached (in the *Critique of Judgment*, section *24* there is a reference to the mathematically and dynamically sublime), but which is hard to interpret in its original context, the more so because Kant himself says (B 201–2/A 162) that he is 'as little concerned in the one case with the principles of mathematics as in the other with the principles of general physical dynamics'. The principles of mathematics and general dynamics here referred to are 'special' principles (B 202/A 162); the principles of pure understanding with which Kant is concerned are more fundamental than these (they apply without distinction to all representations), and indeed render the special principles themselves possible. 'I have named them, therefore, on account rather of their application than of their content' (ibid.). I take this to mean that the propositions Kant wants to prove are not propositions, even highly general propositions, *in* mathematics or dynamics, but propositions which have a bearing on the possibility of the two sciences. The principles of the Axioms and Anticipations underlie applied mathematics, but do not belong to it; the principles of the Analogies underlie general dynamics, but again are not part of it, if only because they are stated in entirely general terms (it turns out that they have counterparts of a more restricted kind in physics: see *Metaphysical Foundations of Natural Science*). The Postulates of Empirical Thought fail to fit into this scheme altogether.

More important, though still somewhat puzzling, are two further distinctions which Kant makes between the two sets of principles. He says that the principles in the first group 'allow of intuitive certainty, alike as regards their evidential force and as regards their *a priori* application to appearances', while those in the second group 'are capable only of a merely discursive certainty'. Certainty is, how-ever, in both cases 'complete' (B 201/A 161–2). Kant further announces that whereas the mathematical principles are *constitutive* of their objects, their dynamical companions (and here he explicitly includes the Postulates) have only *regulative* force. An analogy of experience, for instance, is 'only a rule according to which a unity of experience may arise from perception. It does not tell us how mere intuition or empirical intuition in general itself comes about' (B 222/A 180). I assume that mathematical principles do tell us how mere intuition or empirical intuition in general comes about; they have to do with what might be called the internal structure of what-ever falls within experience, the conditions which any experiential content must meet. By contrast, the dynamical principles concern not the internal constitution of any experiential item, but the relations between one item and another; as Kant puts it (B 221/A 179) they have to do with *existence*. The occurrence of one item in experience is thought on the strength of these principles to demand the existence of some other item, as for example any event demands a cause. But the demand is unspecific, since the causal principle, if we can stick to that, says only that a given event has *some cause or other*; it does not specify any particular cause. It was for this reason that Kant described such principles as merely regulative in character. We need to examine his detailed treatment of the two sets of principles before being in a position to say whether these distinctions have any real validity. Meantime it is perhaps worth remarking that both sets of principles might be said to have both regulative and constitutive force: they regulate empirical enquiries (as we shall see, the mathematical principles, too, license the asking of questions rather than provide specific answers), and they constitute the experienced world. There is no question in Kant's mind of experiences turning up which are not amenable to the dynamical principles as well as the mathematical; something which failed so to conform would not be part of experience at all, but merely 'a blind play of representations' (A 112). In this respect there is a sharp contrast between principles of the understanding *of any sort* and what Kant calls 'principles of pure reason' (B 692/A 664), which according to a theory expounded in the Dialectic regulate the operations of the understanding and as it were point them in a certain definite direction, without however having any certainty that their injunctions will be accepted. The principles of reason urge us to look for system, to take a particular instance, in all our knowledge, but whether or not we find it is an empirical question: it depends on the particular constitution of experience. A world governed by laws which were not systematically connected could quite well be an object of experience, though not, perhaps, a very suitable subject for science. The fact that Kant had this contrast between principles of the understanding and principles of reason up his sleeve makes his description of the dynamical principles as 'merely regulative' (B 296/A 236) confusing to say the least.

That there are some differences between mathematical and dynamical principles need not be denied; there is at least the external difference that commentators have found more sense and appeal in the latter than in the former, despite what Kant says about evidential force. But the differences are in any case differences of detail; the logical function of the two sorts of principle is presented as being the same. I shall therefore from now on largely disregard the distinctions that have been mentioned. I put them in only because Kant himself stresses them, and out of a general conviction that the distinctions he draws, however scholastic they may seem, are never entirely negligible from the philosophical point of view.

§ 19 *Some Problems about Transcendental Proofs*

Before examining Kant's treatment of individual principles it is important to consider his general remarks about the sort of proof he thinks appropriate for them. Previous philosophers had proceeded on the assumption that there were only two ways of proving a philosophical proposition, which Kant called 'dogmatic' and 'empirical'. An empirical proof simply says that the proposition is adequately supported by empirical evidence; an alternative form of empirical proof appeals to its acceptance by common sense. A dogmatic or, as it would be called today, conceptual proof tries to argue that the proposition in question must be accepted, since to deny it would involve one in self-contradiction, immediate or remote. The argument that there must be a God because the idea of God is so widespread is an example of an empirical proof which has actually been attempted; the Ontological Argument for God's existence is an example of a dogmatic or conceptual proof.

According to Kant empirical proofs are entirely out of place in philosophy, which is occupied with necessary, not contingent, propositions, whilst the appeal to common sense in a philosophical context is 'an expedient which is always a sign that the cause of reason is in desperate straits' (B 811–12/A 795–4; compare *Prolegomena*, introduction, on Hume and Beattie). As for dogmatic proofs, they serve only to establish conclusions which are analytically true and so do not advance knowledge. Someone who produces what he says is a conceptual proof of the principle of causality only succeeds in making explicit the assumptions from which he starts out; he does nothing to make us think that the principle is true of the world. It follows that if there are to be adequate proofs of propositions of this kind, which are synthetic as well as necessary, the method of proof must be of a quite special kind. To use the rather crude language of the Introduction, we need here some third thing to connect subject and predicate in the proposition, as experience connects subject and predicate in the case of a true empirical proposition and as construction in pure intuition is supposed to do in the case of a mathematical truth. The third thing is found, if Kant is to be believed, in the idea of the possibility of experience. To show that a principle of the understanding is valid is to show that without its operation experience as we have it would not be possible. This sort of demonstration Kant calls a 'transcendental' proof, the term 'transcendental' being in place because the proof is alleged to legitimise a certain claim to *a priori* knowledge, e.g. that whatever events occur they must all have causes.

The notion of a transcendental proof, as explained by Kant, involves a number of difficulties. We can set aside as unfounded the objection that Kant must be claiming here that there is a form of reasoning which is neither deductive nor inductive. In actual fact a transcendental argument follows a pattern which is straightforwardly deductive. It first lays down that P could not be true unless Q were true. It then goes on to assert the truth of P. Finally it draws the conclusion that Q must be true as well. There is nothing peculiar in the logic here; interest centres rather on the right to assert the premises and hence on the right to assert the conclusion.

There is also a difficulty about the logical status of the conclusion, as I now hope to show.

Principles of the understanding, according to Kant, are at once synthetic and necessary; any argument which purports to prove such a principle must therefore prove it as necessary. Now it is, of course, a principle of elementary logic that a necessary conclusion can follow only from premises which are themselves all necessary. But this requirement is not met in the case of Kant's transcendental proofs, since the minor premise says only that our experience answers a certain description, not that it necessarily wears this form. In the second Analogy, for example, it is said that we have the ability to discriminate objective from subjective successions, and could not exercise this ability unless there were ubiquitous causal connections in the experienced world. An important aspect of experience is thus alleged to be bound up with the operation of the causal principle. But how do we know that this aspect of experience will persist? May it not be the case that we wake up tomorrow and find that we no longer have the ability in question? The possibility may not be serious, but if it is there at all the argument contains a premise which is indisputably contingent. But in that case the conclusion will at most be contingently true, and the claim to have proved a proposition which is *a priori* as well as synthetic cannot be sustained.

Unfortunately this is a difficulty which Kant nowhere discusses. So far as I can see the only thing he could say in partial defence of himself would be to point out that the 'facts' to which he appeals in putting forward his transcendental arguments tend to be facts of an extremely general kind, as that we can date events and processes objectively, or state what is the case as opposed to what merely seems to be the case, or apply mathematics to the world. The 'experience' whose 'possibility' is invoked in a Kantian transcendental argument is thus central rather than peripheral, to use a Quinean way of speaking, and for that reason we are less likely to be wrong about it than we should if the argument depended on reference to a particular fact (say, the fact that it is midday in Los Angeles when it is 3 p.m. in New York). Kant would want to claim that the facts to which he appeals in such arguments are crucial in the further sense that their removal would carry with it the destruction of experience as we know it. No doubt he would be correct in making this claim, as we can see by asking ourselves what it would be like not to possess the abilities mentioned above. What is less clear, however, is that the loss of these and similar abilities would mean that we had no experience at all. If the sole alternative here were to have a 'blind play of representations', we might agree that the case had been made: experience of that sort would indeed be less than a dream. It could be, however, that there were other ways in which experience could be organised, different abilities which might replace those which were to be removed; a being possessing these abilities and not ours would not have experience as we know it, but would not therefore be without experience at all. To make his argument watertight Kant must rule this possibility out. As it is he is forced to admit that it is a contingent fact that we can think and act as we do, and so that the argument he presents has conditional force at best.

There is another and even more serious difficulty in the Kantian notion of a transcendental argument, this time concerning the major premise. The form of this premise is that P could not be true unless Q were true: only if Q, then P. And Kant, if I am not mistaken, takes this as saying not merely that Q is a necessary condition for P, but further that nothing else could produce P: he wants to make out, in effect, that Q is the sole possible condition of P. That this reading is correct is shown, I believe, by the way he develops his individual arguments, for example in the Aesthetic, where he takes it that the experience of space as we have it can be accounted for only by his own theory, and makes the point by ruling out what he takes to be the only conceivable alternatives, the theories of Newton and Leibniz. The difficulty about this is twofold: how he knows that the alternatives are exhaustive, and how he can be sure that those he discards are definitively proved to be wrong. As regards the first point Kant seems to rely on nothing more than unsupported immediate insight: he takes it that 'space' must name either an objective reality or something mental, that if space is an objective reality it will be either a substance or a set of relations and that if it is something mental it will be a form of thought or perception. That these are all possibilities is obvious enough, that they are all the possibilities less obvious. The same must be said of the discussions in the Deduction, where Kant apparently says that the facts to which he draws attention can be accounted for in three ways only: by the hypothesis of transcendental idealism, by that of transcendental realism or by some form of pre-established harmony theory (cf. B 167–8). How he knows that there are no more alternatives is not clear. In general, the problem of how Kant sets up the major premise of these particular arguments is one to which he should have given more attention. So again is the problem of how he satisfies himself that particular possibilities are ruled out. Sometimes he proceeds in what might be called a rigorous manner, arguing that a certain claim cannot be maintained because it involves, or leads to, contradictions; this is what he holds, for instance, of the Newtonian theory of space, which in his view is committed to saying that space is both a substance and not a substance (an *Unding*: B 56/A 39). But elsewhere he is content with an argument which is, on the face of it, much less compelling. His reason for dismissing the Leibnizian view of space is that Leibniz 'can neither account for the possibility of *a priori* mathematical knowledge, nor bring the propositions of experience into necessary agreement with it' (B 57/A 40–1). Again, his objection to the pre-established harmony conception of categories, according to which they are subjective dispositions implanted in us which in fact correspond to features of the world, is that it fails to explain the necessity we attribute to categorial principles (B 167–8). I am not saying that such a point is not pertinent or important, but only that it seems less than satisfactory in a context where the handling of a necessary proposition is involved. And if defenders of Kant reply that it is absurd to claim logical necessity for the propositions in question, since that would commit one to believing that Kant's own conclusions are logically true, the consequence must be that doubt is cast on the status of the major premise of a transcendental argument as well as its minor premise. That in these circumstances such an argument would be taken as logically acceptable seems very hard to uphold.

Kant's transcendental arguments are a good deal better in practice than in theory. His suggestion that we can fruitfully ask what must be true if experience is to be possible sounds unsatisfactory at first hearing, if only because the notion of the possibility of experience is vague. A cynic might say that he only proves that categories and forms of intuition are necessary for the possibility of experience by making them definitory of that which is really possible (cf. B 265/A 218). In fact, however, Kant fixes attention in his actual arguments on features of the world or the human condition which are of obvious and central importance, and both the questions he poses and the answers he gives are at the lowest estimate worth discussion. Despite first appearances, he does not simply *define* experience as what fits in with the requirements of his theory. On the contrary, he puts before us in passage after passage tantalising or alarming possibilities which might be realised, like the suggestion in the first Analogy that there might be a plurality of different streams of time (cf. B 231–2/A 188), and then goes on to claim what must be true if these are to be ruled out. That something significant is at issue here is shown by the close attention which these arguments have commanded, not least in recent years. We certainly cannot rule them out of court because of difficulties in Kant's account of their logical structure. Kant was, in general, clumsy and incompetent as a logician, but this is not to say that he did not know how to deploy an argument in practice.

Kant's fullest discussion of the idea of a transcendental proof is contained not in the Analytic of Principles itself, but in the Transcendental Doctrine of Method at the end of the *Critique*, in a section called 'The Discipline of Pure Reason in regard to its Proofs' (B 810/A 782 ff.). One serious defect of this passage is that it uses the expression 'transcendental proof' to cover philosophical proofs or purported proofs generally, including the arguments used by traditional metaphysicians (compare e.g. B 816/A 788: 'the transcendental proof of the existence of God', meaning the Ontological Argument). Kant reflects here to some extent on his own procedure earlier in the *Critique*, but not exclusively. However, he makes some points on the subject which are of mild interest. First, he reiterates in a very general way his point that it is vital to a successful philosophical argument that the person concerned should know what sort of a principle he is putting forward and what must be done to defend such a principle properly; attention to this will rule out, for example, a metaphysical use of categories or an attempt to exploit the principles of reason to arrive at truths about the world (B 814–15/A 786–7). Secondly, he says that it is a peculiarity of transcendental proofs that only one proof can be found for each transcendental proposition (B 815/A 787). This may come as a surprise to readers of the second Analogy, but Kant says explicitly here that 'the sole possible ground of proof' of the causal principle is to show that 'the determination of an event in time, and therefore the event as belonging to experience, would be impossible save as standing under such a dynamical rule' (B 816/A 788). Other proofs which have been attempted turn out to be verbal, or to presuppose the correctness of Kant's proof. Finally, Kant claims that transcendental proofs must never be apagogic, but always ostensive (B 817/A 789). An apagogic proof is a *reductio*, and it seems clear that what Kant is condemning here is the form of argument adopted in the setting out of thesis and antithesis in the Antinomies, where the procedure is to demonstrate that a view must be accepted because its contradictory is self-contradictory. Kant's objection is that the alleged mutually contradictory pair of propositions may turn out not to be such, but rather to be contraries or even independent of one another. In fact, however, he does not avoid indirect arguments in his own transcendental proofs. In the first Analogy, for instance, he invites his readers to consider what would happen if some substances in the experienced world could come into being absolutely or go clean out of existence, and declares the result to be 'absurd' (B 232/A 188). Similarly in the second Analogy there is a paragraph which begins with the words 'Let us suppose that there is nothing antecedent to an event, upon which it must follow according to rule' (B 239/A 194), which is the contradictory of what Kant wants to prove. Here, and again in B 247/A 201, he seeks to make his conclusion more vivid by removing what he says is a necessary condition of something or other and arguing that the result would alter experience in a fundamental way. I can myself see no reason why such a move should not be legitimate. But in case anyone wants to stand by Kant here I should point out that the argument does not result in a formal *reductio*: we are not shown that the conclusion is incoherent, but only that it conflicts with obvious facts. Nor is it true that Kant in these passages relies exclusively on apagogic proofs. He appeals to indirect arguments only after trying to make his case in a normal straightforward manner.

§20 *Mathematics and the World : General Considerations*
It is a pleasure to turn from these matters of principle to particular cases. Kant introduces his first principle under the title 'Axioms of Intuition', his second under that of 'Anticipations of Sense-Perception', and the first point that must be made is that these labels are misleading. The single principle which corresponds to the three categories of Quantity is not itself an axiom, but at most a principle which lies behind and justifies the application of a certain set of axioms, as I hope to show in detail presently. The single principle which corresponds to the categories of Quality certainly has to do with the anticipation of sense-experience, but only in a particular respect, namely in regard to the degree of any sensation. It would have been better described as a principle of the Anticipation of Sense-Perception in respect of Degree. Axioms, Anticipations and Analogies alike put forward principles which, if correct, enable us to anticipate experience in various significant ways. Indeed, it is this feature in principles of the understanding generally which makes them philosophically important.

The simplest way to characterise the Axioms and Anticipations, as I shall continue to refer to them, is to say that they purport to justify the asking of mathematical questions about the world. The

Axioms section has to do with 'extensive magnitudes', the Antici-pations with 'intensive magnitudes'. Extensive magnitudes are illustrated by such things as length, width, height, area, volume of two- or three-dimensional objects; intensive magnitudes are exhibited in, for example, the depth of a colour or the intensity of a light or illumination. The point Kant is getting at in both cases is that we approach experience with certain assumptions and hence proceed to ask certain questions; the problem is what justifies the assumptions and renders the questions legitimate. In the case of the Axioms the assumption is that whatever falls within external experience, or, more satisfactorily, forms part of an objective external order has determinate dimensions and a determinate size; it is on the basis of these assumptions that we ask of any supposed external object such questions as 'How long is it?', 'What area does it cover?', and so on. In the case of the Anticipations we are concerned not with external objects but with sensations, and the assumption is that every sensa-tion is present in a determinate degree. According to Kant, this assumption alone legitimises questions about the intensity of particu-lar sensations. It should be made clear, however, that it is not just the fact that we ask these questions that impresses him, but rather that we believe it right to ask them no matter what turns up in experience. We dismiss from our minds the possibility that there might be an external object with no determinate dimensions or an internal sensa-tion which was not present in any determinate degree. Or if we allow the latter so far as purely subjective feeling is concerned, we do not allow it when sensation becomes an object of serious scrutiny (see below, section 22). We believe that the degree of a sensation must be, in principle, mathematically expressible even when we are not in possession of techniques for measuring it.

When Kant says that it is a synthetic *a priori* truth that 'all intui-tions are extensive magnitudes' (B 202) or that 'in all appearances, the real that is an object of sensation has ... a degree' (B 207), he is not of course meaning to say that we can know concrete facts about the world without reference to experience. That all intuitions are extensive magnitudes says no more than that they all have *some* determinant magnitude or other; what that magnitude is must be found out by empirical means. Similarly, though the principle that the real that is an object of sensation has a degree enables us to anti-cipate experience in a surprising way, by assuring us for example that whatever is heavy will be weighable, it does not in itself proffer any empirical information. To determine how heavy this particular thing is we have to put it on a scale and weigh it. In other words, the principles of the Axioms and Anticipations concern no more than the form of experience, or certain formal characteristics of an objective order. They license the asking of different ranges of empirical questions, but make no pretence of supplying the answers.

It is useful to emphasise these points at the outset for two reasons in particular. First, to counter the common objection that in sponsoring synthetic *a priori* judgments Kant must have been meaning to say that we can find out necessary truths about the world in a mysterious non-empirical way. The principles dealt with in the sections on Axioms and Anticipations (and the same is true, as we shall see presently, of those dealt with in the Analogies) are not properly described as truths about the world. They are not co-ordinate with everyday facts, or for that matter with the less familiar facts handled by the scientist, however general those facts may be, but function on what can only be described as a higher logical level. They are principles which give rise to questions that admit of empirical answers, and so belong to the framework of enquiry rather than its concrete content. If I know that whatever falls within external experience will have determinate dimensions I do not know anything in particular; I am not in possession of any fact, but simply aware of the form of some possible fact. That I have this knowledge, if indeed I do, is something which, as Kant saw, cannot be passed over without explanation: things need not have been constituted on these lines, and we have at least to recognise the consequences of the fact that they are. But to assume that the only explanation is that I have come by this knowledge as a result of direct insight into the structure of reality is, to say the least, somewhat hasty. Whatever other defenders of the synthetic *a priori* may have thought, Kant never suggested that the principles of the understanding were arrived at by such insight. In his view, human beings have no power of intellectual intuition: they can neither grasp primary data by merely thinking nor use purely intellectual means to establish synthetic (as opposed to analytic) connections between concepts. Those who write as if Kant were committed to the material *a priori* have failed completely to grasp the most elementary points in his theory of the understanding.

The second reason why it is useful to bring out the logical status of Kant's principles by connecting them with assumptions underlying ranges of questions is for the light it throws on what was previously (see section 8 above) described as a test for detecting the presence of categories, or establishing the categorial character of principles. I said before that you can find out whether a proposition functions as a categorial principle by noting the peculiar absurdity which its denial involves. The man who suggests that there might be in the external world objects of no determinate size or no particular volume provokes incredulity or, more often, exasperated indignation because he challenges one of our most central and most cherished assumptions; we think of him as making a misplaced joke, or putting forward a view that is plainly absurd. We might, however, be got to agree that there is no logical absurdity in the suggestion: that some things might be of no determinate size, like Alice only worse, is a perfectly intelligible proposition. To take it seriously is, for all that, very different from taking seriously the possibility that we might be wrong in accepting some well-attested and hitherto unquestioned empirical belief. A law like the law of gravity plays a central part in our understanding of the physical universe; if we had to give it up our whole picture of nature would be radically different. But things would be far worse if we had to abandon the general principle that mathematics applies to the world, with its particular applications in the Axioms and Anticipations For in these circumstances we might find ourselves saying not just that our concept of nature needed radical alteration, but that we simply could form no concept of nature at all. It would not be a matter of having to rethink the answers to particular questions but of wondering whether we had any right to ask questions of that sort at all. Our underlying procedures would be challenged, not any particular application we made of them.

That we are *disposed* to dismiss a suggestion as absurd is not of course a compelling reason for ruling it out of court; it cannot be pretended that recourse to the test of absurdity will just by itself authenticate the principle under discussion. But in fact Kant never claimed that it did. His own procedure was rather to construct proofs of the different principles of the understanding, and to claim on that basis that we have no alternative but to accept each principle as prescriptive to experience as a whole or a specified part of it. The proofs can be considered more and less narrowly: first in Kant's own terms, and then in relation to the aspect of possible experience on which they are supposed to bear. But before considering them in detail we need to look at two objections of a general kind which might be thought to invalidate Kant's whole enterprise.

Philosophers sympathetic to empiricism in its modern forms may claim that, at least in the passages we are examining, Kant was making a fuss about nothing. I described him earlier as concerned with the justification we have for asking mathematical questions about the world. The implication here is that it might be a real possibility that such questions could not be asked with success, and that Kant will come forward with an argument that in fact guarantees that this possibility will not be realised. On this the comment might be made, first that there is a sense in which the possibility is not real at all, and second that in so far as it is real the threat it poses cannot be legislated out of existence by any form of philosophical argument.

To explain: for the critics who take this view the propositions of pure mathematics are either arbitrary postulates or the logical consequences of such postulates, each of which is analytically true given the axioms and definitions of the system. It follows that pure mathematics is entirely self-contained: the question what is true in the sphere of pure mathematics is decided without any reference to anything outside that discipline. It further follows that no truth of fact can either conflict with or lend support to a pure mathematical proposition. In one sense there is no problem about the applicability of mathematics, since every factual truth must be consistent with the existence of mathematical truths, the latter being valid no matter what the facts are and thus holding for all possible worlds. If someone asks how we know that mathematics will apply to our world one answer is 'How could it not?'. But another answer, given from a somewhat different point of view, might be that only experience can show whether it will. In so far as applied mathematics demands that the propositions of pure mathematics be given some specific interpretation, we face in this connection a problem to which there neither is nor can be any *a priori* solution. There are parts of pure mathematics which in fact have at present no empirical application, though that is not to say that they will always remain in that state. But there are other bits of mathematical doctrine whose applications are well known, and the very fact that this is so is enough to show the hollowness of the possibility Kant holds before us.

These criticisms are of course made from a standpoint very different from Kant's, though to say that will not excuse him from answering them, since he too thought of the sphere of pure mathematical truth as self-contained and believed that there could be no conflict between the results of pure mathematics and discoveries about the empirical world. That pure mathematical propositions are *a priori* is more important in this connection than that they are also supposed to be synthetic and to involve concepts which can be constructed in pure intuition. Kant's story about pure intuition would, if correct, put a limit on the possibilities of mathematical invention: it would mean that mathematical postulates were not wholly arbitrary, as some modern writers take them to be. But this difference of detail has no effect on the more general question of the relationship between mathematics and the world. How then could Kant respond to criticisms of the kind outlined above?

One thing he might argue is that the application of mathematics, and therefore the development of a science of physics, requires that at least some things be true of the objects concerned. If things could not be discriminated, they could not be counted; if they were not stable up to a certain point, they could not be measured. In a Heracleitean world, where everything was literally in flux, it would be hard, indeed impossible for mathematics to get a grip. Facts may be such that they cannot conflict with the truths of pure mathematics; equally, however, they may frustrate the application of these truths. There could be a world in which mathematics was true but entirely irrelevant, because inapplicable in principle. Kant's argument in the Axioms and Anticipations seeks to prove that our world does not answer this description, but contains objects which are inherently suitable for treatment in mathematical terms; such, for example, as to be commensurable by reference to common standards. The objects in question may differ enormously in their empirical characters (Kant says nothing to preclude this), but must agree in the formal respect of being measurable. If they lacked this property they could not form part of the common experience.

It must be admitted that the gap between the empiricist and the Kantian view about mathematics and the world is wide. The empiricist insists that the question whether mathematics can be applied is in one sense entirely contingent; in principle it may or it may not. Kant by contrast wants to connect mathematics with space and time, which he regards as fundamental forms of sense-intuition; the effect of his theory is to rule out the possibility that Euclid's geometry should be without application in experience. Kant might have been prepared to allow that, say, a four-dimensional geometry was possible in principle (it would involve no *logical* difficulty: B 268/A 220−1). But he was convinced that such a geometry must be useless, since it is built on axioms which are simply not true of our world. On points like this it is not possible to defend him. But we can see his argument in the Analytic as making better sense if we take him as saying not that pure mathematics *must* apply to the world, but that the world must have certain characteristics *if* mathematics is to apply to it. The former contention is dogmatic and at the lowest estimate highly dubious, the latter is altogether more moderate and at least deserves investigation in detail.

However there is a further difficulty which must be faced before we

proceed: the difficulty that Kant has already discussed the subject before, in the Transcendental Aesthetic. One of the advantages Kant
claimed for his theory of space and time was that it explained the possibility of both pure and applied mathematics. It explained pure mathematics through its theory of the constructibility of mathematical concepts in pure intuition, a theory whose difficulties have been explored
earlier in this book (section 5). It explained applied mathematics by
saying that pure intuition underlies empirical intuition: whatever is
true of the former must be true of the latter. If space and time are
pure forms of sensibility, as Kant claimed they were, nothing could be
intuited by human beings which did not conform to them. It followed,
Kant thought, that nothing could be intuited which might resist the
application of mathematical concepts. If this demonstration is correct, why did Kant raise the subject again in the Analytic?

There are a number of possible answers. One would be that Kant
was simply inconsistent, or simply inattentive. Another, urged by
Kemp Smith among others, is that the Aesthetic, which largely
reproduces the doctrines of the inaugural *Dissertation*, represents an
early stage in his thought which he subsequently outgrew. If we
want to know what the mature Kant had to say on these subjects we
must turn to the Analytic. A third possibility, not wholly separate
from the second, is that Kant deliberately made the Aesthetic one-
sided, by concentrating on intuition in distinction from concepts
(cf. B 36/A 22), and meant to correct the resulting errors at a later
stage in his work. On this view the Analytic supplements the
discussions of the Aesthetic, without invalidating them altogether.
To be charitable to Kant we must adopt something like this third
view. We shall then say that the central doctrine of the Aesthetic,
that nothing can be intuited save under the forms of space and time
(or of time alone in some instances), is carried over into the
Analytic without any further discussion. However, Kant now
realises that the notion of a space-time world, i.e. of a set of objects
in space and time, is far more difficult than was at first suggested.
To show that the things which fall within experience belong to a
single spatio-temporal system, not just as a matter of fact but of
necessity, we need to do far more than simply argue that all our
intuiting is informed by space and time as pure intuitions. We need
to tell a story which involves concepts as well as intuitions, and speaks
of the characteristics objects have to possess, as opposed to their bare
sensory content. It was only in the Analytic that Kant made any
attempt to work out this story in detail, and it accordingly follows
that the discussions of the latter must take precedence over those of

the Aesthetic. The theses put forward in the Aesthetic are in any case unspecific, as can be seen if we ask what it means to say that everything must be intuited under the forms of space and time. Is the view that all intuitions will have spatial and temporal content, or is there some further implication about things being intuited *in* space and time? It is the second of these that Kant requires, yet his arguments for it in the Aesthetic remain highly schematic. If he offers a detailed case in its support anywhere in the *Critique*, it is in the Analytic, and specifically in the Analytic of Principles.

§ 21 *Mathematics and the World : Determinate Size*

In the section entitled 'Axioms of Intuition' Kant first puts forward two alleged proofs of the principle that 'all intuitions are extensive magnitudes' (B 202) or, as he expressed it in the first edition (A 162), that 'all appearances are, in their intuition, extensive magnitudes'. The reason why the subject is treated twice is expository: Kant was dissatisfied with the persuasiveness of his argument as set out in the first edition version of the Axioms, Anticipations and Analogies, and therefore began each of them (and the three separate Analogies as well) with a new summary proof in the second edition. The new proof simply stands alongside the old, and is sometimes unintelligible without the latter. After giving his proofs in the Axioms Kant discourses on the relation of his principle to axioms in the mathematical sense, and discusses the nature of arithmetical propositions (according to him, there are no axioms in arithmetic). Finally, he alludes briefly and not very effectively to the general subject of the applicability of mathematics, and draws from his own account of the subject the conclusion that the world to which mathematics necessarily applies cannot be a world of things in themselves, but must be a world of appearances.

The conclusion Kant seeks to prove is stated least obscurely towards the end of the first edition version, where we read that 'all appearances are . . . intuited as aggregates, as complexes of previously given parts' (B 204/ A 163). In the second edition he speaks about 'intuitions' being extensive magnitudes, but it is clear that the argument concerns what is intuited, not the intuiting. Kant's use of the term 'appearance' in this context is less easy to gloss. Does he mean by 'appearances' whatever comes into the consciousness of some particular individual, or is he talking about things which belong to the common experience, phenomenal realities? The fact that he illustrates the notion of an extensive magnitude by saying that 'I cannot represent to myself a line, however small, without drawing it in thought' (B 203/A 162) argues for the second alternative; lines are public objects. So too does the reflection that bare sensory content cannot be said to possess extensive magnitude. In a later passage summarising his views here (B 300/A 242) Kant writes:

> The concept of magnitude in general can never be explained except by saying that it is that determination of a thing whereby we are enabled to think how many times a unit is posited in it. But this how-many-times is based on successive repetition, and therefore on time and the synthesis of the homogeneous in time.

Magnitude is in question only when we synthesise or combine homogeneous parts to form a whole, as when we produce a line by 'generating from a point all its parts one after another' (B 203/A 162–3). But it is not only spatial objects which are generated in this way, if Kant is to be believed; the same is true of 'all times, however small. In these I think to myself only that successive advance from one moment to another, whereby through the parts of time and their addition a determinate time-magnitude is generated' (B 203/A 163). It seems from this that the 'appearances' of Kant's argument are either stretches of space and time, or phenomenal objects considered as occupying space or enduring through time. What Kant is wanting to say is that determinate spaces and times are not so much there awaiting our immediate apprehension, as produced by us by the successive addition of part to part, and that this is what makes them susceptible to numerical treatment. Spaces and times are *essentially* aggregates, and for that reason are measurable. And since every empirical object has spatial and temporal (or at least temporal) characteristics it follows that empirical objects too can be seen as aggregates or 'complexes of previously given parts' (B 204/A 163). If this is correct it will be possible to ask of them, too, how many times they accommodate a given unit in respect of length, breadth, height, etc.

One difficulty with this argument is that it seems to run directly counter to the indications of the Aesthetic, which spoke of space and time as being wholes which were prior to their parts, particular spaces and times being no more than limitations within them. The difference is perhaps explained by the fact that in the Aesthetic Kant was thinking of space and time as stretching away indefinitely from any given point, whereas here he is concerned with taking cognisance of particular spatial and temporal stretches. The notion of space as a whole was prominent in the Aesthetic, since Kant's interest there was in the status of the idea of space. In the Analytic, by contrast, his attention is directed on spaces, like the space occupied by this room. There need be no conflict between the two points of view, for we can think of any particular space as being carved out of, or delimited in, space as a whole, without implying that this process enables us to grasp it as a determinate amount. We can roughly delimit a region of space by marking it off from its surroundings, but to find out its precise extent we need to do something further. According to Kant, this something further is constituting, or re-constituting, the stretch in question out of homogeneous parts, build-ing it up in such a way that it becomes measurable against an accepted standard. Only if it is possible to treat particular spaces, particular times and the things that fall within them in this way will an applied mathematics of extensive quantity be guaranteed.

Is Kant talking about a process which is regularly gone through in the course of human perception? If so, his remarks would be properly classified as psychological, and his theory would be open to empirical confutation. A person might claim, for instance, that he never found himself engaged in generating determinate lengths in the manner described. To meet this difficulty Kant must say that what he has in mind is not so much a regular proceeding as an ability: a man must be able to think of a line as produced part by part if he is to grasp that line as having a determinate length. He need not actually engage in this process, since he may be satisfied either with a rough estimate ('about the length of a cricket pitch') or with the results of someone else's measurement. Details of his personal history are thus irrelevant to the truth of the theory. What is relevant is that it would not be unreasonable for someone in his situation to think of the line as built up out of its parts and thus as being essentially an aggregate. That he could is not an extravagant claim to make.

The ambiguity between process and ability involved here is one which affects Kant's whole account of synthesis in the Analytic. He writes all too often as if he were describing the course of human cognition, claiming that it begins with the acquisition of bare data which have subsequently to be put together ('synthesised') under concepts in order to arrive at knowledge of things as opposed to mere 'representations'. For reasons given earlier empirical concepts will not suffice to produce this result, and the 'empirical' synthesis has accordingly to be supplemented by a 'transcendental' synthesis. It is natural to ask in these circumstances where these syntheses are supposed to take place and just what is involved in them. Some writers say that they are unconscious operations carried out by the noumenal self, the 'I in itself' which is supposed to lie behind the phenomenal ego with which alone each of us is directly acquainted. Others point out that the very fact that Kant gave an account of them rules this interpretation out, and argue that the syntheses are abstract aspects of processes carried out by the ordinary empirical self. The second theory certainly sounds better than the first, which is indeed totally unintelligible, but does not dispel the impression that Kant is engaging in armchair psychology. To get rid of that we need to see that what is in question is not processes of any sort, but abilities. In speaking of synthesis, whether empirical or transcendental, Kant has in mind not any actual connecting but rather connectibility; he is not concerned with how we actually come by such knowledge as we have, but with what we must be able to do if we are to show that our claims to knowledge are legitimate.

Reflection on these arguments will show that it is not enough to object against Kant that we are sometimes able to grasp stretches of space without generating them out of parts, or are aware of a specious present which involves some internal diversity. Kant himself says in the Antinomies (B 455–6/A 427–8) that 'an indeterminate quantum can be intuited as a whole when it is such that though enclosed within limits we do not require to construct its totality through measurement, that is, through the successive synthesis of its parts'; this corresponds to what was said earlier about the rough delimitation of a region in space or, we may add, a temporal period. It must be left to psychologists to establish the precise facts in this area. But psychologists have surely no jurisdiction over whether Kant was right to claim that awareness of a line as having a determinate length involves the capacity to think of that line as generated out of homogeneous parts. We are concerned here not with what goes on, but with how what goes on may be represented or reconstructed. And this is not a question of fact in the strict sense at all.

It may still be said that Kant begs the question in his own favour by assuming that the synthesis will proceed uniformly, and not in uneven jumps, which generate unequal amounts in equal times. Kant could reply that, since no actual process is at issue, the question does not arise. To get to any point on the line we must in principle be able to traverse all the previous points, and that is all that is necessary to make the theory work. I am not wholly satisfied with this answer, and consequently feel some doubt about whether Kant can be said to have proved his main point in the Axioms section. I also find his attempt to connect his general principle with the part played by axioms in mathematics baffling. Kant says that axioms such as that between two points only one straight line is possible, or that two straight lines cannot enclose a space, 'formulate the conditions of sensible *a priori* intuition under which alone the schema of a pure concept of outer appearance can arise' (B 204/A 163). The idea here is, presumably, that such axioms state or bring out fundamental properties of space, which even the most general thought of anything as being in space must respect. But though this is clear enough, given Kant's general assumption of the connection between space and geometry, it is not in the least clear why Kant says that these axioms find their basis in 'the successive synthesis of the productive imagination in the generation of figures' (same reference). What has the fact, if it is a fact, that every line must be represented as generable out of homogeneous parts to do with whether or not two straight lines can enclose a space? Kant can hardly be meaning to say that the truth of the axioms could be deduced from statements recording synthetic activities, in view of what he says about geometrical concepts needing to be constructed in intuition. But if they are not thus deducible, in what sense does the synthesis constitute their 'basis'?

The bearing of the section's central argument on what Kant has to say about arithmetic is, if possible, even more obscure. In arithmetic, Kant avers, there are no axioms proper, though there are propositions which are 'synthetic and immediately certain (*indemonstrabilia*)' (B 204/A 164). What these indemonstrable propositions are is not explained further. Instead, Kant goes on to claim, first, that such arithmetical propositions or principles as that *if equals be taken from equals, the remainders are equal* are analytic, and secondly that 'propositions of numerical relation', e.g. $7 + 5 = 12$, are synthetic but not general. 'Numerical formulas' of this kind are said a few lines later (the reference is B 205/A 164–5) to be 'only singular'. What Kant means here is explained by an example of his own. If someone says that you can make a triangle out of three straight lines, provided that two of them together are longer than the third, he opens up many possibilities, all of which would satisfy the conditions stated; such a triangle could be right-angled, isosceles or scalene, have a base six inches or six feet long, and so on. By contrast, 'the number seven . . . is possible only in one way' (B 205/A 165), and so is the generation of twelve through the synthesis of seven and five. A geometer confronted with a problem which concerns a general property of triangles can take any triangle he likes as an example or specimen on which to work; an arithmetician with a large sum to work out can only write down the figures and follow the recognised procedures. The difference pointed out here has a bearing on a topic already discussed (section 5 above), that of the contrast between the 'ostensive' and the 'symbolic' construction of mathematical concepts. But what it has to do with appearances, as intuited, being extensive magnitudes is very far from clear.

Despite these criticisms, the general problem raised in the Axioms section remains important and the solution Kant gives to it intriguing. The confidence with which we put questions about the dimensions of physical objects suggests that we do not treat as merely empirical the issue of whether they have a determinate size. We proceed as if we *knew* that physical things or spatial regions are essentially measurable. But what justifies such confidence? To say that the truths of pure mathematics are one and all tautologies, and so of their nature cannot be inconsistent with any truths of fact, is not enough to remove the difficulty, since we can quite well imagine worlds in which mathematical principles could get no grip. Mathematics would retain its validity in such conditions, but would equally be without practical use. Our general procedure is to assume that our world is not of this sort, but that physical phenomena are especially apt for treatment in mathematical terms; the whole science of physics proceeds on this assumption. Kant at least has the merit of having made the assumption explicit and of having tried to produce a rational justification of it. We may not believe his answer, but we cannot simply dismiss his question.

§ 22 *Mathematics and the World : Measurable Intensities*

In the Axioms section Kant is reflecting on certain important applications of mathematics, which however do not exhaust our use of this science in relation to the sphere of nature. If we take an illuminated surface, for example, we can enquire into its extent overall—the area it covers—but equally we can investigate the intensity of the illumination. An astronomer will be interested in the size of a distant object, but he will also think it worth enquiring into the temperature at its surface or the degree of its gravitational pull. We presume that such things as the comparative intensity of colours, degrees of illumination, varying amounts of heat or cold can be given mathematical expression by the use of a scale which extends from zero upwards. If someone asks, 'What is the temperature of this room?', we assume that there is a definite answer. But what is the basis of our assumption in this and similar cases? It is this question Kant tries to answer in the section called 'Anticipations of Sense-Perception'.

As Kant points out, the presumption that sensations must all admit of mathematical treatment is at first sight highly paradoxical. The spatial and temporal properties of external objects connect with the form of experience rather than its matter; they concern features which are constant no matter what physical realities turn up. That we can know in advance of experience that they will all have a precise mathematical expression is thus not wholly surprising. But sensation appears to belong to the matter of experience rather than its form; it falls on the side of the given, and for that reason would seem to be incapable of being anticipated. I have to wait on experience to find out if a bag is heavy or a plate is hot; it is, if you like, a matter of brute fact. Kant has no wish to challenge such claims. He holds, nevertheless, that there is one respect in which I can say something in advance of experience even about sensation, namely that whatever its content it will be present in a determinate degree. As Kant himself puts it (B 207), 'in all appearances the real that is an object of sensation has intensive magnitude'. That sensations have intensive magnitude, if indeed they do, is a formal fact about them; it is a condition alleged to hold without regard to the particular nature of what is sensed. Kant therefore argues that the situation about sensation is precisely parallel to that of spatial and temporal properties: in each case we know in advance of experience that they are determinate in intensity or extent, though in both cases we have to wait on experience to discover in what actual amount they are present.

To clarify his position here Kant should first have offered some elucidation of what he intended by the term 'sensation'. In a passage in the *Critique of Judgment* (section *3*) he distinguishes between 'objective' and 'subjective' sensation, connecting the former with perception and the latter with feeling. The green colour of the meadows, he says, belongs to objective sensation, its agreeableness to subjective sensation, which has nothing to do with cognition. But what about the fact that the meadows seem green to me, brown to you? Sensations can and do vary significantly from person to person, so much so that they might be said to have an essentially personal reference. Kant himself was apparently of that view when he put forward his difficult doctrine of judgments of perception in the *Prolegomena*. Yet in the Anticipations the sensations spoken of are obviously supposed to be invariant from person to person; what Kant is after is, for instance, *the* temperature of the room, not how hot or how cold it feels to you or me. It is this which is determinate and determinable by reference to a commonly accepted scale, not the actual degree of feeling experienced by an individual. 'Sensation' in this connection thus covers what a person should feel, or what he would feel if his faculties were normal and other conditions of perception met standard requirements.

Attention to this point might have removed, or at any rate lessened, a further obvious difficulty in Kant's account: his failure to specify just how widely his doctrine is intended to apply. At first sight he appears to be claiming that any sensation is capable of mathematical treatment, which would imply, amongst other things, that felt pains and pleasures could be compared precisely in respect of intensity. Similarly, the dryness of a wine or the sweetness of an orange should be measurable objectively if the doctrine applies to all sensations. It seems clear that Kant does not intend to apply it to the first of these cases, on the ground that pains and pleasures are purely matters of personal feeling. It makes no sense, in his view, to contrast the real painfulness of a felt condition with its apparent painfulness, and therefore to speak of the true degree in which the pain is present. The second case is more difficult. Kant says at one point (A 28) in the Aesthetic:

> The taste of a wine does not belong to the objective determinations of the wine, not even if by the wine as an object we mean the wine as appearance, but to the special constitution of sense in the subject that tastes it.

He claims in the same passage that taste is 'grounded . . . upon feeling (pleasure and pain), as an effect of sensation'. This would suggest that tastes too are purely personal, and so do not fall within the scope of Kant's doctrine. But the same passage couples tastes and colours together as subjective in opposition to space, which is the same for all percipients, and we can certainly talk about the real colour of an object and determine its intensity. In general, it looks as if Kant meant his principle to apply only to what might be called 'ideal' sensations, which are in point only in situations where it makes sense to distinguish between how things feel or seem to me and how they would feel or seem in standard conditions. The dictum that there is no arguing about tastes would suggest that it could not apply in their case; the fact that we do argue about them may be evidence on the other side. In any case, Kant is altogether too careless on the point, being content to start from the fact that it is part of the task of physics to measure light, sound, heat, etc. He was certainly percipient in seeing that there is a problem about what justifies us in thinking that sensations of a certain kind must all be capable of mathematical expression. Where he fell down was in not specifying, at all exactly, which sensations they were.

The argument Kant produces in support of his principle runs closely parallel to that of the Axioms. It begins by noting that sensation proper is a momentary affair: it is not come by as a result of adding parts to parts, as in the case of the representation of a line. Sensations have in consequence no external magnitude. We can, however, think of any particular sensation as fading away until it vanishes altogether; in such circumstances there would be a 'graduated transition' (B 208) from empirical consciousness to pure consciousness, from a state in which the mind is affected in a particular way to one in which it has nothing before it but the pure manifold of time and space. Every sensation is thus (B 210/A 168)

> capable of diminution, so that it can decrease and gradually vanish. Between reality in the field of appearance and negation there is therefore a continuity of many possible intermediate sensations, the difference between any two of which is always smaller than the difference between the given sensation and zero or complete negation. In other words, the real in the field of appearance has always a magnitude.

The magnitude is in fact an intensive magnitude: it represents the degree of intensity which belongs to the content of the sensation, the strength or weakness of its presence. It is Kant's thesis that it possesses this magnitude thanks to the fact that we can think of any particular sensation as generated by a continuous process in which consciousness is raised from nothing to the degree of intensity the sensation manifests. Every sensation can be seen as generated, or at least generable, in this manner, and this is the formal fact about it which explains why every sensation has a determinate degree.

As with the earlier passage, the main difficulty here is to know what sort of a thesis Kant is putting forward. In places it looks as if he is giving an account of what actually goes on when people have sensations: sensations come into being by a gradual heightening of consciousness from total absence to particular presence. But this would suggest that all sensation takes time, when Kant says that it 'occupies only an instant' (B 209/A 167). In this connection it is important to notice that the passage quoted above speaks not of the actual diminution of sensations, but of their *possible* diminution: the 'graduated transition' spoken of in the second edition proof is a possible transition, and so is the 'synthesis in the process of generating the magnitude of a sensation from its beginning in pure intuition = o, up to any required magnitude' (B 208). In other words, Kant may be discussing not what in fact happens, but rather what could be represented as happening; he may once more have in mind an ability rather than a process. Sensation can be thought of as capable of indefinite diminution, with further possible stages lying beyond any stage reached; conversely, it can be thought of as coming into existence by a gradual heightening of consciousness. But nothing that psychologists have to say on the subject, or that private individuals report about their experiences, can have any bearing on the truth of these claims. They are not meant to state theses in psychology, but belong to transcendental philosophy.

Many people would agree with Kant in repudiating sensations of no determinate intensity. If someone said that he could see an illuminated expanse, but that it was neither bright nor dim nor anything in between, but (perhaps) all and none of these at once, we should treat his report with a good deal of scepticism. We might accept it as an attempt to convey some peculiarly personal experience, without believing that it could serve as a basis for determining how things are. If I belong to a group protesting against the noise made by aircraft the least I can do is allow that the noise is determinate and therefore capable of measurement; governments are not going to be impressed by indeterminate noises which have no particular volume. The principle to which Kant appeals is thus one which is widely accepted in practice. The question is, however, what grounds there are for accepting it. However difficult it may be to accept, or even to understand, Kant's answer to this question, it must be agreed that he shows philosophical acumen of a high order just in asking it.

There is one curiosity about the Anticipations section which deserves a brief further remark. Kant says (B 213/A 172) that his principle is useful not only in enabling us to anticipate perceptions, but also 'by placing a check upon all false inferences which might be drawn from their absence'. The point being got at here is that 'the proof of an empty space or of an empty time can never be derived from experience' (B 214/A 172·). In other words, there can be no scientific demonstration of the necessity of a vacuum. Kant recognised that 'almost all natural philosophers' took a contrary view: it seemed to them that the only explanation of the fact that bodies of the same volume are of widely different weights must be that matter is spread more thinly in some than in others, or again that more empty space is included in the first than in the second. In Kant's own words (B 215/A 173), 'they assume that the real in space . . . is everywhere uniform and varies only in extensive magnitude, that is, in amount'. Against this Kant suggests that there is another possibility which the philosophers in question overlook, namely that two equal spaces can both be filled with matter, but with matter possessing different degrees of intensity. A weak radiation can be said to fill a space just as completely as a strong radiation; it may be the same with matter. Kant concludes (B 216/A 174–5):

> I do not at all intend to assert that this is what actually occurs when material bodies differ in specific gravity, but only to establish from a principle of pure understanding that the nature of our perceptions allows of such a mode of explanation.

Elsewhere Kant works out a dynamical theory of matter in terms of fields of force, as opposed to material particles. In the *Critique* he confines himself to exposing the metaphysical dogmatism of other scientists. Whether we sympathise with his view of matter or not, it is at least instructive to find him turning his philosophical conclusions to account in this way.

§ 23 *General Remarks about the Analogies of Experience*

An 'analogy of experience' is explained by Kant (B 222/A 180) as being 'only a rule according to which a unity of experience may arise from perception'. Analogies in philosophy contrast with analogies in mathematics. In the latter we are concerned with quantitative relations, and the analogy is always constitutive: given A, B and C and the proportion (*analogia* in Greek) 'as A is to B, so C is to D' we can work out the precise value of D. The relations philosophy handles are by contrast qualitative, and accordingly in this area 'from three given members we can obtain *a priori* knowledge only of the relation to a fourth, not of the fourth member itself' (B 222/A 179–80). In other words, the principles handled in the Analogies point to some further existent, but do not determine what it is: it must be left to experience to say what causes what, or what is substance. Why Kant should in these circumstances have grouped his principles under the obscure title 'Analogies' is not apparent, the more so because there is no mention in the main body of his proofs of the four constituents of a relation just referred to. The arguments Kant investigates are not analogical in any obvious sense; they all have to do with the postulation of further existents on the basis of the occurrence of some item in experience. In any case, Kant is not concerned with the type of reasoning here involved, but with the principles or assumptions presupposed in the attempt to apply that pattern of argument no matter what material turns up. He is not engaged in a study belonging to inductive logic, but in a 'transcendental' enquiry into the legitimacy of following certain procedures.

To say that the Analogies give us rules for producing unity of experience out of perception is also unsatisfactory, as is Kant's statement of the 'principle of the analogies' in the second edition: 'Experience is possible only through the representation of a necessary connection of perceptions' (B 218). Both formulas suffer from the defect that they apply too widely: they might be true of categorial principles generally, not just of those categorial principles which fall under the head of Relation. The Transcendental Deduction itself was concerned with 'rules according to which a unity of experience may arise from perception'; its conclusions could well be formulated in the words Kant uses to express the general principle of the Analogies in the second edition. In the first edition (A 176–7) the general principle of the Analogies was stated as being that 'all appearances are, as regards their existence, subject *a priori* to rules determining their relation to one another in one time'. This formula is superior to its replacement in several respects: in making clear that the Analogies have to do with the way in which the occurrence of one item in experience calls for the *existence* of other experienceable items; in emphasising that the rules these principles impose on appearances determine their *relations* to one another; finally and most important, in making clear that the relations in question have to do with the things concerned belonging to *a single temporal system*.

The central point about the Analogies, strangely missed by some commentators, is that they purport to establish what must be true of the experienced world if we are to make objective temporal judgments within a single system of time. Kant starts from what he takes to be a fact, that we do suppose that we can distinguish real from apparent duration, real from apparent succession, real from apparent co-existence. He also takes it, as we all do in our normal thought, that real events and processes belong to a unitary temporal order, so that we can ask of any event whether it was earlier, later or simultaneous with another, and of any process whether it coincided in time with another, overlapped it or was wholly prior or posterior to it. The assumption behind these questions is, of course, that all times are part of one time, a time which is the same for all of us. But how do we know this to be true, seeing that our immediate experience is, apparently, merely of something going on in ourselves? And how are we to feel confident in pronouncing on real temporal properties or relations, when we reflect that time is not the sort of thing that can be perceived? Events do not come to us with their true dates stamped on their backs, nor processes with their real duration: we have to work out dates and lengths of processes, on the basis of an experience which is primarily personal. It is Kant's contention that we do this inside a framework of principles which specify conditions that have to be met by any item that can belong to an objective temporal order; the effect of our so doing is that we make demands on the experienced world which are to say the least surprising. We proceed as if it were a necessary truth that nothing is absolutely created or annihilated in that world, but that all change is transformation. We take it as axiomatic that it is a world in which events are not 'loose and separate' in the way Hume took them to be, but that the situation is rather that the very fact that something occurs means that something else *must* have occurred and that something further *must* follow, in other words that there are necessary connections between events. Finally, we take it to be a world in which different physical things do not operate in causal independence of one another, but form part of a system all of whose members are in thoroughgoing causal interaction. Kant would allow that, in one way, there is no necessity in the principles here involved: to deny them validity is not to fall into logical self-contradiction. He believes all the same that he can show them to be necessary in a different sense, necessary 'for the possibility of experience'. If we are to make the time-discriminations and temporal ascriptions that we do—if we are to have a viable system of objective time-judgments—we must organise our experiences according to the principles stated in the three Analogies. Failing that, coherent time-experience would be impossible.

It should be noticed at once that, so interpreted, the principles of substance, causality and reciprocity have a strictly restricted application. They are not the metaphysical principles, valid of 'things in general', which their names may suggest. On the contrary, they have to do only with 'appearances', i.e. with what can form part of the common *experience*. As Kant says himself (B 223–4/A 181), they 'have no other purpose save that of being the conditions of the unity of *empirical* knowledge in the synthesis of *appearances*' (Kant's italics). It follows that the concepts which underlie them are not so much the pure concepts of the understanding, the categories themselves which preside over 'synthesis in general' (B 224/A 181), but rather the transcendental schemata. Kant *says* that 'in the principle itself we do indeed make use of the category' (ibid.), without indicating at all how we are supposed to do so. But he adds that 'in applying to it appearances we substitute for it its schema as the key to its employment, or rather set it beside the category as its restricting condition', and it is certainly true that the concepts which figure most prominently in his detailed discussions are those of permanence of the real in time, invariable or regular succession and coexistence of empirical properties in different substances (see B 183–4/A 143–4). That principles embodying these concepts are declared to be synthetic *a priori* need cause only the mildest of qualms to the convinced empiricist. If we say that these are truths of reason, they are truths of a reason which is empty except when directed on material that has temporal aspects or connections. Remove the reference to time and they lose all authority, indeed all definite meaning. The wider implications of Kant's solution of the problem of pure concepts of the understanding are nowhere so clear as here.

As was mentioned earlier, the Analogies section is peculiar in that Kant there undertakes to prove both a general principle (the one already quoted in its two versions) and three particular principles. The particular principles are needed because there are three 'modes' (B 219/A 177) of time, duration, succession and coexistence, each of which has to be dealt with if the general problem of knowledge of a unitary objective time-system is to be solved. Kant has to enquire into the conditions which make judgments possible, first about the objective duration of things and states of affairs, second about the objective succession of events, third about the objective coexistence of things and their properties; and these are separate problems. They are, nevertheless, closely connected, as can be seen from the fact that arguments presented under one head turn out to have very close counterparts under another. It might even be claimed that the first two principles at least are intimately bound up together: it is hard to imagine a world in which the Kantian principle of substance held, but not the principle of necessary connection, or again one which was governed by the second principle but not the first. The principle of reciprocity seems at first sight to be another matter, since it looks on the face of things as if there could be a sphere in which substance was permanent and necessary connections ubiquitous without its being true that all particular substances were in reciprocal causal connection (there might be wholly independent causal lines). But however the three principles are related in practice, they must all be self-subsistent on the logical level, or Kant's claim that they each rest on a category will break down. Categories are one and all 'elementary' concepts (B 109), 'fundamental' and not 'derivative or composite' (B 89/A 64), and although 'the third category in each class always arises from the combination of the second with the first' (B 110), Kant goes out of his way to insist on its primary and hence basically independent character. If the principle of reciprocity could be deduced from those of substance and causality it would not have the interest Kant ascribes to it and would not figure separately in the *Critique of Pure Reason*.

We shall have to return to this question of the relation of the three Analogies (see section 26 below). Meantime, I must refer briefly to Kant's supposed proof of his general principle, set out most fully in the paragraph added at the beginning of the second edition discussion (B 218–9) and to some extent anticipated in A 177–8. The added paragraph follows the general lines of the argument in the second edition Deduction, with one important omission. It begins by asserting that empirical knowledge or experience proper requires the synthesising of perceptions in one consciousness; without such 'synthetic unity' there can be no knowledge of objects. It then goes on to claim that in our private experience 'perceptions come together only in accidental order'; such connections as there are between them are merely personal or subjective. It follows that there is a problem about arriving at how things are, as opposed to how they seem to each of us individually. It is a problem which is particularly urgent when our concern is to determine what exists objectively in time, since time 'cannot itself be perceived'. The problem is solved, if Kant is to be believed, by recognising that (B 219)

> the determination of the existence of objects in time can take place only through their relation to time in general, and there-fore only through concepts that connect them *a priori*. Since these always carry necessity with them, it follows that experi-ence is only possible through a representation of the necessary connection of perceptions.

The major defect of this argument, as compared with that of the Deduction, is its failure to mention judgment: we do not know if Kant is saying that objectivity is achieved in judgment, or arrived at by imposing *a priori* principles on data which are essentially private. The ambiguities of the word 'perception' leave both possibilities open, though it must be admitted that the second, less palatable, solution appears to fit the text better. But even if this difficulty were removed the argument would not be entirely satisfactory. It is, in truth, no more than a sketch of a general line to follow: at this stage the reader can hardly be expected to know what phrases like 'relation to time in general' or even 'representation of the necessary connection of perceptions' can be taken to mean. The old difficulty of the Deduction argument, about whether it shows that *necessarily* perceptions are connected or connectible, or that perceptions are connected or connectible *necessarily*, i.e. according to *a priori* principles, (the difficulty of the position of the modal operator), is not solved in the passage. We need, in fact, to go on to the particular principles if we are to find anything specific to debate.

It is often said that what Kant set out to do in the Analogies was provide a rational basis for Newtonian physics; since the latter is now outmoded, the implication here is that Kant's claims in the Analogies must be wrong. They may of course be wrong quite apart from the supposed connection with Newton. As for that, it is certainly true that Kant's whole conception of empirical reality is deeply coloured by his allegiance to the physics of his time, the main lines of which had been shaped by Newton. Kant was not wholly uncritical of Newton, as can be seen from the strictures he cast in the Anticipations on the notion of a vacuum, as well as from the arguments of the Aesthetic. But he obviously thought that Newton had produced definitive solutions to many physical problems, and would himself have counted it a merit in his own work that it underpinned Newtonian ideas. Even so, he would have denied that the *Critique* itself had such underpinning as one of its main objects. If we want to know where and to what extent Kant supports Newton, we have to turn to his treatise *Metaphysical Foundations of Natural Science*, published in 1786 and purporting to deal with the most general principles of physics on the basis of the results of the *Critique of Pure Reason*. This treatise begins by taking for granted the empirical concept of the movable in space, and then with the help of the Analytic of Principles deduces such laws as that 'with regard to all changes of corporeal nature, the quantity of matter taken as a whole remains the same, unincreased and undiminished' and 'in all communication of motion, action and reaction are always equal to one another' (Berlin edition IV, 541, 544; Ellington translation, pp. 102, 106). There is undoubtedly a very close connection here between the Analogies in particular and certain Newtonian laws. It remains true, nevertheless, that the argument of the Analogies moves on a different level from that of Newton, and that the considerations to which it appeals do not on the face of it have much, if anything, to do with physics. The first Analogy undertakes to prove that something is permanent, not that matter is permanent, the second Analogy that every change has a cause, not that 'every change of matter has an external cause' (Berlin edition IV 543; Ellington, p. 104). We ought therefore to consider the arguments of the Analogies without regard to the use Kant subsequently made of their conclusions. If it turns out that they are complete sophisms we can look again at the suggestion that a major object of the *Critique* was to do obeisance to Newton.

§ 24. *Kant's Defence of Substance*

The easiest way into the first Analogy is to look at the paragraphs which immediately follow the 'proofs' with which Kant begins each version of his discussion. In B 227/A 184 Kant says that the principle that something permanent persists through change has always been taken as indubitable not only by 'philosophers' (i.e. natural philosophers), but also by the common understanding, though neither has seen the necessity to attempt a proof of 'this obviously synthetic proposition'. In B 228/A 185 the point is illustrated and reinforced with the help of a homely example:

> A philosopher, on being asked how much smoke weighs, made reply: 'Subtract from the weight of the wood burnt the weight of the ashes which are left over, and you have the weight of the smoke'. He thus presupposed as undeniable that even in fire the matter (substance) does not vanish, but only suffers an alteration of form.

What was presupposed here was that something permanent persisted through the change, namely an underlying matter which was transformed in the process. The thesis in which Kant is interested, and which he says has been accepted without proof, is that an underlying substance persists through *all* change, change as such thus being essentially transformation. That this thesis is or has been widely taken for granted he supports by citing the constant appeal to the principle that nothing arises out of nothing, along with the more complex dictum of the ancients '*Gigni de nihilo nihil, in nihilum nil posse reverti*'. Some modern writers, says Kant, are inclined to separate the two propositions here, rejecting the first on the ground that it is inconsistent with the doctrine of creation. But there is no need to make the separation provided that we make clear that the principle is intended to apply only to the world of appearances. Whatever may be true of things in themselves our attitude as regards the experienced world is that nothing comes absolutely into existence or goes clean out of it. The question is what justifies us in maintaining such an attitude.

A sceptic may wonder whether Kant has represented the facts fairly here, whether he has given an accurate account of what philosophers and ordinary men take for granted. He could urge that it is one thing to believe that in any particular change something persists, another altogether to claim that an identical substance persists through all change whatsoever. Many modern commentators say that Kant has shown the necessity for something relatively permanent, but not for something whose permanence is as it were absolute. We shall discuss this issue below. Meantime it is important to insist that he would not lightly abandon his claims about what is commonly taken for granted, though he might agree that the common man is not always clear about the distinction which the sceptic seeks to draw. We can imagine him in this connection pointing out that a question such as that asked of the philosopher about smoke could be asked about any one of a series of changes, the implication being that the same something persisted through the whole lot, and then going on to try to make out that all changes whatever could be regarded as belonging to a singly highly complex series, adding that if such a view seems bizarre to the common man, it sounds a good deal less odd to the scientist, with his ambition to explain everything in terms of the properties of fundamental particles. A lot of argument would be needed to make the case anything like persuasive, but perhaps enough has been said to show that Kant was not simply careless in putting it forward.

Whether he was or not, it is in absolute permanence, the unbroken persistence through time of a single substance, that he is himself interested; it is permanence of this kind which he believes to be necessary for a unitary temporal system. Why? The direct arguments invoked in support of the idea are to say the least elusive. In the second edition proof (B 224–5) Kant begins by saying that all appearances are in time, in which alone coexistence or succession can be represented. Time constitutes a framework in which all change of appearances has to be thought, a framework which is not itself subject to change. But time itself cannot be perceived, and there must therefore 'be found in the objects of perception . . . the substratum which represents time in general'. The substratum of all that is real is substance, which in the shape of the permanent is that 'in relation to which alone all time-relations of appearances can be determined'. The meaning of this last sentence is clarified in the paragraph which follows (B 225–6/A 182–4). All our apprehension is successive, and that means that we face a problem about what is coexistent and what successive in objective reality. 'For such determination we require an underlying ground which exists *at all times*, that is, something *abiding* and *permanent*, of which all change and coexistence are only so many ways (modes of time) in which the permanent exists'. 'In other words', Kant goes on, the permanent is the *substratum* of the empirical representation of time itself; in it alone is any determination of time possible.

This argument has sometimes been read as saying that we can descry changes only against a permanent background; it is then objected that the background need not remain permanently what it is, provided that it is stable for a sufficient period. It seems clear enough, however, that Kant's meaning is quite different. The permanent which provides an underlying ground existing at all times is presupposed, not perceived; belief in it amounts to the conviction that what we have before us now is a modification or rearrangement of something which existed earlier in another form. Kant's contention is that we must believe in an underlying substance, capable of unending transformation, if there is to be genuine *continuity* in our experience. For past, present and future to belong together as parts of a single time we have to think that a single subject of predicates is concerned in all of them, a subject whose roots are in the past and which will survive to undergo fresh vicissitudes in the future. There can be no question of such a subject's going right out of existence, as opposed to being transformed, perhaps out of all recognition, nor again of its coming into existence out of nothing. So far as the experienced world is concerned we are compelled to accept it as something which is 'unchangeable in its existence' and such that 'its quantity in nature can neither be increased nor diminished' (B 225).

Kant attempts to reinforce the case here stated by considering what would happen if his principle were abrogated. In one passage (B 229/A 186) he says that 'the unity of experience would never be possible if we were willing to allow that new things, that is, new *substances*, could come into existence'. In these circumstances we should lose 'the identity of the substratum, wherein alone all change has thoroughgoing unity' (ibid.). In fact, however, the situation is worse than this suggests. 'A coming to be or ceasing to be that is not simply a determination of the permanent but is absolute, can never be a possible perception': absolute creation and absolute annihilation are not experienceable events. Kant proceeds to give his reasons (B 231/A 188):

> If we assume that something absolutely begins to be, we must have a point of time in which it was not. But to what are we to attach this point, if not to that which already exists? For a preceding empty time is not an object of perception. But if we connect the coming to be with things which previously existed, and which persist in existence up to the moment of this coming

to be, this latter must be simply a determination of what is
permanent in that which precedes it.

If substances could come into or go out of being in the absolute sense,
'the one condition of the empirical unity of time would be removed.
Appearances would then relate to two different times, and existence
would flow in two parallel streams—which is absurd' (B 231-2/
A 188).

These indirect arguments have attracted little attention; they
appear nevertheless to add up to something important. If the coming
into being of a new substance, or the going out of existence of an old
one, cannot be witnessed or thought of as part of the objective order
of things, considerable doubt is cast on whether these notions could
have any application. But why should they not be witnessed? In
asking this question we think of ourselves as inhabiting a world in
which there is general continuity, but in which from time to time
unheralded events occur, like the appearance of a new star to the
eye of a layman, or in which unaccountably a few things fail to have
their usual consequences. In these conditions, we assume, there
would be no difficulty in taking cognisance of these wayward
happenings. But is it as easy as this? Suppose someone argued that
events of this kind, events without proper antecedents or proper
successors, were not events at all but simply illusions: how should
we set about refuting him? It might be said that the reality of a
newly created substance would be palpable enough because of its
effects on other things whose existence was not in doubt. But would
this show that it was *created*, indeed *created out of nothing*? When a
new planet swims into their ken even naive watchers of the skies
are apt to ask in what form, or where, it existed before; confronted
with an apparently new creation, we should start investigating past
conditions in the hope of finding its antecedents. We might of course
be disappointed, but that in itself would not show that the procedure
was wrong. Similarly with things supposed to go clean out of
existence. We might suppose that the annihilation of a substance
could certainly be observed, since the thing in question would be
part of the natural order up to a certain point, and would then just
suddenly cease to be. But how should we know that it had been
annihilated, in the required sense of the term? If it blew up in a
species of cosmic explosion, what would prevent us continuing to ask
the question what became of it? It is not obvious that any combination of facts could logically compel us to agree that the asking of that
question was illegitimate. Even if it were agreed that annihilation
is witnessable in principle, it would always be possible in any

particular case to refuse to allow that it is real, on the ground that there was nothing to distinguish it from illusion. And once it had been conceded that the continuity of the universe might be broken in one or other of these ways, there would be no limit to the possibilities of disorder. We have been considering the question on the assumption that continuity is general and new creation or absolute annihilation rare. But when it is allowed that they are possible, how do we know that they will be rare? Nothing in these circumstances would guarantee that general continuity would be maintained: new creations and fresh annihilations could be occurring all the time. But if they were, or even might be, our own sense of the unity and continuity of time must inevitably be lost.

Kant's point can be put in a different way if we enlarge on his somewhat cryptic remarks about how existence would flow in two parallel streams if substances could come into being or cease to be absolutely. The first thing to note here is that talk about *two* parallel streams is too modest: there would be as many streams as there are unrelated substances. Every newly created substance would begin a fresh history, a history which, for reasons already stated, could not be integrated into any existing order of events and which would hence constitute a time-series of its own. The career of substances which ceased to exist would similarly have to be withdrawn from what in our terms would be the common temporal order, and allowed to belong in each case to a time of its own. In these circumstances we should confront two alternatives. One would be to follow Kant in maintaining stoutly that 'there is only one time in which all different times must be located' (B 232/ A 188–9); to take this path would involve dismissing new and vanishing substances as illusory, and interpreting the phenomena as continuous modifications of what was there already. The other would be to pursue a policy of maximum liberality, and recognise all time-series as real, despite their having no relation one to another. This second course might seem to have the advantage of offering us a welcome increase of diversity, rather as if we suddenly learnt that we could move not just in the dull world of everyday fact, but had only to close our eyes to transfer ourselves to one or another of a whole series of worlds with equal claims to reality. The difficulty in these conditions is that we should at once encounter too much that was real and encounter no reality at all. Imaginary worlds remain intriguing just because we can contrast them with acknowledged fact; we have always got that to hang on to if we feel we are losing our way. But in a situation where there was an acknowledged plurality of times and orders of existence, no such advantage would be available to us. The consequences Kant predicted, namely total loss of continuity of consciousness and therefore of all sense of self, would seem all too probable in the circumstances described.

For these reasons I find Kant's central argument in the first Analogy impressive, indeed unanswerable. I would agree that his talk about 'the substratum which represents time in general' (B 225; cf. A 183) is extremely unsatisfactory; I would agree too that his claim that all apprehension is successive, which also plays a large part in the argument of the second Analogy, requires elaboration and defence. But on the main point about the connection between recognising the continuity of time and believing in an underlying substance which can undergo endless transformations but remains the same through all of them, he seems to me to have a powerful case. It is certainly no answer to it to maintain, as do so many of his critics, that to measure objective durations we need only objects that are enduring, not an object which is sempiternal. Although duration is the 'mode of time' supposed to be handled in the first Analogy, its real concern is broader: what Kant is after are the conditions in which we can provide for continuity in a unitary temporal system. The question, what has to be true if all coexistences and all successions are to fall within a single time-series, is clearly separate from the question, what has to be true if we are to observe changes at all. When Kant says that only the permanent can change, it looks as if he might be answering the second question: change can be observed only against a background of things that persist unchanged. But attention to his actual words shows that it is not this problem which concerns him, but the much broader problem of how we are to think of all changes as belonging to the same time-order, as constituting episodes in a single history. The first problem is empirical: it is answered by referring to relatively permanent objects like the sun and the earth. The second problem is of another order altogether: it cannot be solved by the mere citation of empirical facts.

The conclusion for which Kant argues in the first Analogy is that 'in all change of appearances substance is permanent: its quantum in nature is neither increased nor diminished' (B 224). Substance is here spoken of in the singular; although there is nothing in the argument to require that it take the form of matter, there seems little doubt that Kant thinks of it on these lines. Now matter is not so much a thing as a stuff, of which ordinary physical things are temporary configurations. Kant's argument for substance is an argument for a continuing stuff out of which all things are made. It seems odd in these circumstances that Kant should talk not just about *substance*, but about *substances*, as for example when he says at the end of his discussion in the first Analogy (B 231/A 188) that 'substances, in the field of appearance, are the substrata of all determinations of time'. The third Analogy professes to prove that 'all substances, in so far as they can be perceived to coexist in space, are in thoroughgoing reciprocity' (B 256; compare A 211). What can these substances be, if not collocations or (to put it crudely) dollops of substance? What Kant seems to have in mind in the third Analogy is, quite simply, enduring physical objects like the moon and the sun. But of course these bodies, although long-lasting, are very far from being sempiternal: they came into existence at a particular time and will go out of existence at a particular time. It is certainly no part of Kant's programme to prove that objects of this kind cannot come into existence or go clean out of it: they are constantly doing both. We shall have to return to this question in discussing the third Analogy; meantime, it must be admitted that Kant's move from singular to plural in his talk of substance is undertaken without explanation, and so far as it can be understood seems to be entirely without justification.

§ 25 *Kant on Causality*

I come now to the second Analogy, which has received more attention from commentators and provoked more controversy than any other part of the *Critique*. The existence of the controversy shows at the lowest estimate that Kant has not expressed himself in a very convincing way. One feature of the section which is highly puzzling is that Kant apparently offers not one proof of his principle, but a whole succession of them (see Paton, *Kant's Metaphysics of Experience* II 224–5, summarising Adickes, for details). It is as if he thought that he had something very important to say, but was not sure that he had managed to get it across, and therefore decided to put the point repeatedly in slightly different terms. The addition of yet another proof at the beginning of the second edition version clearly fits in with this policy. Unfortunately the new proof is no more definitive than the others, and we are reduced to taking points from a variety of passages if we are to make Kant's case at all convincing.

The principle to be proved was formulated in the second edition (B 232) as 'All alterations take place in conformity with the law of the connection of cause and effect'. In the first edition (A 189) the wording was 'Everything that happens, that is, begins to be, presupposes something upon which it follows according to a rule'. Once more there is reason to prefer Kant's first version to his second, if only because it fastens on to something which is central to all his thinking in this part of the *Critique*, the notion of an event. Kant is concerned with what has to be true, first if something is to constitute a real as opposed to a mere seeming event, a happening which is part of the objective order, and second if such an event is to be perceived. In much of what he says he seems to be concentrating on the second of these issues, struggling with what he takes to be the fact that all human apprehension is successive and suggesting that we can sort out real from apparent successions by realising that the first are irreversible whereas the order of the second is not fixed. But it is quite wrong to give exclusive attention to these passages. As is made clear repeatedly, Kant's central preoccupation is with events as such, that is with the recognition of happenings as occurring objectively at a determinate point in time. All three Analogies have to do with the assigning of objective dates and durations, processes which Kant believes to be far more complex and difficult than is commonly assumed. To leave this aspect of the argument out of account, or to push it into the background, as many commentators do, is to load the dice against Kant from the start.

An event is a happening at a determinate point in time; it is something which belongs not just to the private experience of a single individual, but to the common experience. It is part of the objective order, the order which is the same for each of us, or for each of us in so far as he is rational. But how does an event get a definite date? What ensures that it occurs as and when it does? Kant's answer to these questions is that every event must be seen as the successor to some previous event, upon which it follows according to a rule; it occurs at this determinate point of time because something else occurred previously. Obviously more is intended here than the empty tautology that nothing could be described as happening now unless it were also appropriate to describe something else as having happened in the past, though Kant's talk about the preceding time necessarily determining the succeeding ('since I cannot advance to the succeeding time save through the preceding': B 244/A 199) is muddling in this connection. The something else that occurred previously has got to answer a definite description and be of a certain sort; this is why Kant puts in the reference to a rule. What he has in mind is plainly that when one sort of event occurs, another follows with causal necessity. What kinds of events are linked in this way has to be established empirically. But that every event points backward to *some* preceding event is a principle which can be laid down *a priori*. It is the principle that all alterations take place in conformity with the law of the connection of cause and effect.

The question may be asked why we should allow ourselves to be thus pushed into determinism. That every event occurs at a definite date is a tautology; that every event has to occur at the date it does is an obviously synthetic proposition, and one that on the face of things seems to be quite untrue. It is my intention now to go on working on this book tomorrow, and to start at or soon after 9 o'clock. Suppose I in fact start at 9.10 precisely: do I have to say that the event of my starting had to take place at that hour? Might I not have read the paper a little longer and begun at 9.15, or wasted less time beforehand and begun at 9.00? Unfortunately Kant does not consider questions of this sort in the second Analogy. He does take them up in his discussion of the third Antinomy, where he makes clear that his commitment to the universal rule of causal law as regards nature is not intended to rule out human responsibility for actions. The details of his complicated theory can hardly be considered now. All that we need note is that he believed that only if there were necessary connections between events would it be possible to speak of an objective natural order, and that the existence of free will in the ethical sphere did not show this to be false.

According to Kant, it is a necessary condition of something's being an event occurring at a definite time that it should have been preceded by some other event of a particular kind, on which it followed according to a rule. Suppose now we look at the process from the opposite point of view: can we say that the occurrence of the first event was a sufficient condition for the occurrence of the second? It will not of course be a sufficient condition unless it is taken along with appropriate background conditions, some of which may fail to be present, with the result that the customary effect does not follow. But in the case we are considering the effect did follow, and the background conditions were presumably therefore complete. It seems clear that in these circumstances Kant would say that the occurrence of the first event was a sufficient condition for the occurrence of the second, and that this is the standard situation throughout nature. His commitment to the law of causality thus involves not just the belief that every event will have its proper causal antecedent, but also that, other things being equal, it will also have its proper causal successor. In Kant's phenomenal world necessary connection holds forwards as well as backwards; in fact every item that occurs in that world is linked causally with something in the past and something in the future.

One reason for accepting this tightly deterministic position is that it is taken for granted in scientific practice; another that people treat as absurd the idea of an uncaused event, as in my example of the car that broke down for no reason at all (*Metaphysics*, p. 155). Kant gives neither of these reasons in the second Analogy. Instead, he concentrates on the contrast between the way in which things strike each of us individually and the way in which things really are, as that contrast applies to successive happenings. The very fact that all our apprehension is successive means that the order of our experiencing cannot always coincide with the order of existence, and this sets us a problem about how to sort out the objective from the subjective. If we could simply find out what was objective fact by looking and seeing, the problem could be solved without difficulty. But 'time cannot be perceived': events do not come to us with objective dates upon them. We have to *establish* that something is really happening; we cannot just *observe* it, since it essentially involves reference to something no longer present. Further, our perception of reality is unavoidably mediated by our cognitive apparatus, with the result that knowledge of things as they are in themselves lies beyond our powers. In these circumstances we have no alternative but to think that what is really there is what we take to be there when we judge impersonally. According to the argument of the Transcendental Deduction, judgment of that sort is informed by *a priori* concepts, with the consequence that the world constituted in judgment is a world governed by necessary principles. In the second Analogy Kant makes this theory more concrete by confining his attention to a single aspect of phenomena and the operation of a single such principle.

Too much stress has been laid by commentators on Kant's examples of the house whose different features can be perceived in a variety of orders, and the ship moving downstream whose movements can be perceived in one order only (B 237/A 192). The order in the first case is reversible, whereas in the second it is irreversible. But Kant is not pretending that irreversible succession must be causal succession, as many of his critics seem to think. Irreversibility of perceptions is at most a sign or symptom of the presence of causal necessity. That events in nature are causally connected is for Kant an *a priori* proposition; it is not a conclusion to which we come by observing that this kind of thing and that are constantly conjoined in experience. Otherwise there would be no difference of importance between the positions on this topic of Kant and Hume, when Kant himself thinks the difference fundamental. Kant goes out of his way to attack the view that we come by the concept of cause by noticing that certain events are always followed by certain others (see B 240–1/A 195–6): this derivation, in his view, takes away all necessity from the causal principle. The position as he sees it is that necessary connection is presupposed in our thinking about the experienced world, and thus lies at the basis of the regularities which are actually found. From one point of view it is true to say that the regularities are there because we demand that they be exhibited: we postulate necessary connection, and look about unceasingly for it. If someone tells us that in some particular case there is no such connection, we simply refuse to believe him. The Humean view that confidence in causality is instilled into us by custom and habit is thus mistaken in principle. As the point was put in the Deduction, association presupposes affinity: regular and irreversible successions point to causal connections, but do not constitute them. It is not in any case very flattering to Kant to take him as offering the example of the ship going down stream as an instance of a causal transaction, as if its being in one position were the cause of its being in another. We have to do here with an objective succession, but though for Kant objective succession depends on the operation of causality it is not itself straightforwardly causal. There must be something in the preceding situation which stands in a causal relation to each element in the situation that comes about. But that is not to say that the whole preceding situation must be the cause of what ensues, or night would be the cause of day.

In the Analogies generally Kant makes much of the contrast between the subjective order of an individual's experience and the objective order of events, and some critics allege that he relies unduly on an unacceptable premise in these arguments, the premise that 'the apprehension of the manifold of appearance is always successive' (B 234/A 189). That this premise is false is shown, we are told, by the simple fact that there are some wholes we can take in at a glance. Defenders of Kant try to rescue him at this point by distinguishing between determinate and indeterminate apprehension: they admit that we can gain an immediate grasp of, say, the amount of ground covered by a field, but argue that it is necessarily vague and unspecific; to convert it into a determinate apprehension we need to go through its parts one by one in the way Kant suggests (see B 455–6/A 427–8 note, and the discussion in section 21 above). But we do not need to make good this argument in order to make

Kant's general position watertight. Even if it is false that 'our apprehension of the manifold of appearance is *always* successive' (B 225/A 182), it at least *sometimes* is; even if there are wholes which we can take in at a glance, there are others which we can not. This being so, the discrepancy Kant finds between the subjective order of experiencing and the objective order of events remains a real possibility: it is always possible that things do not exist as they seem to do because of the serial nature of some of our apprehending. And this is all Kant needs to persuade his reader that there is a genuine problem about what is objectively there.

As in the case of the first Analogy, many critics of the argument of the second Analogy say that Kant claims too much in his conclusion. He wants to say that *all* alterations take place in conformity with the law of the connection of cause and effect, or that *everything* that happens presupposes something upon which it follows according to a rule, on the ground that only if necessary connections are ubiquitous will it be possible to distinguish objective from subjective successions. His critics retort that no such ubiquity is required: if nature were generally orderly, and most objective successions conformed to the Kantian pattern, we should have at least a good chance of separating what was really going on from what merely seemed to be. We do not need an absolutely orderly world, but only a moderately orderly one, in order to be able to assign objective dates. The critics here are clearly thinking of Kant as confronting a practical problem, when he is in fact concerned with the theoretical foundations of a process; they also allow themselves too many easy assumptions, above all that if there are exceptions to the rule of natural law they will not be numerous. If we did live in a world in which nearly everything that happened conformed to law, though a few things did not, and if we could be assured that this is and will remain the situation, no doubt we could make a fair guess at what successions were objective and what not. The trouble about the critics' position is that we can have no such assurance, once it is allowed that alterations may take place which are not in accordance with the law of cause and effect. If there are some breaches of law, why may there not be indefinitely many breaches? And if the reply is that so far at any rate things seem to have gone on in a generally orderly fashion what guarantee does that offer that this relatively happy situation will continue? Kant's commitment to complete causal determinism involves him in severe embarrassments so far as his ethics is concerned, but at least it is entirely false to suggest that he entered into it lightly, without due consideration of what he was saying, or could have stuck to his main claims in the second Analogy without going nearly so far. When it comes to choosing between Kant and his critics here, it is Kant who turns out to have thought more carefully and argued more effectively, just because he has treated his problem in more depth and seen far more of its complexities.

Kant's main concern in the second Analogy is to offer a proof of the causal *principle*; we look in the section in vain for a detailed exposition of his views on the causal *relation*. We know of course from earlier passages that he took regular sequence or unvarying succession ('the real upon which, whenever posited, something else always follows': B 183/A 144) to be the schema of cause. The schema of a category is not identical with the category itself; it should therefore follow that the causal relation for Kant was more than a matter of constant conjunction. What more? The category of cause, according to the Analytic of Concepts, has an intimate connection with the hypothetical form of judgment, which in turn is concerned with the relation 'of the ground to its consequence' (B 98/A 73). If this means anything, it should imply that a Kantian cause is, if not exactly the ground of its effect, related to it on the analogy of ground and consequent. Such a cause would be active in producing its effect rather than its mere regular antecedent. Towards the end of the second Analogy Kant says that 'causality leads to the concept of action, this in turn to the concept of force, and thereby to the concept of substance' (B 249/A 204); he adds that 'action signifies the relation of the subject of causality to its effect' (B 250/A 205), before going on to argue that action is a sufficient empirical criterion of substantiality. Causal agency is shown in the exercise of force of various kinds. In making these remarks Kant is probably thinking of his own dynamical theory of matter, where every part or nodule simultaneously attracts and repels all others. But whether he intended them to support an 'activity' analysis of the causal relation is less certain. In theory he should accept such an analysis. But the facts he adduces here do not require it; they can be interpreted without difficulty along Humean lines. We are therefore left in doubt about how exactly he thought cause related to effect. The indications of his writings on philosophy of science are that he thought the relation intelligible so far as effects could be calculated mathematically; he would have distinguished cases of this kind from those where the cause merely triggers off the effect, without our having any understanding of the mechanism concerned. But he would probably have agreed that the intelligibility involved was limited, in so far as it is a matter of experience, and only of experience, what things there are in the world and what powers they exercise (compare B 269–70/A 222–3; B 798–9/A 770–1). When we get down to fundamentals, we have just to accept that certain kinds of things produce certain kinds of effects. If this was Kant's standpoint, it is only marginally different from Hume's.

There is one passage in the second Analogy which is of some interest in connection with the problem of the causal relation, the one in which Kant points out (B 248/A 203) that 'the great majority of efficient natural causes are simultaneous with their effects'. Most empiricist analyses of causality say that the cause precedes the effect, and Kant himself accepts this view in much of what he writes. But he also sees that in many cases, and particularly in the scientific instances he was himself apt to take, there is no gap between the time in which the cause is complete and the time in which the effect begins to appear. 'If I view as a cause a ball which impresses a hollow as it lies on a stuffed cushion, the cause is simultaneous with the effect' (ibid.). Kant comments that what matters in the causal relation is not the *lapse*, but the *order* of time. 'The time between the causality of the cause and its immediate effect may be vanishing, and they may thus be simultaneous; but the relation of the one to the other will always still remain determinable in time'. It will do this because producing the cause will immediately produce the effect, whereas producing the effect will not immediately produce the cause. The idea that an effect could produce its cause is dismissed by Kant as obviously impossible. But even if we sympathise with him on this point, as I do myself, it can hardly be claimed that what he says on the general topic in this context is wholly satisfactory. The implications of the previous discussion are that a cause is a previous event; in this passage a cause seems to be conceived as the sum of the necessary and sufficient conditions needed to bring something about, the completion of which conditions is simultaneous with the appearance of the effect. Collingwood in his intriguing essay on causality in *An Essay on Metaphysics* (pp. 285–343) was right to point out that different senses of the word 'cause' may here be involved. We need a much fuller discussion than Kant offers of what causality comprises if we are to have any hope of sorting these difficulties out. Meantime, however, his calling attention to cases in which cause and effect appear to be simultaneous, if not entirely original (it had been considered by Hume: *Treatise*, I iii 2, p. 76 ed. Selby-Bigge), is at least useful. It suggests that there are aspects of the problem of causality which were simply not thought of in standard discussions of the subject.

§ 26 *Kant on Reciprocity and Coexistence*

The third Analogy was doubtless as important to Kant as the other two, but has received much less attention from commentators. This is partly because the argument appears to run closely parallel to that of the preceding section, and thus not to introduce any fundamentally new point. But it also has something to do with a certain fuzziness both in the problem Kant professes to be tackling and in the solution he offers for it.

At the end of his second edition proof (B 256–8) Kant writes:

> Thus the coexistence of substances in space cannot be known in experience save on the assumption of their reciprocal inter-action. This is therefore the condition of the possibility of the things themselves as objects of experience.

The first thing to note here is that Kant is discussing substances and not events, as he was in the second Analogy; he is concerned with what must be true if we are to know that these substances coexist. The substances in question coexist in space, and there is every reason to think that they are simply enduring material bodies like the moon and the sun. Kant gives no indication of what he will allow to count as a substance in this sense (could we, for example, reckon Mount Everest as well as the earth among substances?). On the basis of what has gone before he would presumably say that nothing could count as a substance unless it exercised causal agency. But since every bit of matter exerts force in attracting and repelling every other bit this would make every bit of matter a substance. Nor does Kant explain what the substances which coexist in space have to do with the permanent which persists through change and is not itself in space though it is continually manifested there. As was pointed out before, the relation of substance to substances in the *Critique* remains a matter of great obscurity.

At the very beginning of the third Analogy Kant says that there is an empirical criterion of the coexistence of substances, namely that 'the perceptions of them can follow upon one another reciproc-ally' (B 256–7). I can look at the moon and then look at the earth, or look at the earth and then look at the moon, and because the order of my perceptions is indifferent, the things concerned 'exist in one and the same time' (B 258/A 211) and so are coexistent. Kant does not ask what the position is if I look first at the moon and then at some distant star, many light years away, which may now no longer exist. Instead he accepts the empirical criterion as reliable and simply asks what lies behind it. His thesis is that the reversibility of the perceptual order in cases like the one he gives must be seen as a consequence of the fulfilment of a transcendental condition: the things concerned must stand in a relationship of thoroughgoing causal reciprocity. As he puts the point himself (B 257): 'a pure concept of the reciprocal sequence of their determinations is required, if we are to be able to say that the reciprocal sequence of the perceptions is grounded in the object, and so to represent the coexistence as objective'. The 'determinations' of a substance are its qualities, characteristics or modes; to speak of their 'reciprocal sequence' is, I think, a loose way of referring to the manifested series of mutually determined characteristics. Each substance is thought of as exercising causality on every other, and so as determining how and when it shall manifest itself. In the second Analogy Kant took irreversible succession to depend on sequence which was causally determined; the objective order of events is one in which the happening of each one has to come about at a certain point. In the third Analogy the same principle is invoked to account for reversible succession, except that Kant now considers causal agents which interact instead of confining himself to single causal chains. His claim that when different substances interact they can be said to belong to one and the same time is easy enough to accept. What is difficult is to see why their coexistence is possible only if this condition is fulfilled.

Perhaps we can get at the point he is trying to make if we restate the argument in a freer form. Suppose there were to be things in the universe which did *not* stand in a relationship of causal interaction with the remaining things, but as it were each pursued its own course and enacted its own history. The way in which such things manifested themselves might well be rule-governed: it could be the case that each of the manifested states was causally related to some preceding state. But would it be possible in these circumstances to handle the appearances of the different substances in terms of a single time-system? Could one date their different vicissitudes, and so say that the things themselves fell within one time? The answer must surely be 'no', for reasons which Kant indicated in the first Analogy in his talk about substances which might spring into being out of nothing. As he put it there, the appearances of such substances would belong to a time-series which could simply not be correlated with the general time-series. Similarly here: if there were to be substances which were in the literal sense loose and separate, we should confront not a single history, but a plurality of histories which could not be brought into relationship one with another. There would be not one time, but as many times as there were non-interacting substances or groups of substances. To talk about the substances concerned as coexisting (or for that matter as not coexisting) would in these circumstances make no sense. It is thus a condition of the empirical unity of time (something which Kant says we take for granted in all our thinking about the experienced world) that whatever substances there are should be in mutual causal reciprocity.

One reason for thinking this argument less than wholly satisfactory is that Kant does not indicate the limits within which he takes his principle to hold. The earth and the moon are in reciprocal causal interaction, and as a result there are events on earth which depend on the influence of the moon and events on the moon which depend on the influence of the earth. But there are also, of course, many events on both in which the influence of the other is minimal or nonexistent. The earth and the moon each has a constitution of its own, and this determines many of their characteristics either wholly or partially. Is it Kant's thesis that no empirical substance is fully self-determining, but owes at least some of its characteristics to the influence of other substances? This would seem to be the implication of B 259/A 212, where we read that 'each substance . . . must . . . contain in itself the causality of *certain* determinations in the other substance, and at the same time the effects of the causality of that other' (my italics). The question this passage raises is how many mutually affected determinations there have to be for the reciprocity to be described as 'thoroughgoing'. Alternatively we might try to say that, where mutual interaction is in place, each substance affects the other to an extent which is potentially unlimited, with the result that it is not possible in principle to draw an absolute distinction between what might be called free and dependent characteristics. But here too there will be degrees of freedom and dependence, and a question could be asked about the limits of their extent. Perhaps all that can be said in general is that for mutual interaction to prevail there must be at once some degree of freedom and some degree of dependence. Kant is of course concerned with a requirement of a highly general kind, and would be quite justified in pointing out that it is for empirical enquirers to specify the nature and extent of the reciprocity found in any particular situation. But clearly there are aspects of the principle of reciprocity itself which he has left insufficiently discussed. He should in particular have said something about the internal nature of substances as well as about the effects of their external relations; had he done so his thesis might have been both more intelligible and more palatable. And of course he should have discussed what qualified as a substance for the purposes of his theory.

We are naturally brought back at the end of the Analogies to the question how Kant's three principles are related. I suggested in section 23 that, though the three must be logically independent one of another if Kant's account of categories is to be preserved, there is at least a very close connection in practice between the first and the second Analogies, if only because an event which could not be interpreted as involving a modification of something already existing would also be an event standing in no rule-governed relation to some preceding event. That there should be a world which obeyed Kant's principle of substance, but not his principle of causality, or one which conformed to the principle of causality but not that of the permanence of substance, was accordingly difficult to believe. But at this stage I added that the third principle was on the face of things different: there might be a world conforming to the principles of substance and causality, but in which there were wholly independent causal chains. The results of our present discussion show that this verdict needs modification: the principle of the third Analogy is as closely bound up with the other two principles as they are bound up with each other. What we have here, in fact, is not three separate ways of thinking, but a set of interconnected ways of thinking, which owe much of their force and power to the fact that they do thus go together. Critics have tended on the whole to take Kant's contentions piecemeal and to behave as if he might be right about some of them even if he was wrong on others. Kant himself sanctions—indeed, encourages—this procedure, and I have certainly not avoided it altogether in my own discussion. It is, however, only fair to point out that a good deal of the plausibility of Kant's argument in this part of his work derives from its cumulative effect: the story about substance both gains support from and lends support to the story about causality, and the same is true *mutatis mutandis* of the story about reciprocity in its relation to each and both of the others. So much is this the case that we may wonder if Kant is really dealing here with three separate ideas, as he officially supposes, and not rather with a single complex concept which has components which are distinguishable but not ultimately distinct. Such components would be involved with one another in a specially intimate way, in somewhat the same manner as are the members of a Hegelian triad, but without the developmental overtones of the latter (reciprocity is surely not a development of substance). It is regrettable that Kant did not address himself explicitly to the question of the relationship of the three categories of Relation. It is regrettable, again, that he passed over in silence the question how the categories of Quantity and Quality on the one hand relate to those of Relation on the other, except for what he says about the former being 'mathematical' and the latter 'dynamical'. By failing to raise such issues he gave the impression that his categories form an unconnected heap, when to all appearances they belong together as parts of a connected point of view. Kant simply assures us that they are one and all necessary for experience as we have it; he should have gone further and shown how commitment to one carries with it commitment to all the rest. Failing any such attempt there is substance in Hegel's complaint (*Encyclopaedia*, section 42) that Kant 'did not put himself to much trouble in discovering the categories'. As his readers know to their cost, he strove hard and long to discover a 'clue to the discovery of all pure concepts of the understanding'. But the clue he found was at best an external clue, and Kant's preoccupation with it distracted him from investigating something more important—the internal or systematic connections of the individual categorial concepts he had to put forward.

§ 27 *Modal Concepts and Matter of Fact*

The Postulates of Empirical Thought are obviously very different from the Axioms, Anticipations and Analogies. I have expounded these as giving rise to principles which license important ranges of questions about the experienced world. The Axioms and Anticipations have to do with what might be called our inveterate tendency to put questions about such things as the precise extent of an area or the precise intensity of a sensation. The Analogies relate to the kind of questions we ask when changes take place in nature; they make clear the presuppositions which underlie these questions and purport to show that they are justified. If Kant is right in his main arguments in these sections (and I have been taking it that he is) experience can be anticipated in a number of important, though always formal, respects. Alternatively, we can say that the unspecific concept of an 'object in general', prominent in the Transcendental Deduction, is here filled out with at least some concrete content. The concept of an object in general is the concept of an object thought according to the principles expounded in the three sections with which we have been concerned. It is, if you like, the form of a possible empirical object; the characteristics it possesses must be found in every actual empirical object, and nothing can be an empirical object which lacks those characteristics.

By contrast the Postulates do nothing to enlarge our concept of anything, nor do they license questions at all like those with which we have been dealing. They simply consider what it means to say that something, i.e. something the concept of which is already determinate, is possible, actual or necessary. As Kant himself puts it (B 266/A 219), 'the principles of modality are nothing but explanations of the concepts of possibility, actuality and necessity, in their empirical employment'. Kant includes the last four words because he wants to concern himself not with thoughts but with things. He is not content to confine his attention to possibility, actuality and necessity as they figure in logic; his idea is to go beyond logic and consider these notions as they apply to the sphere of fact. It is his contention that we can form a concept of what it is for something to be possible, actual or necessary in a real as opposed to a merely logical sense, the real sense being part, though not the whole, of what is meant by describing something as empirically possible, actual or necessary. Real possibility as Kant sees it is what is essential in empirical possibility; to grasp it is accordingly to know both what can be actual and what can not.

The sting of this doctrine lies in its tail: it is Kant's claim to be able to rule possibilities out which is the most striking part of his theory. He says for instance that, though there is no internal contradiction in the idea of a two-sided figure enclosing a space and though such a figure is thus logically possible, it is not really possible. 'The impossibility arises not from the concept in itself, but in connection with its construction in space, that is, from the conditions of space and of its determinations' (B 268/A 221). I find in fact that no such figure can be constructed in pure intuition, and hence that it does not agree with the formal conditions of intuition and so of experience generally. Nothing can be actual which is not consonant with what Kant calls (B 265/A 218) 'the conditions of intuition and of concepts', i.e. the requirements set out in the Aesthetic and Analytic of Principles as so far explored. Kant illustrates this doctrine still more strikingly by referring to what look at first sight like respectable empirical possibilities, but which he says are not. He argues that even the concepts of substance, cause and reciprocity define possibilities only so far as they relate to experience: what substances, forces or reciprocal actions there are in the world must always be found out empirically. To imagine that the world contains substances or forces of radically different kinds from those met with in experience is to occupy oneself with fancies: the possibility of such things 'must either be known *a posteriori* and empirically, or it cannot be known at all' (B 269–70/A 222). As Kant puts the point later (B 798–9/A 770–1):

Thus it is not permissible to invent any new original powers, as for instance an understanding capable of intuiting its objects without the aid of senses; or a force of attraction without any contact; or a new kind of substance existing in space and yet not impenetrable. Nor is it legitimate to postulate a form of communion of substances which is different from any revealed in experience, a presence which is not spatial, a duration that is not temporal.

In the Postulates section itself Kant's examples of things which are logically but not really possible include precognition ('a special ultimate mental power of *intuitively* anticipating the future (and not merely inferring it)') and telepathy ('a power of standing in community with other men, however distant they may be': B 270/A 222); he dismisses them by saying simply that they are 'concepts the possibility of which is altogether groundless, as they cannot be based on experience and its known laws'. Without such a basis they remain nothing but 'arbitrary combinations of thoughts', free from contradiction indeed, but quite unable to lay claim to objective reality.

There can be little doubt that the main motive behind these remarks is antimetaphysical. In the Analytic as a whole Kant conducts a sustained polemic against the idea that we can arrive at the most fundamental of truths about the world by pure thought, and this polemic comes to a head in the Postulates, the appended note on the System of Principles and the first part of the succeeding chapter on Phenomena and Noumena. If we want to know why Kant selects precognition and telepathy for attention, we have to turn back to his essay of 1766 *Dreams of a Spirit-Seer* which, in the context of a comparison between the ideas of metaphysicians and those of the mystic Swedenborg, expatiated on the concept of a community of spirits and argued that in such a community, 'distance in space and time, which forms in the visible world the great cleft severing all communion, would disappear' (Berlin edition, II 332; Goerwitz translation, p. 60), leaving precognition and telepathy the order of the day. In Kant's mind precognition and telepathy were associated with a form of speculation which was essentially idle; they could not be taken for serious possibilities. But though Kant's antipathy to bare speculation would command wide sympathy, it may be objected that the case he states against it in the Postulates is weak. It may also be argued that, if we do accept his case, we shall be committed not merely to dismissing metaphysics, but also to ruling much potentially useful empirical theorising out of court. We must now examine these objections.

When it comes to discussing substances, fundamental forces and types of interaction, says Kant, we can be guided only by experience. Possibility has to be defined by actuality in this sphere, or it cannot be defined at all. Why? It cannot be said that Kant offers any reasons in support of this opinion; he simply declares for it as a matter of ultimate conviction. He might however argue that we were not justified in positing fresh substances, forces, etc, unless we could do more than simply suppose them to exist; we should have to show, or at least make plausible, how they could operate, by what mechanisms and through what media. So far as I can see Kant does not explicitly invoke this argument in the present context, but perhaps he makes an implicit appeal to it. We can imagine him saying of telepathy, for instance, that those who subscribe to it simply do not know how persons at a great distance from one another could communicate in this non-natural way, or again that they leave the discrepancy between communication of this sort and normal physical communication unexplained. These are legitimate objections, and Kant is right to say that we must not allow ourselves to be so dazzled by what appears to be empirical evidence into neglecting them as unimportant. But if he is to take this line, he needs to work it out much more fully than he does in the Postulates section. It is not enough to say that what is really possible must agree with the formal conditions of experience; he must show, in particular instances, how what look like genuine possibilities are not such because they conflict with those conditions. Otherwise Kant runs the risk of appearing to be merely dogmatic, dismissing speculation of one type on the basis of convictions which are equally speculative and equally unargued.

That more needs to be said here is also important in connection with the second objection. On the face of things it seems arrogant and absurd to suggest that empirical possibility has to be defined by actuality, or that the only possible forces in the physical world are those which are known to be actual. Have no new forces been discovered since Kant's time? The answer is of course that all sorts of new agents and agencies have been discovered. But Kant might say that the discoveries were all made within a framework of accepted presuppositions; the new fits in with the old, and conforms to the same general requirements. If this is true, he might turn such developments to his own account, by arguing that the only new possibilities that can be taken seriously are those that fit in with the general conditions of experience. But here again it would be necessary to specify those conditions more carefully than he does. When, for instance, in the passage quoted from the Discipline of Pure

Reason Kant says that it is not permissible to postulate 'a force of attraction without any contact', is that metaphysical wisdom on his part or simply metaphysical prejudice? No doubt he would himself connect it not only with the continuity of space, but also with what was said in the third Analogy (see B 260−1/A 213−4): he would say that a reasoned case could be made in favour of the ban. That physical disputes about such things as the possibility of a vacuum or that of action at a distance often involved the parties concerned in unconscious metaphysical assumptions would be hard to deny; Kant pointed out one such set of assumptions in his remarks about empty space in the Anticipations. But to show that other people are dogmatic in this way is not to demonstrate that you are free of dogmatism yourself. Had Kant set out his case in detail in each of the instances quoted, instead of just saying that the supposed possibilities 'cannot be based on experience and its known laws', his views on the subject would have been very much more persuasive.

It may be argued that, if we are to work with a concept of real, as opposed to empirical, possibility, we must define it in terms of the most general principles accepted at any one time by the scientific community, instead of invoking the supposedly timeless apparatus of pure reason. This would give us a shifting notion of what is really possible—things dubbed impossible at one time might be thought within the bounds of possibility at another—but the disadvantages of this would be offset by the advantage of greater contact with actual scientific work. Kant's proclamations and prohibitions in this field seem to spring from nothing better than armchair philosophising; the new concept of the really possible would not be open to that charge. It might even be said that Kant himself could accept the change, provided that he stuck only to the general assertion that some categories are necessary if experience is to be possible and avoided specifying any particular categories. Against this, much of the interest of Kant's work comes, as Collingwood somewhere remarked, from his combining a passion for generality with a passion for detail: remove the detail, and the contentions of the *Critique* become thin and uninteresting. It is not in any case obvious that one could stick to the main contention of the Deduction, that we must operate concepts of an object in general if we are to have shared experience, and go on to contend that the answer to what concepts qualify for this description depends on the state of particular knowledge at the time. I have already denied that it is a main function of the Analytic to defend or sanctify the principles of Newtonian physics, and have pointed out that Kant believes that his argument moves at a higher level of abstraction. There seems little doubt that Kant would fight hard to defend the indispensability, in any conceptual scheme which was to define an objective order, of *all* his categories and categorial principles; without their operation, he would argue, experience as we have it would simply not be possible. When Kant talks about 'experience' he certainly has general scientific attitudes in mind, though he is not thinking exclusively about science. He is not, however, committed to any particular scientific conclusions in his capacity as a transcendental philosopher, even if he believes it an advantage of his system that scientific principles can be brought under it. If all this is correct, Kant's doctrine that real possibility must be understood in terms of the formal conditions of experience becomes not only intelligible; it becomes highly plausible as well. If we are to take it that it makes sense to talk about the bounds of possibility, when something more than mere logic is at stake, it will be hard to avoid a theory constructed along these lines.

The actual or, as he puts it elsewhere, what exists is explained by Kant (B 266/A 218) as 'that which is bound up with the material conditions of experience, that is with sensation'. Mere thinking cannot determine what exists, not even in the case of the concept of God; only with the help of sense-experience can we determine what is actual. Kant mitigates this apparently dogmatic empiricism by stressing that the real is not simply what is sensed, but also what is 'bound up' with it, bound up in this context being explained in terms of the principles set out in the Analogies. Thus from seeing the behaviour of iron filings attracted by a magnet I can infer 'the existence of a magnetic matter pervading all bodies', a matter which I could in fact encounter empirically if it were not for the grossness of my senses. Generally, however, 'our knowledge of the existence of things reaches . . . only so far as perception and its advance according to empirical laws can extend' (B 273/A 226). In other words, *esse est aut percipi aut posse percipi*. To establish this Kant needs to consider apparent exceptions, notably the cases of God and the soul. He goes into both in the Dialectic, and I propose to defer any discussion of them until I comment on that part of his work (see sections 38 and 31 respectively). I also intend to leave his remarks on the Refutation of Idealism, inserted in the second edition into the actuality section of the Postulates, for consideration at a later stage (see section 33 below).

Kant has proved so persuasive on the subject of real necessity as to appear now to have little of importance to say about it. He defines the really necessary (B 266/A 218) as 'that which in its connection with the actual is determined in accordance with universal conditions of experience'. His main aim in this part of his work is to play down a concept which had figured prominently in rationalist metaphysics, and which he himself was prepared to use for the characterisation of noumena as late as 1770 (see *Dissertation*, sections *8, 9*). He now tells us (B 280/A 227–8) that

> Necessity concerns only the relations of appearances in conformity with the dynamical law of causality and the possibility grounded upon it of inferring *a priori* from a given existence (a cause) to another existence (the effect). That everything which happens is hypothetically necessary is a principle which subordinates alteration in the world to a law, that is, to a rule of necessary existence, without which there would be nothing that could be entitled nature.

It follows that it is not the existence of substances but that of their states which is necessary; it follows, again, that such necessity as there is is conditional rather than absolute. It is a case of *if this exists, then that must exist*. But nothing in the experienced world exists through the necessities of its own nature; there are no necessary beings there. The old metaphysical concept of necessity has here all but disappeared.

In a curious discussion at the end of the Postulates Kant asks whether it is correct to say that the sphere of the possible is wider than that of the actual, which in turn is wider than that of the necessary. One might very well think that it is platitudinous to say that they are. Kant, however, announces that the question is equivalent to asking whether 'my perceptions can belong, in their general connection, to more than one possible experience' (B 282–3/A 230), and then goes on to claim that we cannot make such alternative kinds of experience 'conceivable and comprehensible to ourselves' (B 283/A 230). So far as we are concerned there is only one possible experience, the one defined by the categories and forms of intuition; possible worlds of another kind are phantoms of the brain. Clearly Kant is here once again pursuing his polemic against metaphysics, without however considering the paradoxes his argument generates when the subject is thought of on a more mundane level. There may be, as far as we are concerned, only one possible experience, but within that it must be allowed that the sphere of the possible is wider than that of the actual, though that is not of course to say that possibles *exist* in some attenuated sense. In any world conceived of by discursive consciousness there must be unrealised possibilities. It hardly seems likely that Kant meant to deny that, and the explanation must be, as suggested, that he was treating the question at a higher level. As for his own point, it is paradoxical to read that other forms of possible experience are inconceivable and incomprehensible when Kant talks about them so often. Apart from his frequent references to the thinking of an intuitive understanding, particularly important in the Deduction, he says more than once that there could be beings whose minds were like ours in being discursive, but were different in having other forms of intuition than space and time. He may even have thought of the minds of animals as answering this description. Whether this is so or not, he certainly seems to possess the concept of an intelligence not like the human. When he says that we do not know whether such things are possible, he must mean that we cannot make their *real* possibility clear to ourselves: we cannot say in any detail what it would be like to have that sort of mind, but have to be content with a schematic description, mostly couched in negative terms. Our predicament here is somewhat like that of theologians when they come to speak of God, and find that they can say what he is not, but not directly what he is. If this was Kant's point it is both valid in itself, and could not be made without reference to the concept of real possibility, to defend whose authenticity was a major object of the Postulates section.

§ 28 *Metaphysics and Meaning*
In the remainder of the Analytic Kant puts forward no new positive doctrines, but occupies himself, first with spelling out the anti-metaphysical implications of the views he has advocated, second with elaborating and defending the contrast between phenomena and noumena on which so much of his previous argument has depended, lastly with writing a critique from his own point of view of what he takes to be the central doctrines of Leibniz (in 'The Amphiboly of Concepts of Reflection': B 316/A 260 ff.). The critique is, as so often with Kant, at once acute and unsympathetic; I shall take it that its interest is largely parochial, and shall not comment on it here. Nor shall I say very much about Kant's anti-metaphysical conclusions, in view of the fact that these are already apparent in the Deduction and Schematism and have hence been sketched and discussed above (section 15). My main attention here will be given to two points only. The contrast between phenomena and noumena is, however, one of great internal importance for Kant's philosophy and will need separate treatment despite the attention which has already been given to Kant's concept of a world of appearances.

It must be allowed that the force and vigour with which Kant states his conclusions in this part of his work are remarkable by any standards. Making crystal clear his original dichotomy of concepts and intuitions, he shows with devastating clarity that no concept, whatever its origins, can be of any concrete use until brought to bear on intuitive data, a fact which in the human case means that pure concepts of the understanding can, as he puts it in slightly misleading language (B 303/A 246), '*never* admit of *transcendental*, but *always* only of *empirical* employment'. Principles of 'the pure understanding' can be applied only to 'objects of the senses under the universal conditions of a possible experience, never to things, in general without regard to the mode in which we are able to intuit them'. As a result

> The Transcendental Analytic leads to this important conclusion, that the most the understanding can achieve *a priori* is to anticipate the form of a possible experience in general. And since that which is not appearance cannot be an object of experience, the understanding can never transcend those limits of sensibility within which alone objects can be given to us. Its principles are merely rules for the exposition of appearances; and the proud name of an Ontology that presumptuously claims to supply, in systematic doctrinal form, synthetic *a priori* knowledge of things in general (for instance, the principle of causality) must, therefore, give way to the modest title of a mere Analytic of pure understanding (B 303/A 246–7).

The importance of this passage lies in the striking way in which Kant relates his own philosophical results to those of earlier philosophers, arguing that the categories are the counterpart of the concepts handled in traditional ontology, the first part of metaphysics as presented by Wolff and Baumgarten, but going on to claim that their significance is totally different from what those writers supposed. Ontology as an account of the necessary characteristics of whatever is to be a thing—ontology as a doctrine of being as such—is impossible, and all that can be put in its place is Transcendental Analytic, which sets out the properties of objects in general, but at the same time makes clear that such objects are restricted to the sphere of possible experience. There are critics who cite this passage in support of the view that Kant had abiding metaphysical interests; in my opinion it shows beyond any dispute how remote he thought himself from the metaphysics of the past. As he said in the *Prolegomena* (Berlin edition, IV 366; Lucas translation, p. 135), 'Criticism is related to ordinary school-metaphysics exactly as *chemistry* to *alchemy*, or as *astronomy* to the divinations of *astrology'*. Admittedly here the reference is to *Schulmetaphysik*, i.e. to metaphysics as presented in academic textbooks. But what Kant has to say about major metaphysicians such as Plato and Leibniz, both of whom are mentioned relatively often in the *Critique*, does not suggest that his verdict about metaphysics generally would have been different. He had greater respect for Plato than for Wolff, but no higher opinion of his ability to arrive at knowledge of things in general by purely intellectual means.

I wish now to refer to my two points of detail, each of which has been touched on briefly before. First, Kant's account of meaning. In the Schematism chapter (B 178/ A 139) we read that 'concepts are altogether impossible, and can have no meaning, if no object is given for them, or at least for the elements of which they are composed'. Elsewhere in the same chapter (B 186/ A 147) Kant says that 'there certainly does remain in the pure concepts of understanding, even after elimination of every sensible condition, a meaning; but it is purely logical, signifying only the bare unity of the representations. The pure concepts can find no object, and so can acquire no meaning which might yield a concept of some object'. In both these passages the word translated as 'meaning' is *'Bedeutung'*. The subject is taken up again at the beginning of the chapter on Phenomena and Noumena, B 298–9/ A 239–40. Kant first says there that

> We demand in every concept, first, the logical form of a concept (of thought) in general, and secondly, the possibility of giving it an object to which it may be applied. In the absence of such object, it has no meaning (*Sinn*) and is completely lacking in content, though it may still contain the logical function which is required for making a concept out of any data that may be presented.

He goes on to argue that an object can be given for a concept only in intuition, indeed in empirical intuition, for

> though a pure intuition can indeed precede the object *a priori*, even this intuition can acquire its object, and therefore objective validity, only through the empirical intuition of which it is the mere form.

All concepts accordingly relate to empirical intuitions and without them lack all objective validity. Kant proceeds to illustrate his point by reference to mathematical concepts, saying of principles such as that space has three dimensions that they

> would mean (*bedeuten*) nothing, were we not always able to

present their meaning (*Bedeutung*) in appearances, that is, in
empirical objects. We therefore demand that a bare concept be
made sensible, that is, that an object corresponding to it be
presented in intuition. Otherwise the concept would, as we say,
be without sense (*Sinn*), that is, without meaning (*Bedeutung*).
The mathematician meets this demand by the construction of
a figure.

A line or two later there is a reference to the concept of magnitude
seeking its 'support and sensible meaning' (*Haltung und Sinn*) in
number, 'and this in turn in the fingers, in the beads of the abacus,
or in strokes and points which can be placed before the eyes'. What
are we to make of all this?

The first thing that must be said is that the terms '*Sinn*' and
'*Bedeutung*' are synonymous for Kant; there is no hint of any
anticipation of the Fregean distinction between the two. More
important, there is no evidence of any clear recognition of the
distinction between sense and reference itself. Kant says sometimes
that a concept for which no object is given has no meaning, sometimes that it lacks objective validity (e.g. B 298/A 239). It seems
clear that what he is talking about here is the application of concepts, a process which has to do with finding a reference for them.
You cannot intelligibly enquire into whether a concept has a
reference unless it has a sense, i.e. a content of its own. There seems
no doubt that Kant was very confused on this point. It could be,
however, that in the discussions with which we are concerned he
was troubled about two separate matters: the question whether
certain concepts have application, and the question how their content is to be made intelligible. In cases where the content of the
concept is very remote from everyday experience, as happens over
the pure categories, there is a problem of bringing the concept down
to earth and making it more palpable. The doctrine of Schematism
is introduced as having to do with the subsumption of particulars
under universals, i.e. with the application of concepts; what Kant
says about the schemata of empirical and mathematical concepts
concerns the problem of finding their referents, the particulars to
which they apply. But when he passes to transcendental schemata
Kant may well have something different in mind, namely providing
an immediately intelligible model for an idea whose content is
remote from sense. As was argued above (section 13), at least one
description of the transcendental schema suggests that Kant thought
of it as itself a concept, one that was superior to the pure category in
that its content could be sensibly grasped. Other phrases used by

Kant make the transcendental schema a sort of phenomenal embodiment of the category, its counterpart in the empirical world. What
Kant says about mathematics in the passages quoted above might be
interpreted as meaning that the figure gives body to the geometrical
idea, though equally it could be seen as a standard instance. Which-
ever is right, it is clear that in some of his remarks on these topics
Kant was dealing with a problem which really has to do with sense
rather than reference, the problem of getting one's audience to
understand the idea one is trying to convey. Unfortunately Kant
himself is extremely unclear on these points, and this means that
his otherwise impressive treatment of pure concepts and metaphysics
is constantly marred by verbal infelicities.

As regards empirical concepts Kant appears to hold a version of
the Humean view that they or their elements must all be derived
from (intuited) impressions, and are meaningful in so far as they
are so derived. Meaning is here connected with intuition because
(basic) empirical concepts reflect or mirror what is given in
intuition. Kant's account of how pure concepts get meaning is less
crude, though here again much stress is laid on the importance of
intuitions if the concepts concerned are to have significance. I shall
take it that the ambiguities of this general claim have been
sufficiently explored. What requires comment now is something
already touched on in a previous discussion, the thesis that to
demonstrate the objective reality of categories we need not just
intuitions, but external intuitions.

Kant's reason for thinking that we need intuitions to demonstrate
the objective reality of categories is, roughly, that the latter remain
indeterminate, and indeed incomprehensible, without the former.
To understand causality we must invoke the idea of alteration, and
alteration is 'combination of contradictorily opposed determinations
in the existence of one and the same thing' (B 291). To show 'how
it is possible that from a given state of a thing an opposite state should
follow' (B 292) we need to think in concrete terms of the suggested
situation, first by bringing in time (the contradictorily opposed
features are not both present at the same moment), and then by
adducing the idea of the movement of a point in space. 'The
presence of the point in different locations (as a sequence of opposite
determinations) is what alone first yields us an intuition of alteration'; alterations in the mental world become intelligible only after
physical alteration has been grasped. Similarly with other categories,
all of which have to be interpreted in terms of outer intuitions, i.e.
with reference to physical situations. The question that must be

asked now is whether this is a necessary or a contingent fact. Does it just happen to be the case that we can see sense in the categories when we envisage certain spatial conditions, or must we have recourse to space if we are to see sense in them at all? That Kant accepted the first alternative is suggested by his official account of schemata as determinations of *time*, and by the priority which he assigned to time over space in many parts of the *Critique* (time is the only truly universal form of our intuiting). That he favoured the second could be inferred from his argument in the second edition Refutation of Idealism, which maintained that we can make determinate statements about mental events only against a persisting physical background, from his frequent remarks about there being nothing stable in inner sense and from the low opinion he had of the possibilities of a science of psychology (*Metaphysical Foundations of Natural Science*, preface; Berlin edition IV 471, Ellington translation, p. 8). To arrive at a firm decision about what Kant would have said on the point is perhaps impossible. But if we ask ourselves what he *should* have said, the answer seems to be that he should have seen physical interpretation as necessary. The shared experience with which Kant connects the categories is primarily experience of persisting, causally active and interacting physical things; it is not only that, but is all the same shapeless without that. Kant keeps saying that without the categories we should have no grasp of nature, and nature here means first and foremost physical nature. To have appreciated the epistemological primacy of the physical over the mental was one of Kant's boldest philosophical innovations. It is an idea which connects closely with the somewhat esoteric doctrine we have been discussing.

§ 29 *The Contrast of Phenomena and Noumena*

That the experienced world is a world of appearances or phenomena is the central thesis of the Analytic. It has the enormous advantage of enabling us to explain how we can anticipate experience in certain important respects, something which would be quite unintelligible if the things we know were independently real, whilst still leaving open the possibility that there is another order, one which consists of realities as opposed to appearances. In order to secure the structure of science Kant has to say that we know only appearances; except on these terms he cannot see how scientific truths, and above all fundamental scientific truths, could possess necessity. For the purpose of his ethics he needs to add that there may be a world of realities distinct from the world of appearances, though in some way manifesting itself in the latter. Only if the moral agent removes himself from the phenomenal order, in considering what ought to be done and acting upon it, will it be possible to treat him as initiating a series of events and therefore as a responsible being. He is condemned to inhabit a world of phenomena, and is indeed a phenomenon himself when seen by a spectator. But in acting he ceases to be a mere phenomenon and takes on another character which Kant describes as 'intelligible' or 'noumenal'. He behaves as if he were an independent intelligence endowed with a will, and not just another empirical object pushed and pulled about by forces over which he has no control.

In previous discussions (see especially section 17) I examined the question how Kant could claim that the world of appearances was a common world, seeing that sensing is something which goes on in individuals. I argued that the main difficulties here could be overcome if, first, we agreed that sensation is not a form of knowledge by acquaintance but a type of experience which is *sui generis*, and second, maintained that the experienced world is a world of facts constituted in judgment. The activity of judgment arises on a basis which is personal, namely the occurrence of sensory content in this or that mind, but proceeds by rules which hold without distinction of persons; its products are accordingly impersonal. But even if all this is correct we are still left with the difficulty of describing what is taken to be the case as phenomenal. Why should natural science, to which Kant attached such evident importance, have to confine itself to the realm of appearances or, in so far as it deals with realities, deal only with what is empirically real? What would it be like for an enquirer, as opposed to an agent, to go beyond appearances and apprehend realities? On what basis can we apply the terms 'appearance' and 'reality', 'phenomenon' and 'noumenon' in these connections? If Kant attempts to answer these questions anywhere, it is in his chapter on Phenomena and Noumena.

Before considering what he says there it is worth mentioning that Kant introduced the distinction of phenomena and noumena on the basis of a philosophical position which was significantly different from that of the *Critique*. In the 1770 *Dissertation* he argued that objects of the senses must be described as phenomena on the grounds that they are all presented within a framework which is either spatio-temporal or barely temporal, and that space and time themselves are forms of the human sensibility, not features of independent reality. Physics and mathematics (which has a special connection with space and time) must accordingly be said to concern phenomena. But at this period Kant wanted to vindicate metaphysics as well as to defend mathematics and physics; he did so by claiming that metaphysics reveals truths about a different kind of object, intelligibilia or noumena. Metaphysics has nothing to do with the senses or with things sensible; its instrument is the intellect and its aim to arrive at knowledge of noumenal or intelligible reality. It cannot achieve this aim to the extent of gaining face to face knowledge of such a reality, for intellectual intuition is an impossibility for human beings. But it can go some way towards satisfying its aspirations, thanks to its possession of a range of concepts of its own, including necessity, substance and cause. The fact that we have such concepts enables us to arrive at descriptive knowledge ('symbolic cognition') of the supersensible; it also makes possible a grasp of the idea of the perfect being, God, who is 'the common measure of all other things as far as real' (*Dissertation*, section 9). Kant's language on this latter subject is obscure: it is not clear whether he is saying that we can come to know that God exists, or merely form the concept of a perfect being, on the strength of possessing pure intellectual concepts. It could be that he believed that to form the idea would itself be to guarantee the reality of its object, along lines sketched in his earlier essay *The Only Possible Ground of Proof of God's Existence*. But even if he had abandoned the *a priori* argument there stated, he was in any case claiming substantial knowledge of a reality which lies outside ordinary sense-experience. Nor was there anything amiss in describing that reality as noumenal, in view of its being known by intellectual means.

The position in the *Critique of Pure Reason* is, however, substantially different. True, the story about space, time and mathematics is preserved largely unchanged, and objects of the senses are still described as 'phenomena'. But the crude idea that pure intellectual concepts open up a non-phenomenal world is given up, and in its place comes the theory of categories, whose function is seen as being to relate or organise the data of the senses. Categories are like the pure concepts of the *Dissertation* in having a purely intellectual origin, but they differ from them radically in having full significance only in relation to things phenomenal. The difference comes out most plainly in connection with Schematism, which is of central importance in the *Critique*, but absent altogether in the *Dissertation*. Categories without their corresponding schemata are empty forms of thought, incapable of determining any object. And every schema has an essential connection with time, which means that categories apply properly only to phenomena.

The difficulty about all this is to know what justifies Kant in continuing to employ his vocabulary of 'phenomena' and 'noumena', given his new assumptions. For Plato phenomena were objects of the senses, noumena objects of the intellect. For Kant in the *Dissertation* much the same was true, except that Kant thought the powers of the intellect limited as Plato had not. For Kant in the *Critique*, however, senses and intellect had the same objects, being conceived not as rivals but as complementary to each other. The job of the senses was to intuit, that of the intellect to supply concepts, and intuitions and concepts were both necessary if there was to be knowledge. Because he preserved without substantial change the *Dissertation* account of sensing, Kant believed himself justified in continuing to say that sense-objects were phenomena or appearances; he even believed that the case for doing so was improved as a result of the arguments of the Analytic. The truth was, however, that the change in his theory of pure concepts cut the ground from beneath his feet as far as talk about 'phenomena' and 'noumena' was concerned. Unless he could produce new arguments he should in logic have abandoned it altogether and substituted something else for it, as I have myself in this book in talking so much about the 'experienced world'.

The curious thing is that Kant himself took so long to see the difficulty; indeed, it may be doubted if he ever fully saw it, though he was certainly sensitive on the general point, as is shown by his having recast a vital part of the argument in the Phenomena and Noumena chapter for his second edition. In the first edition (see A 249 ff.) he began by saying that the doctrines of the Aesthetic themselves justify the division of objects into phenomena and noumena, for 'if the senses represent to us something merely *as it appears*, this something must also in itself be a thing, and an object of a non-sensible intuition, that is, of the understanding'. The other side of an appearance is of course what appears, and this can be taken as being reality. Kant shows no awareness of begging enormous questions at this point, but goes on to consider whether accepting the argument commits him to saying that the categories must apply to something more than phenomena. His answer to this is negative: categories determine only what he mysteriously calls 'the transcendental object', which is itself 'only the representation of appearances under the concept of an object in general' (A 251). We can think of this as purely intellectual if we like, but it is an abstract schema awaiting application, not a special sort of thing, and what it applies to is the data of the senses. As for the argument that if there are appearances, there must be something behind them which appears, Kant holds that this gives us the concept of a noumenon, but adds that we have to recognise that this concept is 'in no way positive', that it does not give us 'determinate knowledge of anything' and that it 'signifies only the thought of something in general, in which I abstract from everything that belongs to the form of sensible intuition' (A 252). To make the concept positive I should have to fill it out by reference to a different form of immediate awarness from the sensible, by connecting it with intellectual intuition. But I have no positive idea of what intellectual intuition involves, and so no concept of the objects of such intuiting. To say in these terms that over and above the realm of phenomena there is another realm of noumena is clearly to say very little.

In the second edition Kant expresses what are fundamentally the same ideas in slightly different words. He starts once more from the point that 'if we entitle certain objects, as appearances, sensible entities (phenomena)', this commits us to setting certain other things in opposition to them and calling them 'intelligible entities (noumena)' (B 306). There is then a temptation to appeal to the categories to fill out the concept of a noumenon. But to yield to the temptation is a mistake, since here we confuse a concept which is 'entirely indeterminate' (B 307) with one that is fully specified. We need, in fact, to distinguish two separate concepts of a noumenon, one according to which it means 'a thing so far as it is not an object of our sensible intuition', the other according to which it signifies 'an object of a non-sensible intuition'. The former is the noumenon 'in the negative sense of the term', the latter the noumenon in the positive sense. 'The doctrine of sensibility' commits us to noumena in the negative sense, but not to noumena positively conceived; indeed, we have no means of getting at what the latter involve, since we lack intellectual intuition. Kant concludes that we must hang on to the noumenon as a problematic concept which is internally coherent and is needed 'to prevent sensible intuition from being extended to things in themselves' (B 310/A 254). The concept of a noumenon is a limiting concept, admitting only of a negative employment.

The weakness in all this is, of course, in the beginning of the argument. *If* we describe certain things as 'appearances', it follows that certain other things which are not appearances must be at least possible. But why should we import the concept of appearance in the first place, and what right have we to do so? Kant might have said that if space and time are forms of human intuition they constitute a barrier between the percipient and what he perceives, and that this would justify calling the percept an appearance. But this assumes that we have independent knowledge of the constituents of the situation, which on Kant's assumptions we do not. The point becomes still more difficult if we set aside the simplicities of the Aesthetic and consider the problem in the more sophisticated terms of the Analytic. According to the arguments stated above, the activity of judgment results in the constitution of a common world of facts. It might be urged that the notion of fact is itself something which is mind-dependent; if there were no minds there would be no facts, and accordingly what exists in the form of fact cannot be identified with independent reality. On this view the experienced world would be a world of appearances just because it was a world of facts. The difficulty with this is to know what to make of the contrast between independent reality and what exists in the form of fact, to give a proper sense to the former. 'Independent reality' is supposed to be the name of what we judge about, to refer to what is judged considered as existing outside the judging relationship. But since the only use we can make of concepts, including the concepts of existence and reality, is to employ them in judgment, in what terms are we to speak about that? Does it even make sense to say that, over and above the world we elaborate in judgment, there must or may be another realm, which could be within our grasp if we were not impeded by a cognitive apparatus which is clearly defective?

Two critical comments can be made at this point. It can be argued first that it is possible to draw a contrast between what exists in judgment and what might obtain out of it, thanks to our ability to distinguish between a discursive and an intuitive understanding. We know in principle what it would be to have an intellect which originated its own material instead of receiving it from another faculty, and that gives us the idea of a better form of apprehension, one in which there would be no separation between conceiving and intuiting. Independent reality could be understood in terms of what an intuitive understanding might think. It could, but would that be wholly satisfactory? Our concept of an intuitive understanding is, as Kant keeps saying, framed exclusively in negative terms; in one sense of the word, we do not even know that such an understanding is possible. Nor if we did would it take away from the fact that any conception we do form of the supposed reality must be in a form which purports to make it intelligible to a discursive consciousness. But even if these difficulties could be overcome, it is not clear why we must say that what is known in intellectual intuition is real while what is made out in judgment is merely apparent. If what we express in the form of judgments could also be the subject of a wholly different form of apprehension, that would not make our judgments any the less *true*.

A second criticism might be that Kant does not rest his main case on the fact that we judge, but rather on the claim that we judge in accordance with certain pre-existing forms, which can be specified and to which we can think of alternatives, in principle at any rate. We operate not just with concepts but with *a priori* concepts, and this could be held to preclude our grasping independent reality. This argument is really a duplicate of the one stated in the Aesthetic, and suffers from the same disadvantage: it would be conclusive if we had access to reality outside the judging situation, when there is nothing to show that we do. But even if this difficulty is ignored, it is not clear that the argument establishes anything of importance. It may indeed be true that our judgment proceeds on principles which are presupposed as axiomatic and that we can think of beings which would not judge on these lines. But why should these facts, if facts they are, be taken to show that our own judgments are inherently unsatisfactory? Why should they imply that the reality we elaborate in judgment is somehow defective, worthy only of the pejorative description 'phenomenal'? It is worth mentioning in this connection that, though Kant suggests that it is a contingent fact that our thinking proceeds according to these and no other forms of judgment (B 145–6), he goes out of his way to argue that the categories we have are *all* indispensable if experience as we know it is to be possible. There is not the slightest reason to suppose that he so much as considered the idea that we might attain a better grasp of reality if only we had a more adequate set of categories; Hegelian thoughts of this kind were far from his mind. So far as he was concerned we have to employ these and no other categories if we are to have knowledge of an objective world. Kant's arguments in support of this position may be less formidable than he thought, but even if that is agreed nothing follows about the inadequacy of human knowledge or the apparent character of its object. That alternative descriptions of any situation are possible in principle does not in itself falsify the descriptions we ourselves offer.

I conclude that the case for describing the objects of human knowledge as 'appearances' is not good. But if 'appearances' or 'phenomena' fall to the ground, so of course do 'realities' or 'noumena'. There seems in any case to be a difficulty in accepting the latter as properly so called, even on Kant's own terms. If 'appearances' imply 'realities' or things in themselves, that does nothing to show that 'realities' have a special connection with the intelligence. Kant's choice of the expressions 'intelligibilia' and 'noumena' (which are of course equivalents in Latin and Greek) was made in the light of an epistemological theory which he subsequently abandoned; once he had seen that, on the cognitive plane, the intellect essentially co-operates with the senses instead of rivalling them, he had no reason to persist with it. That he did so persist would seem to be due to extraneous factors. He wanted, as we know, to say that in acting morally a man frees himself from the shackles of the natural world and operates as an independent intelligence; it was not wholly inappropriate in these circumstances to describe such a man as taking on a noumenal character or transferring himself in thought to a world of noumena. A moral agent for Kant was essentially an intelligence, possessed of practical reason; it was also the case that he ceased to be a mere thing, part of the empirical order, in so far as he gave heed to moral scruples. In his pre-critical essay *Dreams of a Spirit-Seer* Kant had sketched a contrast between a material order and a world of spirits, and had argued that sensitivity to moral claims constituted empirical evidence for our belonging to such a world (see *Dreams*, Goerwitz translation, pp. 64–5; Berlin edition II 335). In his ethical essay *Groundwork of the Metaphysic of Morals* (1785) Kant still spoke of moral feeling as pointing to the noumenal. There seems no doubt that his continued use of this term is to be explained as due to what he took to be the requirements of his moral theory. But if that is said, it must be added that the theory in its mature form demanded only that the world of the scientific observer and the world of the moral agent be different; strictly, it did not call for the one to be superior in reality to the other. And even if it had, that would not suffice to show that the 'reality' said to be demanded by the arguments of the *Critique of Pure Reason* can be identified with the 'reality' demanded in ethical reflection. There is a large gap in his argument here of which Kant was scarcely aware, and which in consequence he does little or nothing to fill.

In this discussion of phenomena and noumena I have said nothing of an important claim of Kant's, that his doctrine that what we know through our senses is all phenomenal is supported by the existence of the antinomies. It is clearly impossible to consider this properly without going into the whole argument of the Antinomy of Pure Reason, which can be done satisfactorily only as part of a general survey of the arguments of the Dialectic (see sections 34–36 below). I pass to these arguments now, remarking meanwhile that though Kant in my view has made good some of his most important claims in the Analytic, he has not in fact shown that the world of common experience is a world of appearances or mere phenomena.

Reason and Metaphysics

§30 *Scholastic Preliminaries*

After the obscurities and excitements of the Analytic the rest of the *Critique* is at once comparatively straightforward and comparatively dull. The greater part of the Transcendental Dialectic is taken up with a detailed criticism of particular metaphysical doctrines and arguments, arranged in a way which corresponds to their treatment in Wolff and Baumgarten under the headings 'Rational Psychology', 'Rational Cosmology' and 'Natural Theology'. Much of this criticism could have been anticipated by an intelligent reader of the Analytic, though that is not to say that nothing new emerges when the sub-jects are treated in detail. In some cases Kant contrives to elaborate what was said in the Analytic and so to throw further light on con-cepts which were ambiguous or elusive as there presented; this is particularly true of the mysterious 'I think', variously described as a 'representation', a 'concept' and a 'judgment', which is at once the expression of the unity of apperception and the basis on which speculative metaphysicians erect the pseudo-science of Rational Psychology. The section on the Paralogisms of Rational Psychology is of interest not just as an exposure of bad metaphysical arguments, but also for the light it throws on Kant's own views on the nature and knowability of the self, which are referred to in passing at various points in the Aesthetic and Analytic, but get no systematic discussion there. The other two main chapters in the Dialectic are at first sight straightforwardly negative: their aim is to show up metaphysical errors in a systematic way, and thus to discredit philosophising of this sort for all time. It turns out, however, that the negative criticism of the Antinomies prepares the ground for the positive doctrine of the regulative function of ideas of reason which is expounded at the very end of the Dialectic, as well as for the reconciliation of science and ethics which was, for Kant, the most important of philosophical aims. It turns out, again, that the destruction of speculative theology which is the main object of the chapter on the Ideal is an essential propaedeutic to the elaboration of a different and altogether better sort of theology: the 'moral theology' whose main tenets are expressed as 'postulates of pure practical reason' (see *Critique of Practical Reason*, especially v 119ff.). To read Kant as if he were a positivist before his time, interested only in demonstrating that metaphysics is nonsense, is profoundly mistaken; the truth is that he is anxious to recommend a certain set of metaphysical convictions, if not exactly a certain set of metaphysical truths. We can separate the negative and the positive sides of Kant's enterprise in this part of the *Critique* only at the cost of some distortion of his real thought. Nevertheless, it has to be allowed that the negative aspect is the more prominent, and that there are points in the Dialectic where Kant's pleasure in the successful carrying out of his job as intellectual hatchet man is barely concealed. The reputation he had as the man who crushed everything (*der allzermalmende*) was clearly not wholly without foundation.

It should be clear already that, in so far as the Dialectic is properly seen as an exposure of bad metaphysical arguments, it continues the work of the Analytic rather than opens up fresh ground, for the Analytic too has as a principal aim the discrediting of a branch of metaphysics, namely ontology. In the words of a passage quoted a few pages back (section 28 above), that alleged branch of science 'presumptuously claims to supply, in systematic doctrinal form, synthetic *a priori* knowledge of things in general', employing as its basis for this purpose the pure concepts of the understanding whose proper use is to order appearances. I shall say no more now about the grounds of Kant's criticism of ontology; instead, I wish to direct attention to an apparent inconsistency in his thought about metaphysics which is of some importance for the structure of the Dialectic. The Analytic is concerned with the use and the misuse of categories; it tries to show that they must be employed if we are to have objective knowledge or shared experience, but that they lose all significance if we attempt to extend their use outside the empirical sphere. In his preliminary discussion at the beginning of Transcendental Logic (B 87–8/A 62–4), Kant, after mentioning 'elements of the pure knowledge yielded by understanding' and 'the principles without which no object can be thought' as the subject-matter of Transcendental Analytic, says that it is 'very tempting' to use these concepts and principles by themselves. In virtue of this temptation 'the understanding is led to incur the risk of making, with a mere show of rationality, a material use of its pure and merely formal principles, and of passing judgments upon objects without distinction—upon objects which are not given to us, nay, perhaps cannot in any way be given'. In these circumstances 'the employment of the pure understanding . . . becomes dialectical', with the result that we need 'a critical treatment of the pure understanding, for the guarding of it against sophistical illusion' (B 88/ A 64). There is no mention here of any faculty other than the understanding: the whole passage proceeds as if nothing more were in question than the correct and incorrect exploitation of categories, and the same is generally true of the main discussions of the Analytic. But the situation changes radically when we move from the Analytic to the Dialectic, for Kant there speaks as if 'understanding' were exclusively the name of the intellect in so far as it co-operates with the senses, and introduces a further term 'reason' to designate the intellect when prosecuting metaphysical aims. Nor is this a mere terminological shift, since the new faculty is presented as having a special set of *a priori* concepts of its own, and the tendency to frame and hold metaphysical beliefs is explained as a natural though not therefore justified consequence of that fact. Left to itself, the implication seems to be, the understanding would confine itself to empirical investigations, seeking causes for effects and effects for causes, calculating, measuring and so on. But it is not left to itself, since reason too is on the scene, and reason's preoccupation with what Kant calls 'the unconditioned' means that human attention is constantly diverted from the empirical sphere, where every fact or object is conditioned by some other, to the sphere of the supersensible in which, the hope is, the final conditions of everything else, themselves unconditioned, are to be found.

That there is some sort of an inconsistency here could scarcely be denied. According to the indications of the Analytic, the understanding blunders into metaphysics as it were by inadvertence; according to the Dialectic the search for metaphysical truth, whether or not it turns out to be a will o' the wisp, would not even start if it were not for the faculty of reason. Nor is the discrepancy merely a local one. As Kemp Smith emphasised, the Dialectic itself is ambiguous in its treatment of ideas of reason, sometimes speaking as if they were nothing but categories stripped of their restricting conditions, sometimes ascribing to them a nature of their own and a role quite independent of that contemplated for the categories. Here as in other cases it is difficult to produce an interpretation of Kant's text which covers all parts of it with equal conviction. But perhaps in this case it is not important to do so. The account of metaphysics given in the Analytic loses nothing if it is supplemented by the story about reason's search for the unconditioned. We could if we liked take it as valid in itself, at least for the case of ontology, but we do not need to. What the Dialectic tries to add to it mainly concerns the motives which lead men to engage in metaphysical speculation, not what such speculation involves. It enables Kant to present his critique of metaphysics in a systematic way, but makes no fundamental alteration in the charges against metaphysics already preferred in the Analytic.

But is it enlightening in itself? Jonathan Bennett has spoken for many readers of Kant in suggesting that the whole formal setting in which Kant presented his polemic against particular metaphysical arguments in the *Critique* is an artificial irrelevance, and in dismissing the faculty of reason as unworthy of serious philosophical consideration. What Kant says about 'the understanding' can just get by, since the unplausibility of the formal exposition, in sections such as the Metaphysical Deduction, is rapidly obliterated by the great insight Kant shows when he proceeds to more concrete discussions. But 'reason' seems to be a monster from the first, thought up for unworthy purposes and sustained in existence by little more than a series of sophisms. If we ask why Kant was inclined to believe in this faculty, one answer might be as follows. Intellectual activities were divided in traditional logic, e.g. by the 16th-century logician Peter Ramus, who is mentioned in B 173/A 134 note, into the forming of concepts, the making of judgments and the drawing of inferences. These operations were then assigned to different faculties: the understanding formed concepts, 'the power of judgment' made assertions or denials, reason drew inferences or engaged in chains of reasoning. In B 92/A 67 Kant speaks of the 'logical employment' of the understanding, and at B 359/A 303 he has a page on the 'logical employment' of reason. Now he was convinced from an early stage that, where a faculty has a *logical* use, the chances are that it will also have what he calls a *real* or *pure* use; that is to say, that it will not only operate in a formal way, but will further be a source of *a priori* knowledge. In the *Critique of Pure Reason* Kant resisted this inference as far as the power of judgment was concerned, though his resistance crumbled when he came to write the *Critique of Judgment*.

But he went along with it as regards the third operation, and so passed from the activity of reasoning to the postulation of a separate faculty of reason.

This is without doubt a thoroughly bad argument. The assignment of logical operations to different faculties is dubious in any case, and the assumption that a logical use will always be complemented by a real employment is quite gratuitous. If Kant can produce no better case than this he really does deserve to be dismissed without a hearing. What other grounds does he have for separating reason from understanding, which, incidentally, he did not do in 1770? One point he would have stressed himself is that there is a *special* temptation to misuse the categories, which cannot be just taken for granted but needs to be explained as arising out of something healthy. We are subject to what Kant calls (B 354/A 298) a '*natural* and inevitable *illusion*', as a result of which we take it that we can make meaningful and indeed well-founded statements about the reality beyond appearances. In one way the illusion cannot be removed; it is 'inseparable from human reason' and will continue to play tricks with us 'even after its deceptiveness has been exposed'. But it can all the same be uncovered, as Kant proceeds to show. The illusion is produced through the fact that the intellect has about it principles which are indispensable to its effective functioning, but which are readily interpreted as referring to existing things; what has subjective validity is here taken as being objectively valid. The subjective principles concerned are clearly different from the principles of the understanding, and Kant marks the difference by assigning them to a separate faculty.

This argument cannot be assessed properly until we can examine it in detail (see section 41 below), but meantime we can say that, to sustain anything like his conclusion, Kant will first have to fix on a clearly-marked and substantial set of intellectual procedures, different in kind from others handled elsewhere in the *Critique*, and then show why it is natural, indeed inevitable, to misconstrue these as something else. I shall suggest that he meets the first requirement in what he says about the regulative function of ideas of reason, but was less convincing on the second. The illusion of which he speaks was perhaps 'natural and inevitable' to a thinker with Kant's background in rationalist metaphysics, but would be less dangerous for, say, a scientifically-minded positivist. The force of the argument may thus be more personal than Kant supposes. And the same must be said of another set of considerations that undoubtedly weighed with him, that in the sphere of conduct we need to distinguish between the intellect as it works out means to ends and the intellect as an originator of action, and thus need the concept of pure practical reason. If pure reason can be practical, may it not also have theoretical functions? May not there be counterparts in the sphere of enquiry to the ideas and ideals which figure so largely in the thinking of the moral man? Kant had no difficulty in convincing himself that there are such counterparts, and in arguing that just as moral ideas can hope for only partial embodiment, so their counterparts must fall short of full realisation. But the formal case he had to make here was at best thin. Even if we agree with him that pure reason can be practical, which philosophers such as Aristotle and Hume would deny, it is by no means clear that anything follows about reason having a role in enquiry. The parallels Kant sees between moral ideas and theoretical ideas are not particularly impressive, and the case made for saying that the metaphysical ideas of God, the soul, and the world as a whole, function in respectable scientific thinking has little cogency. If what Kant says here is never entirely negligible, it certainly lacks the conviction which Kant himself ascribes to it.

I conclude that the theses that there is a faculty of theoretical reason (as opposed to understanding), and that it has a special connection with the human proneness to embrace metaphysical views, require more support than they initially get from Kant. The passage in which he introduces the idea of the unconditioned is also unsatisfactory, partly because Kant assumes there that all deductive inference is syllogistic, partly because the argument is doubtful at a crucial point. Kant begins by examining the process by which a given contention (a potential conclusion) is justified by means of a syllogism; what happens here, he says, is that we bring the judgment concerned under a wider principle which supplies the condition under which it holds. We say that S is P because it is M and because all M is P. Thus in Kant's own example (B 387/A 330) we argue that all bodies are alterable because all bodies are composite, and whatever is composite is subject to alteration. But the process can obviously be taken further by beginning again with the principle adduced and asking after *its* condition; to answer the question we need to construct a further syllogism (a 'prosyllogism'), and to justify the major premise of that, yet another. There is no reason other than a practical one why this regress should not go on, with the consequence that Kant announces (B 364/A 307) that the principle peculiar to reason in its logical employment is

to find for the conditioned knowledge obtained through the

understanding the unconditioned whereby its unity is brought to completion.

This 'logical maxim' is converted into something very different, and becomes a principle of 'pure' as opposed to merely logical reason

> through our assuming that if the conditioned is given, the whole series of conditions, subordinated to one another — a series which is therefore itself unconditioned — is likewise given, that is, contained in the object and its connection.

Kant is clearly suggesting that the logical process leads on naturally to making what amounts to a most important assumption about fact. But he is equally clear that if the move is made it needs far more justification than the connection with logic can supply, for the principle that the conditioned requires the unconditioned is a synthetic principle, treated here as necessarily holding of *things* as opposed to *thoughts*.

Kant's interest in telling this unlikely story about syllogisms connects with his ambition to produce a definitive list of ideas of reason, just as in the Analytic he thought he had produced a definitive list of categories. There are three and only three kinds of syllogism, and hence three and only three ideas of reason. One can only avert one's eyes from this particular folly, the more so because the suggestion that the logical processes which Kant describes involve the idea of the unconditioned seems to be quite unfounded. Kant himself says that the conditions of a given statement must be pursued through a series of prosyllogisms 'whenever practicable' (B 364/A 309); it by no means follows from this that there is in each case some final condition, itself unconditioned by anything further. If you ask me to justify a given judgment I proceed with the justification until I reach a point at which you are satisfied. I could of course proceed further as far as logic is concerned, but that does not show that I could in principle arrive at some ultimate premise or truth which constitutes *the* justification for what I say. It really would have been better if Kant had not introduced these bogus logical considerations, but had brought in the notion of the unconditioned, which is of real importance for metaphysics, by underlining how the understanding moves inevitably from one conditioned object, fact or state of affairs to another, and then adding the natural thought that, where something conditioned exists, that which conditions it must also exist. Along lines like these the traditional First Cause argument can be made to sound highly plausible; in Kant's view its conclusion can be avoided only by accepting his own thesis that the objects of our knowledge are not things existing by themselves, but only 'phenomena'. An entry into the Dialectic made in these terms would have led on immediately to a discussion of the Antinomies, which as Kant saw represent a major obstacle for the metaphysician. Indeed, one can imagine a shorter and altogether more effective version of the Dialectic which would have begun from the unconditioned, proceeded to the Antinomies and ended with an enlarged account of the regulative function of ideas. 'Reason' would have its part to play in this version, though nothing would be said about its logical employment; ideas in the technical sense, so far from being excluded, might well have become both more intelligible and more compelling. They would not, however, have had to be restricted in number, to be identified with God, Freedom and Immortality (B 395), or to be connected intimately with the alleged metaphysical sciences of Rational Psychology, Rational Cosmology and Natural Theology. It is just possible that Kant once thought of handling the problem of metaphysics in this way, since he touched on the problem of the simplicity of the soul in the second Antinomy (see B 491/A 463, B 494/A 466) and on the proof of God's existence in the fourth. In the end, however, he treated psychological and theological problems in separate sections, and thus did justice to metaphysics as it was actually practised. He in fact had to choose between an account which is systematic and one that is complete. His claim that he can have both, thanks to the connection between syllogising and seeking the unconditioned, cannot be taken seriously at all.

§ 31 *Consciousness and its Implications*

Despite these criticisms we shall follow Kant in examining metaphysical claims under the separate headings of the Self, the World and God. Whether or not metaphysical error is generated by the mechanisms Kant invokes, we do not need to refer to those mechanisms in order to expose it.

The word 'paralogism' simply means 'fallacy', and the primary object of the chapter on 'The Paralogisms of Pure Reason' is to argue that the speculative thinking about the self which issues in Rational Psychology is vitiated by formal mistakes. Speculative thinking here contrasts with empirical thinking, the sort of thinking we do when we reflect on the data of consciousness, observe their various relations and attempt to establish the structure which underlies them. Kant had no quarrel with the idea that the phenomena of the self should be studied empirically, though he thinks there are obstacles standing in the way of a viable science of empirical psychology, for example that we are liable to distort the deliverances of inner sense in the very act of giving attention to them (he does not consider the possibility that psychology should study *behaviour*). What he contests is that there is any other way to arrive at knowledge about the self. The thinkers he was concerned with argued that there is: in their view a number of fundamental truths about the self can be established on the basis of purely rational considerations. Thus Descartes in the *cogito* passage claimed not only that the existence of the self is undeniable and is indeed the most certain of all truths, but further that the self is distinct in kind from the body, a substance with a wholly different nature. Plato again had argued in the *Phaedo* that soul and body are respectively immortal and mortal on the ground that soul is single and simple where body is multiple and composite; it makes sense to speak of the parts of the body, but not of the parts of the soul. The issues raised by Plato in this and other dialogues and by Descartes in his metaphysical writings were repeatedly discussed by subsequent philosophers, and the doctrines they proclaimed constitute the live philosophical background against which Kant's criticisms of Rational Psychology should be read. It is important that this should be borne in mind, since it is all too easy to think of Rational Psychology as nothing but the product of the confusions of second-rate thinkers like Wolff and Baumgarten. When Kant wrote about it his immediate attention was directed on Wolff and Baumgarten, but he clearly had more formidable opponents in mind as well. The very fact that he makes such free use of the Cartesian expression 'I think' shows as much.

According to Kant, we have in Rational Psychology 'what professes to be a science built upon the single proposition "I think"' (B 400/A 342). Because of its claim to be 'rational' the partisans of this supposed science cannot appeal to any empirical evidence; the doctrine of the soul they put forward has got to rest on purely intellectual considerations. Where then can it make its start? Kant argues that there is only one possibility, that it should start from the special fact or phenomenon of *consciousness*. This is what Descartes did in talking about the *cogito*. Descartes took the *cogito* to be or express a kind of inner *experience*, one in which the mind concerned became aware of its existence as a 'thinking thing'; for him consciousness was at bottom a fact like any other, though a specially privileged fact. Kant believes this to be radically mistaken: if the fact of consciousness were a fact like any other, any knowledge built upon it would necessarily be empirical. The truth, as Kant himself puts it in his clumsy way (B 404/A 346), is that 'Consciousness in itself is not a representation distinguishing a particular object, but a form of representation in general'. A 'representation' is an item in consciousness, and consciousness itself cannot be such an item. It is not so much a fact as the form of a fact or, at most, a formal constituent of every fact. It follows that any study which attempts to build on consciousness must run into difficulties.

Before exploring these difficulties we must observe that Kant himself is in some embarrassment in referring to this subject: he does not know quite how to describe the referents of the expressions 'I' and 'I think'. He usually speaks of 'I think' as a *judgment* or *proposition*; in the second edition version of the Paralogisms, he even says that it is an *empirical* proposition (B 421, B 422 note). But elsewhere he refers to it as a *concept*, and then more plausibly as 'the vehicle of all concepts' (B 399/A 341). If the 'I think' is a proposition, it must be said to be an incomplete proposition; it is, as Kant allowed in B 421, 'quite indeterminate' because it awaits a content. It should be written in the form 'I think. . . .' Similarly with 'I', of which Kant correctly says in A 382 that it is 'as little an intuition as it is a concept of any object; it is the mere form of consciousness'. If it is neither an intuition nor a concept it cannot be a 'representation' of any sort. Nevertheless Kant commonly speaks as if it were, for example in his description of it (B 408) as 'the poorest of all representations'. In an earlier passage he had come nearer the truth when he said that there was no other basis for the teaching of Rational Psychology than (B 404/A 345–6) 'the simple, and in itself completely empty, representation "*I*"', and had added that

> we cannot even say that this is a concept, but only that it is a bare consciousness which accompanies all concepts. Through this I or he or it (the thing) which thinks, nothing further is represented than a transcendental subject of the thoughts $= X$. It is known only through the thoughts which are its predicates, and of it, apart from them, we cannot have any concept whatsoever, but can only revolve in a perpetual circle, since any judgment upon it has already made use of its representation.

But even here the misleading term 'representation' is used. What Kant is really talking about, as the passage makes clear, is the subject of consciousness which is indicated but not revealed in certain uses of the term 'I'. Already in the Deduction (B 131) he had said that the 'I think' must be capable of accompanying all my representations: nothing can count as an experience for me unless I can identify it as *my* experience. The whole world of experience as elaborated in judgment is experience for a subject; it presupposes, and exists in relation to, the transcendental unity of apperception. But the unity of apperception, as was explained earlier, is nothing personal; it is to be connected not with my consciousness or yours, but with 'consciousness in general'. Further, and more important in this connection, it is not an existent but an abstraction. It is a form which, when taken apart from its content, remains essentially empty. When Kant talks about 'the unity of apperception' he is referring to a constituent of experience, but not a material constituent, not something whose existence or occurrence could be established by looking into oneself in the way Hume pretended to do. That this is so is shown by the fact that any looking must be done by a subject; what is being sought is already presupposed in the seeking. But we cannot conclude from this that it is presupposed as known in some other way. When I use the word 'I' in what might be called a neutral epistemological context (as opposed to when I use it to mean myself in distinction from someone else), I indicate the subject of consciousness without characterising it. The 'I think', as Kant puts it, 'expresses the act of determining my existence', but does not itself amount to a form of self-intuition. 'In the synthetic original unity of apperception I am conscious of myself, not as I appear to myself, nor as I am in myself, but only that I am' (B 157). Kant adds the confusing words: 'This *representation* is a *thought*, not an *intuition*'. What he needs to say is that we are dealing here with a logical presupposition of there being any experience, a necessary condition of our making any claims about fact. The Rational Psychologist takes the 'I think' as the record, or expression, of an experience; he believes that the term 'I' properly refers to a special kind of existent, the self which is distinct from everything material. These assumptions are radically mistaken. But they are encouraged if we speak of 'I' as the name of a representation, even one which is 'simple' and 'poor', or if we think of 'I think' as a judgment or proposition, when in truth it is the form or vehicle of judgments in general.

Once these points are appreciated Kant's criticisms of the doctrines of Rational Psychology become not merely intelligible, but compelling. In surveying them briefly I shall refer to both editions of the *Critique*, but with rather more emphasis on the shorter and more effective second edition version. The Rational Psychologist tries first to say that the soul must be conceived as a substance; his evidence for that is that 'I, as a thinking being, am the *absolute subject* of all my possible judgments' (A 348). Kant allows that this is so; it is, as he points out, an analytical truth that 'the "I", the "I" that thinks, can be regarded always as subject, and as something which does not belong to thought as a mere predicate' (B 407). But he adds that this does not mean that 'I, as *object*, am for myself a *self-subsistent* being or *substance*'. It might be thought that this misses the point: the Rational Psychologist is claiming to tell us about the subject self, not the self as an object. But Kant's objection that the proposition that the self is substance is synthetic when the premise from which it is alleged to be drawn is analytic, remains even when attention is transferred to the subject self. What intuition do we have of that subject self, and what is there in that intuition which is permanent? Kant put the case well in the first edition when he said that though 'the "I" is indeed in all thoughts . . . there is not in this representation the least trace of intuition, distinguishing the "I" from other objects of intuition'. The 'I' is formally present in all thought, and for that matter in all intuiting, but this does not mean that it is 'an abiding and continuing intuition' (A 350). It is a permanent framework for experience, but not a permanent item in experience.

The next claim to consider is that the soul is essentially simple in its nature, a conclusion which is supposed to be proved by the reflection that a composite being could not produce unitary thought. 'For representations (for instance, the single words of a verse), distributed among different beings, never make up a whole thought (a verse), and it is therefore impossible that a thought should inhere in what is essentially composite' (A 352). Again, Kant allows that there is a sense in which this is not just true but necessarily true: the 'I' of apperception is a unitary point to which all experience must relate. It is a logically simple subject (B 408). But nothing follows from this about the simplicity or otherwise of the subject of knowledge itself, the 'I in itself' which the metaphysician takes to be the thing that thinks. The argument that soul and body are essentially different because body is composite and soul simple will not stand examination. Souls and bodies as parts of the experienced world are certainly different; 'extension, impenetrability, cohesion and motion . . . neither are nor contain thoughts' (A 358). But that is not to say that the things that lie behind them also differ fundamentally; it could be that the 'substratum' of matter, as Kant sometimes calls it, was in fact spirit. Kant here clearly lets his own speculative impulse run away with him; on his own view we know nothing of what lies beyond experience, and so cannot profitably enquire into its qualities. But he is right all the same to say that the metaphysical argument for simplicity is fallacious.

The third paralogism concerns personality: it turns on the claim that the subject of consciousness must be numerically identical at different times. Kant says that it is analytically true that 'in all the manifold of which I am conscious I am identical with myself' (B 408): the unitary point to which all my experiences relate must by definition be one and unchanging. But it is one thing to say this, and quite another to claim that I as a person must remain identical whatever changes I undergo. From the proposition that the same formal 'I' is presupposed in everything that is to count as my experience, nothing can be inferred about whether I shall be the same tomorrow as I am today. I might wake up tomorrow and begin a new series of experiences which would have no relation to those I have had today; a formal point of unity would be demanded for these too, but it would be another person who was saying 'I'. It might even be the case, Kant argues in the first edition (A 363 and note), that a subject acquired experiences that he thought were his but were not; there would here be a change of persons with the illusion of continuing personality. In any case, the dictum of the ancients that everything is in flux cannot be refuted by referring to the unity of consciousness. Questions about self-identity depend on material considerations; they cannot be settled in the high-handed manner proposed by the Rational Psychologist.

It may well be true that Kant himself is a trifle arbitrary on this subject. He fails to appreciate the extent to which problems about self-identity involve points which are properly philosophical, and which turn on the logical implications of the language used (can I seriously wonder, as is suggested in A 364, whether *I* as subject of experience may in fact be constantly changing?). He also says little or nothing about the relevance of bodily identity to personal identity. But it should be emphasised that the real object of his discussion in the third Paralogism is to expose a bad metaphysical argument. He is not putting forward his own ideas about self-identity, but simply showing that certain ideas advanced by other philosophers rest on inferences which are invalid.

The fourth paralogism takes very different forms in the two editions. In the first it is concerned with 'ideality', i.e. with the question whether the existence of external objects is uncertain as that of mental objects is not (for this see section 33 below). In the second edition Kant addresses himself to the more obviously metaphysical problem whether the human mind is distinct in substance from the human body, and so might continue to exist in the absence of the latter. Descartes in the sixth *Meditation* had announced that, though mind and body might be conjoined 'very intimately' in this life, it was nevertheless certain that 'this I is entirely and absolutely distinct from my body, and can exist without it' (Haldane and Ross translation, I 190). His reason was that he had a 'clear and distinct' idea of himself as a 'thinking and unextended thing', together with a 'distinct' idea of the body as 'an extended and unthinking thing', and the two are plainly different. If Descartes were asked for the source of his clear and distinct idea of himself as a thinking thing, his answer would be in the experience of the *cogito*, which he took as establishing not just the existence of the mind, but also its essential nature. He thus in Kant's terminology argued to a metaphysical conclusion of major importance from the bare fact of the 'I think'.

But the argument as Kant saw it was fallacious. It was indeed analytically true that I as 'a thinking being', that is to say I as the subject of consciousness, am distinct from other things outside me, including my own body, since '*other* things are such as I think to be *distinct* from myself' (B 409; Kant's italics). To put the point less cryptically, the 'I' of the 'I think' is not to be identified with any of its objects: it stands over against them as the subject with which they are correlated. But this fact proves nothing about the substantial difference of mind and body or about the capacity of the former to exist apart from the latter. That I as thinker am distinct from whatever I experience does not show that I could have experiences if I were only a thinking thing. The form of consciousness is one thing, the content of consciousness another, and it might be the case that a body was needed to supply the latter. In any case the subject of consciousness is an empty abstraction, and no inference from it to the character of any real existent is legitimate.

Once it is accepted that 'I think' is formal and not experiential, as Descartes thought it was, Kant's conclusion follows here with the same cogency as in the three earlier arguments. The only difficulty is whether Kant himself sticks to the conclusion consistently. In the long note to section 25 of the second edition Deduction from which I have quoted above he says correctly that the occurrence of the 'I think' does not allow me to 'determine my existence as a self-active being', but only to 'represent to myself the spontaneity of my thought' (B 158). He then adds the words 'But it is owing to this spontaneity that I entitle myself an intelligence', and this might be taken as implying that I can properly think of myself as an intellectual and not merely a natural being. A more striking passage still is to be found in the Antinomies (B 574–5/A 546–7), where we read that 'man, who knows all the rest of nature solely through his senses, knows himself also through pure apperception', and is 'thus to himself, on the one hand phenomenon, and on the other hand, in respect of certain faculties the action of which cannot be ascribed to the receptivity of sensibility, a purely intelligible object'. On the face of it this says that human beings are not just parts of nature, and says it on the evidence of apperception: precisely the sort of metaphysical inference whose propriety is challenged in the Paralogisms.

The problems raised by such passages will be discussed, so far as I can discuss them at all, in the next section. Meantime, it is worth asking after the general effects of Kant's criticisms in this part of his work. At first sight they appear to be devastating: Rational Psychology has all but disappeared from the philosophical scene. But it might be claimed that the philosophy of mind which now flourishes is simply Rational Psychology under another name. The problems raised by Descartes and others, about the essential nature of mind, the relations of mind and body, personal identity, the differences between men and machines, the differences between men and animals, continue to be vigorously discussed by philosophers, and much of the discussion turns, as it did for the metaphysicians of the past, on conceptual points rather than matters of fact. Admittedly there is little tendency on the part of the philosophers concerned to present their conclusions in what Kant called 'systematic doctrinal form' (cf. B 303/A 247): the idea that we can arrive at the full truth about these subjects by pure thinking is not much in favour. But the less extravagant claim that philosophical as well as empirical considerations are relevant in this area continues to be made, and to be made with good effect. There are few philosophers even among professed opponents of metaphysics today who would reject it out of hand.

It would seem from this that though Kant's criticisms are valid as far as they go, they do not go as far as he thought. It is not true that 'I think' is the sole text for the metaphysician who wishes to pronounce on mind and body, though it is true that Descartes and others have argued largely if not exclusively from it. The fallacies of the *cogito* have been definitively exposed: in future no philosopher will be able to base a substantial metaphysical argument on the bare fact of consciousness with any hope of succeeding. But there are other issues here which Kant has not raised, or not raised with any degree of clarity. With some of these issues I shall be concerned in the discussion which follows.

§ 32 *Kant on Self-Knowledge*

As well as criticising the views about the nature and knowability of the self expressed or implied by others, Kant puts forward theories of his own on the subject. One such theory maintains that self-knowledge is exactly like knowledge of external objects in being confined to appearances. The space-time world which we know when we bring the understanding to bear on the data of the senses is a world of phenomena; there are lots of things in it which are *empirically* real, but from the transcendental point of view they are none of them *independently* real. Experience is all experience for a subject; remove the subject, and space, time and their contents simply vanish. Kant's readers found themselves the more ready to swallow this unlikely story because they had heard similar things from other writers such as Berkeley. But when Kant added that it was not just in the case of physical reality, but also in that of mental life, that we know only appearances, they found his arguments hard to take seriously. In the second edition of the *Critique* Kant made important additions both to bring to the fore what he clearly thought of as the paradox of self-knowledge (B 67–9) and to render it acceptable (B 152–9). That he succeeded in meeting the doubts of many of his readers seems extremely unlikely.

Part of the difficulty here is simply a matter of terminology. Kant wants to say that knowledge of the self is exactly like knowledge of the physical world in so far as it demands both intuitions and concepts. He also holds that all human intuiting proceeds in a framework of *a priori* forms and all objective thinking in a framework of *a priori* concepts. It follows that nothing can be known by human beings in what might be described as its pure state; we know things not as they are, but as they appear. In the case of things physical something appears to the knowing mind, and though this idea has its difficulties these do not seem absolutely insuperable. But when it comes to knowledge of minds, what appears and that to which it appears stand on the same side: it is the self which both serves as subject and is intuited as object. How can it be present in this dual capacity, and above all how can it be *known* to be so present? These difficulties are lessened, if not quite removed, if instead of saying that I know myself only as I appear to myself I say that I know myself only as an object of experience. The advantage of this way of speaking is that the subject for which objects of experience exist or obtain need not be conceived as personal, but is more intelligibly thought of as the subject of consciousness in general, the impersonal 'I' to which individual experiences must relate if they are to count as real. Whatever it is that is made manifest in my inner life, it is not consciousness in general or an impersonal 'I'. As for the question how mind in any form can take cognisance of itself as an object, that, as Kants says, (B 68), is 'a difficulty common to every theory'. For Kant the presence in human beings of internal intuition or inner sense is a fact, a fact he expresses by saying that in certain respects each of us stands in a passive relation to himself. No doubt it is a less straightforward fact than Kant realised, as more recent philosophers have argued; no doubt again there are problems even inside Kant's assumptions about what should be taken as falling within inner sense. Kant himself announces that utterances expressing pleasure and pain, or having to do with the will, should not be counted as matters of knowledge; just what that leaves as genuine knowledge of the self as an object remains a matter of some controversy (see T. D. Weldon, *Kant's Critique of Pure Reason*, part III). But despite these difficulties the theory of inner sense, which Kant himself took over from Locke, is still widely accepted in one form or another. So long as it is, Kant's claims about the subject's standing in a passive relation to itself, and about this being something which has to be generally acknowledged, are at any rate far from absurd.

But even if it is true to say that, in virtue of possessing inner sense, I have knowledge of myself as an object of experience, is that all the knowledge of myself that I have? So far as I know, Kant shows no awareness of the possibility that I might learn something about myself by reflecting on my own behaviour. His own concern is rather with the suggestion that I enjoy a special form of access to myself in self-consciousness, and am because of that in a position to make additional statements about myself as the subject of know-ledge. How he deals with that suggestion we have already seen in considering his criticisms of Rational Psychology. He does not deny or play down what might be called the fact of self-consciousness, expressed in the ability to say 'I'; he allows that this is a feature of the situation which falls entirely outside the province of inner sense. But he claims, surely correctly, that 'the consciousness of self' is 'very far from being a knowledge of the self' on the ground that 'for knowledge of myself I require, besides the consciousness, that is, besides the thought of myself, an intuition of the manifold in me, by which I determine this thought' (B 158). Only if I had another form of self-intuition, over and above what is available in inner sense, could I 'determine my existence as a self-active being' (B 158 note). Inner sense gives me intuition of myself as passive; the new form of self-intuition would have to give me intuition of myself as active. But though I am conscious of what Kant in the same passage calls 'the spontaneity of my thought' and so can properly entitle myself an intelligence, the fact is that I have no direct access to myself in this capacity, with the result that 'my existence is still only determinable sensibly, that is, as the existence of an appearance'. I can think of myself as a self-active being, but I cannot know myself as such.

The obvious comment on this might be that I constantly claim such knowledge in so far as I speak of myself as a thinker or practical agent. I do not merely stand in a passive relation to myself and wait for perceptions of one sort or another to occur; I continually initiate changes in my mental life, setting myself to think about problems, trying to draw inferences, deciding in the light of evidence what the facts are, deciding in the light of evidence what to do. And I know, or at least am in a position to know, what I am doing when I engage in these activities. I know, for instance, that I am at present occupied in a conscious attempt to clarify Kant's views on self-knowledge. But I do not know it, or do not appear to know it, through reflection on data provided by inner sense. It is not the case here that I first experience certain sensations and then interpret them, as I might in coming to know that I was jealous of some other person. My grasp of what is going on seems to be much more direct than that: if someone asks me what I am doing I can say straight off what it is. I know myself *to be* think*ing*, rather than *as qualified* in this way or that. But if I do, will it not follow that Kant's account of self-knowledge is seriously incomplete?

That Kant's account of self-knowledge *is* seriously incomplete is shown by the fact that he fails to discuss these questions in the passages where he talks about knowing the self as a subject. It would not, however, be fair to suggest that he is entirely silent about it. In general, he tries to draw a sharp distinction between what belongs to the will and what belongs to the intellect as an instrument of knowledge, and to argue that the activities under consideration fall under the heading of the former. I know myself as an object of experience, but I also engage in a large number of practical activities, including the activity of thinking. As an object of experience I am part of the phenomenal or natural world and, like everything else in that world, am caused to behave as I do by forces outside my control. But I can see myself in a wholly different light, one in which I am a self-active being, and this is what I do when I act. As independent agent or (though Kant does not stress the point) as independent thinker I present myself to myself as free of the bonds of natural necessity and as governed by the self-imposed law of reason; I take myself to belong to a non-natural order and so as something more than appearance. This is what Kant means when he says that qua agent, or at least qua moral agent, man thinks of himself as noumenon. But though he has no doubt of the correctness of this doctrine, he insists that what is involved here is not knowledge, but only a point of view. I do not *know* myself as noumenon, even when I engage in moral activity; I simply conceive myself as such and behave as if I were part of a noumenal order. It follows that consciousness of myself as agent or thinker cannot for Kant amount to knowledge, any more than consciousness of myself as in pain amounts to knowledge. To be conscious of pain is simply to feel pain; pains are things to be undergone rather than objects to be observed. Similarly to be conscious of doing something or other is not to have a special form of knowledge about myself; it is rather to engage in the activity in question in a special way. To be aware that I am giving you my word, or that I am puzzling myself about self-knowledge, is on this account supervenient on the activities concerned. When I consciously promise, or consciously hazard a guess, I do not do two things, namely promise or guess on the one hand and catch myself promising or guessing on the other. Rather, as Ryle would put it, I engage in an activity in a certain frame of mind, ready to turn to other things if occasion should call for it.

In ascribing these modern-sounding doctrines to Kant I admit that I have gone beyond the text of the *Critique*. The latter declares explicitly that what has to do with pleasure and pain on the one hand and the will on the other do not fall within knowledge (B 66); it does not, so far as I know, discuss how to understand the claim to know that I am in pain or to know that I am engaged in this or that activity. I feel reasonably confident, however, that Kant would say, like Wittgenstein, that pain is not so much known as felt; I can know that I am in pain only in so far as I can be conscious of my pain, a fact which falls under the heading of 'affection' rather than 'cognition' in the overall trichotomy which Kant makes the basis of the three *Critiques*. And if this is correct it seems not unreasonable to suppose that he held a parallel doctrine about knowledge of mental activity. He need not, and of course could not, deny that we are conscious of acting in this way or that, but he could, and in my view did, deny that such consciousness amounted to knowledge. For this to be possible Kant must commit himself to a view of the kind briefly sketched above. Only if he makes consciousness of mental activity continuous with mental activity itself will he be able to avoid awkward questions about what self it is that I know when I know what I am about.

Let us take it that the interpretation given is well founded: what conclusion are we to draw about Kant's general treatment of this subject? It seems to me that we should conclude that Kant's account of self-knowledge is in important respects seriously misleading. I have already suggested that the paradoxical thesis that we know ourselves only as appearances should be replaced by the milder-sounding claim that we know ourselves only as objects of experience. What needs to be added to this, in the light of the foregoing discussion, is that though we can *know* ourselves only as objects, that by no means exhausts the ways we have at our disposal for referring to and talking about ourselves. Man is not just a subject for science; he also appears on the scene as the possessor of feelings, and again as an agent and thinker. Kant's language about knowing myself only as appearance suggests that there is some other me, the real me, which mysteriously remains unknown and unknowable; the rational psychologist promises information about this other me, but lacks the power to make good his promise. The doctrines outlined above show that Kant did not leave the matter in this unsatisfactory state, but realised that lack of intellectual intuition did not rule out meaningful discourse about the self as agent. True, the metaphysical contrast between the natural world of 'appearances' and a non-natural world of 'reality' was never far from his mind; he was inclined to take the very existence of agent language as pointing to the existence of an 'I in itself', for all his conviction that such an 'I' could not be known. We should, however, try here as generally in the talk about phenomena and noumena to separate out what is philosophically tenable from what is due to nothing more than inveterate metaphysical prejudices of Kant's own. I suggest that what Kant has to say about knowing myself as an object is broadly correct, though subject to amendment in detail; that his criticism of metaphysical claims to provide knowledge of the subject self is entirely correct; and that there is at the lowest estimate a lot to be learned from what he says about utterances concerning the will and pleasure and pain. Knowing what I am thinking or doing are, if properly named, less simple forms of knowledge than Kant's predecessors supposed; when I have such knowledge I am not aware of either subject or object self. To have seen this much is enough to make Kant's far from perspicuous pronouncements on this topic worth continuing study.

I have scarcely referred in all this to the complicating circumstance that Kant drew a sharp distinction between moral and non-moral action, downgrading the latter to the status of a mere phenomenon and arguing that reason is only truly practical when it is pure. Kant's stress on this distinction had the effect of preventing him from developing any general theory of action in the modern sense of the term. He thought of action proper, i.e. of moral action, as flowing from pure practical reason, whilst other human activities, however apparently refined, were one and all the product of desire, which was all fundamentally sensuous (see *Critique of Practical Reason*, Berlin edition v 24). It seems reasonable to suppose that such a view would not be without a bearing on our present subject; it could be that Kant would say one thing about consciousness of myself as morally active, another about consciousness of myself as, for example, plotting the overthrow of a rival I envy. However, it seems best to leave these difficulties out of account here and to concentrate on what might be called a generally Kantian view. By following that procedure we can probably get the main issue better into focus, even if we lose sight to some extent of the overall position which the historical Kant wanted to establish.

§33 *The Refutation of Idealism*

In arguing that we know ourselves only as we appear to ourselves Kant took up a position which was decisively different from that of his rationalist predecessors. He also broke with them radically in his attitude to idealism, where that term refers to the thesis that the existence of minds is absolutely certain, that of external things always subject to doubt. According to Descartes, it is logically possible that I and my experiences are the only things in existence. I cannot deny my own existence without implicitly reaffirming it, and I cannot deny that I have certain ideas. But though these ideas seem in many cases to point beyond myself—they are, for instance, ideas of material things—they are strictly no more than occurrences in my mental life, and could be what they are even if there was nothing beyond me. In point of fact Descartes did not think that he was alone in the world: he argued first that the existence in him of the idea of God would be unintelligible unless there really were a God, and second that something really corresponded at least to that part of his ideas of material things which was clear and distinct. But he purported to establish these points by independent considerations on the basis stated above, namely that the sole absolute certainty is the existence of the self and of the ideas which constitute its experiences.

In the first edition of the *Critique* (A 367 ff.) Kant made a lame attempt to refute idealism by arguing that our awareness of physical things is as direct and as certain as our awareness of our own mental states, since physical things are like mental states in being 'nothing but representations, the immediate perception (consciousness) of which is at the same time a sufficient proof of their reality' (A 371). This theory had the disadvantage of precluding any common public world. In the second edition Kant proposed a much more radical disproof of the idealist position, in the section explicitly headed 'Refutation of Idealism' which was added to the chapter on the Postulates of Empirical Thought (B 274–9). Here he argued for the thesis that 'the mere, but empirically determined, consciousness of my own existence proves the existence of objects in space outside me' (B 275). To be in a position to say what is going on in myself I must stand in relation to something which is not myself. Determinate inner consciousness, the datum from which the idealist starts, involves, as a minimum, ability to order the occurrence of ideas; for this to be possible I must be able to assign objective dates, or at least an objective order of occurrence, to different mental events. But 'all determination of time presupposes something permanent in perception': I can measure change only against a background which does not change. There is, however, nothing in the flow of mental states which answers this description: as Kant had put the point in the first edition Deduction (A 107), 'no fixed and abiding self can present itself in this flux of inner appearances'. The phenomena of consciousness are constantly changing, and though they all relate to the unchanging 'I' of apperception, the latter is 'not an intuition, but a merely intellectual representation of the spontaneity of a thinking subject' (B 278); not an item in consciousness, but the bare subject to which all such items belong. It follows that if I am to put internal events in an objective temporal order I must do it by reference to something permanent outside me. It will not do in this connection to say that I could get by with no more than the *apparent* experience of external things, by *seeming* to perceive something outside me, for this would merely land me with extra items of inner experience (with more 'representations'), when the problem is to sort out such items. If I had only the impression of having an external experience I could not distinguish what is real and what is illusory in my inner life. For that I need to know that external experience is, in general (cf. B 278–9), veridical; I need to stand in relation to physical bodies in space, themselves thought of as more or less temporary collocations of an underlying stuff which is permanent.

That this celebrated argument establishes something of real importance is not in doubt. At the lowest estimate it makes clear the dubious character of the assumptions on which the idealists proceeded. Descartes had said that he could suppose that he had no body, but not that he had no mind; he believed that external things generally might be no more than imaginary, but was sure that the same thing could not be said of his mind. In speaking of his mind in this connection he meant the mind he took to exist as part of the objective order, a particular mind about which he believed certain things to be true and certain things to be false. One way of putting Kant's central point in the Refutation is that, if the facts were as Descartes described them, he was not warranted in speaking in this way. If he were indeed alone in the world, he could not begin to characterise his mind as 'empirically determined', i.e. as something which had a real history. He would not in these circumstances have the power to distinguish what was really happening to or in him, but would have to accept whatever came into consciousness as having an equal claim to reality. That we do not do this—that, for example, we mark off idle fancies from genuine experiences or genuine memories—connects with two features of the situation about which Descartes says nothing: that we live in a public world of physical bodies, and that we are normally in the company of other people. Kant's handling of the problem of idealism is deficient in so far as he says nothing about this second point. But he grasps the importance of the first point with admirable clarity, and brings out the central objection that the Cartesian position was incoherent simply because it took for granted the essentials of the thesis it attempted to deny. It assumed without warrant that a mind which was alone in the world would be indistinguishable from a mind which was not, when everything goes to show that access to external things in space affects our minds fundamentally.

But though the Refutation is thus sound in essentials, there are many points of difficulty in its details. One such point concerns exactly what Kant thinks he has proved. Is it his view that the mere consciousness of my existence as empirically determined shows that I am directly aware of things in space, that where external sensation is concerned they and not 'representations' are the immediate objects of my intuition? That this is his view might be read into his declaration in B 275 that 'perception of this permanent is possible only through a *thing* outside me and not through a mere *representation* of a thing outside me', with the parallel claim in B xli that the 'something permanent' must be 'an external thing distinct from all my representations'. But Kant does not say explicitly in either passage that I can *intuit* physical objects; he says only that inner experience is not possible without outer experience, and that the latter must be genuine and not merely apparent. If I have a genuine outer experience this will mean that I have a basis on which to make judgments about physical objects: I have external intuitions which will not mislead me if only I interpret them properly. The trouble about this is that the idealist can say much the same: he can claim to have ideas which ostensibly point outwards, and to use these as a reliable basis on which to predict the occurrence of further ideas. To avoid finding himself in this position Kant must insist on two points. First, he must argue, as was argued above, that though intuition is an essential component in knowledge it is not a form of knowledge in itself. I confront neither things nor my own representations in intuition, since I confront there nothing at all. That there are physical things is a conclusion to which I come in judgment, on the basis of intuition but not by intuition alone. Secondly he must say that outer experience ensures contact with external reality, without being able to specify what form that reality takes. Descartes was wrong to treat the experience of material things as, in essentials, no more than the having of ideas. External intuitions occur in a being which not only has a mind, but is situated bodily in a physical world. Outer intuitions are in general reliable only because people have sense organs and through them a means of getting information about external reality. The senses give me contact with this wider world, but to determine what it is really like I have to supplement sensing with judgment.

How near does Kant come to accepting these requirements? I have argued in earlier sections (see especially section 17 above) that in the second edition at least he recognises the importance of judgment in specifying what is the case, without however fully divesting himself of the view that sensation is in itself a form of knowledge. He continues to speak as if the content of our intuitions could be described at the level of intuition itself, when this is obviously impossible. As for the nature of external intuitions, it seems to me that in the Refutation he recognised that they are not merely mental, but ensure contact with what lies beyond ourselves, without having any explanation of how this is possible. He was precluded from finding such an explanation because, for all his differences from Descartes, he worked generally within Cartesian assumptions about the relations of mind and body. He rejected the claim that the two are, or rather must be, metaphysically distinct, but committed himself to the view that on the empirical level 'dualism alone is tenable' (A 379). Empirically at any rate, the mind is one thing, the body another. It follows that nothing that occurs in the mind can have more than a contingent connection with anything that goes on in the body, and thus that the activity of sensing is in principle describable without any reference to sense-organs. Descartes himself had done better than this, in so far as he had argued that sensing could occur only in a being in which mind and body are intermingled as they are in human beings. Kant on the indications of the Refutation might have done much better. But in fact he never thought sufficiently clearly about the wider philosophical implications of the ideas he here put forward.

What does Kant mean by 'perception of the permanent'? It seems clear enough that the argument of the Refutation proceeds on the basis of what Kant thinks he has established in the first Analogy, which also said that 'all determination of time presupposes something permanent in perception'. In the Analogy, however, the permanent is *only* presupposed. The argument is that we have to interpret what goes on in the world on the basis of the principle that all change is transformation: we have to assume that there is a single underlying stuff whose configurations are constantly altering but which remains unchanged in quantity throughout its various metamorphoses. We can never experience this stuff as it is in itself, but only in one or other of its modifications. The point of postulating it is to enable us to connect diverse phenomena, to show that phenomenon B is intelligible because it represents, in whole or part, what became of phenomenon A; this, incidentally, is why substance figures among the concepts of *relation*. But in the Refutation, though Kant clearly looks back to this theory (cf. particularly B 277–8), he sometimes speaks as if the permanent had to be *perceived* if we were to date internal happenings. 'Perception of this permanent', as Kant puts it in his formal statement of the proof (B 275), 'is possible only through a thing outside me'. This curious wording may, however, be taken to imply that, if the permanent is perceived at all, it is only in an indirect way. What I perceive are physical things, and physical things must all be thought of as modifications of a permanent substance. Kant states the position correctly in the second note he appended to the proof (B 277–8):

> Not only are we unable to perceive any determination of time save through change in outer relations (motion) relatively to the permanent in space (for instance, the motion of the sun relatively to objects on earth), we have nothing permanent on which, as intuition, we can base the concept of a substance, save only matter; and even this permanence is not obtained

from outer experience, but is presupposed *a priori* as a necessary condition of the determination of time.

When Kant talks about the permanent, as was argued above (section 24), he is not concerned with the empirical question of how we actually determine time-relations, but with the transcendental question what has to be true of the world if we are to determine time-relations at all. Kant's case is that our particular questions proceed on the basis of assumptions, or an assumption, which are taken as unquestionable. But just because they have this character they can neither be established nor confuted on empirical grounds. Accordingly, if *that there is a permanent underlying change* is such an assumption, the permanent cannot be literally perceivable. If it were we could say that it was there on the basis of experience alone.

If we ask how the Refutation of Idealism in the first edition of the *Critique* relates to the Refutation of Idealism in the second, the answer must be that the latter simply replaces the former. Kant himself in the second edition preface (B xxxix note) pretended that the change was one 'affecting the method of proof only'. In fact it is much more radical than that. In the first edition Kant tried to show that we have as much reason to claim to have knowledge of bodies as we have to claim to have knowledge of minds. In the second edition he argued that we could not have knowledge of minds unless we also had knowledge of bodies. There is a change in conclusions here, as well as in arguments used. Further, the position maintained in the first edition version closely resembles that taken up by Berkeley, however much it diverges from the views Kant attributes to that philosopher. It seems clear that, in the mood in which he wrote the second edition Refutation, Kant could have found no more satisfaction in the theories of the historical Berkeley than he did in those of Descartes. The only thing we can do with his first attempt to refute idealism is accordingly to ignore it. The full value of his philosophical contribution in this area lies in the later Refutation alone.

It need hardly be added that Kant's antipathy to idealism is directed against what he himself calls 'empirical' idealism, the view that empirical external objects are or may be unreal. As he said in the Aesthetic, space, time and their contents are empirically real; spoken of at the everyday or scientific level they must be said to be undoubtedly there. But this of course does not prevent Kant from adding that they are transcendentally ideal, such that, if abstraction were made from all possible observers, they would not be there at all. Similarly Kant can combine hostility to empirical idealism with subscription to formal or transcendental idealism. The experienced world exists in essential relation to mind, though not to my mind or yours; this is the truth which the critical philosopher must proclaim. But when he ceases philosophising and reverts to the everyday point of view his doubts about external reality should disappear. To get his views clear he needs to insist throughout on the importance of thus distinguishing levels. It was because he thought that Berkeley made no such distinction that Kant was so indignant at being confused with him.

'The dialectical illusion in rational psychology', writes Kant at the end of his second version (B 426), 'arises from the confusion of an idea of reason—the idea of a pure intelligence—with the completely undetermined concept of a thinking being in general'. Similarly in the *Prolegomena* Kant summarises the results of the Paralogisms chapter under the heading 'Psychological Ideas' (in the plural: sections *46–9*). The idea of a pure intelligence is not obviously identifiable with that of 'the absolute (unconditioned) unity of the thinking subject', of which Kant had spoken in his general introduction to the Dialectic (B 391/A 334). But in any case the formal apparatus invoked by Kant is quite irrelevant to his argument in this part of the *Critique*. It is just not true that we are snared into Rational Psychology because of the fascination exerted by an irresistible idea, nor that we are misled by an illusion which is entirely natural and for that reason hard to avoid. We are tempted into it rather as a result of a series of intellectual mistakes, which principally turn on confusion about the role of the 'I think' and the implications of its use. We treat the bare subject of consciousness as if it were a substantial existent, and mix up the ability to say 'I' with a supposed experience of the subject self. That these confusions can be avoided is plain. We have only to read and understand Kant's own criticisms in the Paralogisms chapter to lose all incentive to embrace them.

§ 34 *The Antinomy of Pure Reason : its Formal Constitution*

If Kant's formal apparatus makes sense anywhere, it is in the chapter on the Antinomies, to which we must now turn. 'The Antinomy of Pure Reason' is the name Kant gives to the result produced when human reason is given its head and allowed to think about the world, its nature and conditions of existence without any restrictions; what happens in these circumstances, he says, is that we find ourselves driven to contradictory conclusions each of which appears to be intellectually compelling. The chapter entitled 'The Antinomy of Pure Reason' explores this 'strangest phenomenon of human reason', as Kant calls it in the *Prolegomena* (section 52), first setting up the antinomy under four main headings, then discoursing on the phenomenon in general, finally suggesting that the contradictions can be removed if we drop a premise in, or presupposition of, the argument which both parties to the conflict take for granted but which is in fact false. It is entirely natural to think, as these metaphysicians do, that the world of the senses is a world of things existing in or by themselves. But if we do accept this idea, and proceed to investigate the ultimate conditions of the world in question, we find ourselves entangled in the antinomy, having equal reason both to affirm and to deny that the world has a limit in space and time, that everything in it that is composite is made up of simple parts, that among the causes operative in it are some that are spontaneously active, and that there belongs to it, either as a part or as its cause, a being which is absolutely necessary. To say that this result is produced in pursuit of the unconditioned and under the influence of a natural illusion is certainly not absurd.

Taken at its author's estimate, the Antinomy chapter must count as the boldest, most provocative and most original in the whole of the first *Critique*. In it we find Kant confronting an important group of metaphysicians with a major challenge which, if securely based, must prove absolutely fatal to their enterprise. Other critics of metaphysics have denounced metaphysical aspirations as unscientific and have seen metaphysical pronouncements as lacking in literal significance; Kant himself proffers criticisms of this sort in other parts of his work. But in insisting that pure reason falls into antinomies when it tackles cosmological questions he advances a graver charge against this type of speculation. If it is indeed true that, whenever a student of cosmology puts forward a particular thesis, it is not only found that he can make out a good case in support, but further that someone else can make out an equally cogent case for the precise opposite, the whole enterprise of engaging in cosmological enquiries of a philosophical kind must be abandoned. What makes Kant remarkable in this part of his work is that, alone among critics of metaphysics, he not only hints that metaphysics may be incoherent, but undertakes to demonstrate that it is. He produces what he says are definitive proofs of a series of pairs of propositions which have every appearance of being mutually contradictory, and so puts the spectacle of reason falling into contradictions before our eyes. No other philosopher has undertaken so radical an attack as this. But it should be emphasised that Kant's motive in mounting the attack is not just to discredit a form of speculation which he saw as equally seductive and unprofitable. It is also to provide an indirect proof for his own thesis of transcendental idealism, a thesis which is central in his attempt to show that the sphere of knowledge is limited to possible experience and that when it comes to talking about God, freedom and immortality the most we can attain to is conviction based on moral experience. If what Kant says about the parties engaged in cosmological conflicts is correct, the explanation of their differences is that they both accept a principle which they take to be obviously true, but which is in fact false, indeed self-contradictory: the principle that the world of things in space and time exists on its own, in complete independence of mind. In the Aesthetic and Analytic Kant had suggested reasons for discarding this principle as untenable; in the Antinomy chapter he purports to show that it is not only incorrect but incoherent. In assessing the arguments of the chapter we must bear this extra ambition of Kant's in mind and ask ourselves, if we are unable to accept his conclusion, how otherwise the facts he points to are to be explained.

It must be admitted that Kant's claims in this part of his work have not been taken with entire seriousness by his critics. One charge frequently made against him is that he cheats in constructing his supposedly watertight proofs of the propositions of Rational Cosmology, usually by appealing to doctrines of his own to eke out what would otherwise be an entirely unconvincing case. Another common complaint is that he argues against straw men rather than real metaphysicians. He nowhere quotes from any actual metaphysical writer, or even claims to be summarising real metaphysical arguments, but prefers to argue for thesis and antithesis alike in his own way, thus presenting the conflict in a way which must seem schematic and artificial. Asked why he proceeded on these lines he might have said, as Karl Popper did in the somewhat similar case of his *Poverty of Historicism*, that his object was to state the argument to be examined as convincingly as he could. But he could also have claimed that the conflict he set out schematically could be readily documented in actual metaphysical controversy. In this connection it should be mentioned that a recent writer, Mr Sadik Al-Azm, has argued not only that the antinomies were suggested to Kant by reflection on the Leibniz-Clarke correspondence, but further that the positions represented in the formal statement of the antinomy in section 2 of Kant's chapter are those taken in the correspondence by Newton (through the person of Clarke) and Leibniz respectively (see *The Origins of Kant's Arguments in the Antinomies*, Oxford, 1972). As Al-Azm demonstrates, there are many parallels between the arguments Kant deploys and arguments advanced by Clarke on the one side and Leibniz on the other. Al-Azm's interpretation runs counter to the usual assumptions of Kant's English-speaking commentators, who tend to hold that Leibniz is the author of the thesis propositions, a position supported by Kant's own description of them as constituting a form of Platonism (cf. B 499/A 471, with B 882/A 854). It could be, however, that what began as an argument between Newton and Leibniz was later seen by Kant in a very different light, as a result of developments which were not envisaged when the original conflict was set out. My own inclination is to say that this is indeed so, and thus to support the Al-Azm reading, which is far too convincing in detail to be dismissed as entirely wrong. If this is correct, the antinomies as set out by Kant can be seen to be founded in real metaphysical conflict, and the suspicion that the whole chapter concerns an insignificant game can be removed. There will also in these circumstances be more incentive to treat the arguments advanced in support of thesis and antithesis as being what they purport to be, namely cases which real metaphysicians might have advanced, rather than to dismiss them without serious examination as essentially dependent on principles to which no real metaphysician could or would make appeal.

Let us therefore take it that the antinomies constitute a serious challenge and consider what Kant has to say about them. It will be best to begin by looking at his account of the formal structure of the antinomies and the way of escaping from them as given in *Prolegomena*, sections *50–4*, where he comments on the arguments set out in the *Critique* instead of merely repeating them. The main points made are as follows.

1. The object of the Antinomy is to unmask the pretensions of metaphysicians in a decisive way. Because nothing they say is capable of being verified or falsified in experience, metaphysicians might have gone on indefinitely without anyone being able to offer them a decisive challenge. But if it can be shown that when they do this in the field of 'cosmical concepts' there results a situation in which there is equal warrant for asserting both a certain metaphysical thesis and its precise antithesis, they will never be able to hold up their heads again.

2. The formal argument of the Antinomy establishes that this is the actual situation as regards Rational Cosmology. We find here

that, from the point of view of the dogmatic metaphysician, thesis and antithesis alike can be supported by proofs which Kant describes as 'equally clear, evident and irresistible' (section *52*). In each case the argument starts from a principle which is 'universally conceded', proceeds to a conclusion in the thesis with rigorous logic, starts again in the antithesis from 'another equally well-attested principle', and proceeds to the opposite of the thesis conclusion with precisely the same rigour. Each of the proofs is internally watertight ('I pledge myself for the correctness of all these proofs': section *52*), and hence the result cannot be blamed on faulty logic.

3. But how is any such result possible? Kant writes as follows (section *52b*):

> Of two contradictory propositions both cannot be false, unless the concept that lies at the ground of both of them is self-contradictory. For example, the two propositions *a four-cornered circle is round* and *a four-cornered circle is not round* are both false. For as concerns the first it is false that the said circle is round, because it is four-cornered; but it is also false that it is not round, i.e. has corners, because it is a circle. For the logical mark of the impossibility of a concept consists precisely in this, that when it is presupposed two contradictory propositions are both false.

To explain the existence of the antinomies he must accordingly find some self-contradictory concept which is presupposed as coherent and applicable by both parties to the conflict. Kant says that the concept in question is that of 'a world of the senses existing for itself' (section *52c*), or existing absolutely. It is entirely natural for people generally, and therefore for metaphysicians, to 'think of the appearances of the world of the senses as things in themselves', or again to 'take the principles of their connection as principles universally valid of things in themselves and not merely valid of experience' (section *52*). But to make this assumption or proceed on this presupposition is to generate contradictions, and accordingly it follows that the assumption in question is impossible.

4. To solve the problem of the antinomies we must therefore recognise that the world of things in space and time, the world which is discussed by Rational Cosmologists, has a peculiar status: it exists not absolutely but in essential relation to mind, which means in effect only so far as it is constructed or constituted in judgment. Once this is realised we are in a position to see that, in the case of its first two antinomies, thesis and antithesis are not, as they initially appear to be, true contradictories, but rather what Kant calls in the

Critique (B 532/A 504) 'dialectically opposed judgments'; in simpler terms, logical contraries. Pairs of contrary propositions cannot both be true, but they can both be false. And this is in fact the situation as regards the extent of the world and its divisibility into parts: it is false both that the world is infinite and that it is finite in spatial and temporal extent, false again both that it consists of indivisible simple parts and that it can be divided *ad infinitum*. For in each case there is the further alternative that it is indefinitely extensible or indefinitely divisible, and reflection on the status of the space-time world shows that it is this possibility which must be accepted.

5. Formally this solution applies to all four antinomies: if we insist, for example, on treating the world of things in space and time as independently existent or, in Kant's own words (B 571/A 543), 'yield to the illusion of transcendental realism', nature and freedom must both be abandoned. We cannot then say either that everything happens according to natural causality or that some things do not, since there are convincing arguments against either view. But Kant insists that there is a difference of a vital kind between the first two and the last two antinomies. In the first two the items in question (objects in space and time, parts of matter) are all formally homogeneous: in moving from one to another we there necessarily advance from like to like. But this condition need not hold when we pass to the consideration of causes and effects and of necessary and contingent being; here entities of entirely different kinds could be concerned in the relationship, though equally it could hold between entities of the same sort. Kant draws the conclusion that, in the case of the last two antinomies, thesis and antithesis might both be true, provided that they were true of different sorts of object. Thus it could be true that everything in the space-time world happens according to natural causality, without our having to deny that a different kind of causality might be effective in a noumenal or non-natural order which connects with, but is distinct from, that world. If this is correct thesis and antithesis in the third and fourth antinomies would turn out to resemble sub-contraries rather than contraries or contradictories in the traditional Square of Opposition, in being such that they could be true together.

To restate Kant's main point more formally: according to (2) above, supporters of the thesis propositions start from premises which are undoubtedly true and argue with impeccable logic to the truth of a certain conclusion c, whilst supporters of the antithesis begin from a different set of true premises and, again employing impeccable logic, infer the truth of not-c. Each party establishes its case by showing that the negation of the conclusion it favours must be ruled out. Schematically then the position is as follows:

Thesis	*Antithesis*
e f g . . . are true	p q r . . . are true
If e f g . . . are true, not-c is false	If p q r . . . are true, c is false
therefore c.	therefore not-c.

In the light of (3) Kant proposes to explain the contradiction by saying that the argument in each case proceeds on the basis of a certain presupposition m, which is unstated, common to both parties, but also, as it turns out, self-contradictory. A first step in resolving the antinomy is thus to abandon m and replace it by something different. In the case of the first two antinomies there is only one alternative n, the making explicit of which shows that the two original conclusions are not contradictories but contraries. On the presupposition of n, neither inference goes through. But the situation is different when we turn to the third and fourth antinomies. Here if n is presupposed the conclusion of the antithesis is true and that of the thesis false. There is, however, an alternative to n in these cases in the shape of o, and given this presupposition the thesis conclusion can also be true.

§ 35 *The Antinomy of Pure Reason : Kant's Solution and an Alternative*

We must now raise some questions about this impressive-sounding scheme. Consider first the status of m: is it really a presupposition, or is it an additional, unacknowledged, premise? As Mr J.E. Llewelyn pointed out in a brief but enlightening article ('Dialectical and Analytical Opposites', *Kantstudien*, 1964), Kant in fact treats it as a *statement* in the *Critique*, when he remarks (B 532/A 504) that 'of two dialectically opposed judgments . . . one is not a mere contradictory of the other, but *says something more* than is required for a simple contradiction'. In the *Prolegomena*, by contrast, he consistently presents m as a presupposition. I think there are two things to be said about this difficulty: first, that Kant himself would hardly have seen it as a problem, since he shows little or no awareness of the significance of the distinction between stating and presupposing; second, and more important, that it may be the case that m is more complex than Kant realises, and contains an element which is presupposed *together with* an element which functions as an unacknowledged premise.

A second question about the status of m is whether it is really self-contradictory or only false. Again, there is an apparent conflict on the point between the *Critique* and the *Prolegomena*. In the latter, as we have seen, m has got to be self-contradictory. But in the *Critique* Kant introduces his discussion of the formal structure of the antinomy (B 531/A 503 ff.) by referring to the proposition *All bodies are either good-smelling or not good-smelling*. This proposition expresses a true disjunction only if it is accepted that *all bodies have some smell or other*, which might conceivably be challenged on empirical grounds. Does this mean that m too might be empirically false? If this question had been explicitly put to Kant his answer could only have been negative, in view of the account he gives in the *Prolegomena* about the generation of mutually contradictory conclusions. But if it emerges that m is complex it could be that what Kant thought was self-contradictory was in fact no more than false. To generate the contradiction we need to adduce something which is self-contradictory. But in the case of the antinomies the self-contradiction may not lie precisely where Kant found it.

What precisely is the proposition which constitutes m, or, if m is complex, lies at its heart? Typically Kant himself answers this question, as already mentioned, by pointing not to a proposition but to a concept, that of 'a world of the senses existing for itself' (*Prolegomena*, section *52c*). Elsewhere in the *Prolegomena* (section *52*) he speaks of thinking of 'the appearances of the world of the senses as things in themselves', whilst in the *Critique* (B 535/A 507) we hear of 'the supposition that appearances, and the sensible world which comprehends them all, are things in themselves', and again (B 565/A 537) of 'the inevitable consequence of obstinately insisting on the reality of appearances'. Sometimes Kant calls what is here insisted on 'transcendental realism' (B 519/A 491; B 571/A 543; A 369). Now it is clear that to describe appearances as things in themselves is to fall into contradiction, since the term 'appearance' in this context means precisely something which cannot exist by or for itself. But for Kant to assume at this point that a world of the senses must be a world of appearances is surely not legitimate. The idea of a world of appearances existing absolutely is plainly self-contradictory; the idea of a world of the senses existing absolutely seems at first sight quite intelligible. If Kant denies its intelligibility he is evidently in some difficulty, since a main object of the *Critique* is to show the unacceptability of transcendental realism, which must be an intelligible doctrine if it is to be confuted. Kant is in fact in an awkward dilemma here: he must either say that transcendental realism is necessarily false, which would imply that his own doctrine is necessarily true, or agree that his account of the generation of the antinomies is unacceptable. I think myself that the way out of the dilemma is to show that the proposition that *the world of the senses exists for itself* does not generate the antinomies unaided, but only when used along with other premises, one of which is incoherent. How this might in fact have worked out I shall now try to show.

Let us take it that Al-Azm is right in saying that Kant first set up the antinomy on the basis of the Leibniz-Clarke correspondence, and thus that the conflict formally set out in section 2 of the Antinomy chapter is one between Newton and Leibniz. These philosophers were both men of ability and integrity; they each no doubt thought their premises true and their arguments watertight. But there is one respect, at first sight trivial, in which what Kant says about the parties to the antinomies does not apply to them: it is not true that they based their case on wholly different sets of premises. Kant speaks as if the champions of the theses on the one hand and of the antitheses on the other had nothing in common apart from their unstated assumption about the independent reality of the space-time world. But Newton and Leibniz in the correspondence not only agreed in formal principles of argument; they were further ready to acknowledge the truth of other principles of a less formal kind, among them the principle that there must be a sufficient reason for every happening or state of affairs.

Their agreement about this principle was, however, in some respects peculiar: they both paid lip-service to it, but differed about its application in particular cases. How this came about we can see from a part of the correspondence to which there are close parallels in the first Antinomy. Leibniz asked Clarke why, if the physical world was finite, bounded by empty space, it was placed as it was and not in some other position; again he wanted to know, given Clarke's conclusion that it came into existence at a particular point of time, why the beginning occurred just when it did. Behind his questions lay the conviction that, as Kant put it in developing the case for the antithesis of the first antinomy (B 455/ A 427):

> No coming to be of a thing is possible in an empty time, because no part of such a time possesses, as compared with any other, a distinguishing condition of existence rather than non-existence.

If the universe were, as Newton supposed, bounded by empty space and empty time there would be no sufficient reason for it to be where it is and to have begun when it did. Presented with this argument Clarke replied that though

'tis very true, that nothing is, without a sufficient reason why
it is . . . , this sufficient reason is oft-times no other, than
the mere will of God.

For him it was enough of an explanation of the universe's existing
as it does that God chose that it should. And when the question was
put why God should choose thus Clarke simply brushed it aside with
the comment that, if God could not act without a predetermining
cause, 'this would tend to take away all power of choosing, and to
introduce fatality' (Clarke's second reply, section 1).

One way of interpreting this exchange would be to say that agreement between Leibniz and Clarke on the Principle of Sufficient
Reason is no more than verbal. What Clarke regards as a proper
application of the principle is for Leibniz wholly contrary to it; conversely, the demand Leibniz makes for further reasons when offered
an explanation in terms of God's will seems to Clarke quite unacceptable. It could be argued on this basis that they were not
moving within the same ambit of ideas. But another possibility is
that they were, and that their differences arose from ambiguities
internal to the Principle of Sufficient Reason itself. That principle
can be seen as at once demanding and precluding that there be in
the universe some fact, event or existent which is ultimate and self-
explanatory. It demands such an item because it claims that whatever exists or occurs has a *sufficient* reason; the implication here is
that the chain of reasons can be brought to an end. But at the same
time it precludes it, since it also insists that there must be some
further reason for whatever is put forward as sufficient. If there are
such ambiguities in the principle, it would certainly explain why the
two parties argued as they did. Newton and Clarke take their stand
on what might be described as the positive side; for them God's
choice represents a sufficient reason beyond which they find it
neither necessary nor possible to go. Against them Leibniz argues
negatively that to stop at this point is to abrogate the central element
in the principle, by arbitrarily picking on an item which is allowed
to evade the demand for a reason. Each party uses arguments which
he thinks his opponent must acknowledge as correct, and is indignant
when he finds that the acknowledgement is withheld.

If Leibniz and Clarke got into difficulties because of ambiguities
in the Principle of Sufficient Reason, and Kant originally set up the
antinomy on the basis of their correspondence, there are obvious
implications for our subject. Kant as we know believed that the contradictions the antinomies reveal sprang from illegitimate acceptance
by both parties to the dispute of a presupposition which is self-

contradictory, the presupposition that the world of things in space and time exists absolutely. We saw before that there are difficulties in this position: Kant has on the face of it no reason for pronouncing this proposition internally incoherent (even the arguments of the Aesthetic and Analytic do not establish this much), whilst the very fact that he sought to make out that transcendental realism is false argues that it must at least be intelligible. It is possible to avoid these difficulties if we say that the presupposition on which Kant fixes attention is relevant to the antinomies but not the true source of the contradictions they contain. The true source of the contradictions lies in a premise to which both parties to the conflict make continuous appeal, a premise which contains latent contradictions and whose contradictions are brought to light when it is applied on the assumption of transcendental realism. The Principle of Sufficient Reason is just such a premise. And though it cannot be argued that it is explicitly invoked by the two parties in all four antinomies, it nevertheless figures prominently in antinomies 1, 3 and 4. In these cases, at any rate, it could well be responsible for the impasse into which the contending parties get themselves, an impasse in which each side is convinced of the correctness of what it asserts and yet finds it difficult if not impossible to ward off the attacks of its opponents.

It should be noticed that the solution here suggested differs only marginally from Kant's own. It agrees with Kant in taking the antinomies seriously, holding that they represent positions to which actual metaphysicians can and do subscribe, and finding the key to the difficulty, as Kant does, in a concept or principle whose internal incoherence is not at first apparent. It goes along with Kant further in accepting the importance of the question of the ontological status of the space–time world when it comes to seeking a solution of the conflict. Kant was not wrong in believing that the assumption of transcendental realism played an important part in the thinking of Rational Cosmologists. For it is only when this assumption is accepted that the latent ambiguities of the Principle of Sufficient Reason come out, a conclusion which is confirmed by the fact that they disappear on its removal. To move from m to n, that is from a realist to an idealist view of the status of things in space and time, allows the transformation of the dogmatic principle of Sufficient Reason into the 'critical' principle of the second Analogy, and in so doing removes any temptation to posit uncaused causes. The argument of the Antinomy as here reinterpreted thus lends support to the case for transcendental idealism, without amounting to an indirect proof of that doctrine. If the Antinomy did all Kant claims for it, we should have to say that transcendental realism is necessarily false and transcendental idealism necessarily true. Fortunately we can preserve all that is essential in Kant's position without having to commit ourselves to such unpalatable conclusions.

In all this I have said nothing about a highly important topic— whether Kant cheats in his statement of the antinomies by introducing his own philosophical views in what are supposed to be independent metaphysical arguments. About this I can only say summarily, first that there is no doubt that he does in places mention or expound views peculiar to himself (a particularly flagrant case occurs in the footnote to B 457/A 429, which sets out the Kantian view about space and the objects which fill it), but second that this may not matter as much as might at first appear. It will not matter, or at least not matter much, provided that the main arguments are unaffected by the intrusions. I cannot argue the point in detail here, but my inclination is to believe that the main cases for thesis and antithesis in antinomies 2, 3 and 4 can stand when all the special Kantian passages are excised. The same is true of the argument for the antithesis in the first antinomy, but not of that for the thesis, which turns on what Kant himself calls 'the true transcendental concept of infinitude . . . that the successive synthesis of units required for the enumeration of a quantum can never be completed' (B 460/A 432). Throughout this argument Kant's tendency to connect the concept of number with the activity of numbering (see B 182/A 142–3; also *Dissertation*, section *12*) is very much to the fore. But since the issue discussed is one which was prominent in the dispute between Clarke and Leibniz, I do not see that there is any difficulty of principle about substituting for Kant's statement of the thesis argument another in which 'critical' considerations play no part.

§36 *The Antinomy of Pure Reason: Further Critical Considerations*
The Antinomy of Pure Reason is the longest chapter in the *Critique*; to comment on it in detail would require a book in itself. What can be attempted here is necessarily far more modest. I shall confine myself to two main tasks. First, I shall explain, in more detail than has so far been possible, how Kant develops his general argument in the different parts of the chapter; this will be largely a matter of simple exposition. But when exposition is complete I shall turn to criticism, and in particular to a critical examination of Kant's grounds for offering radically different solutions to the first two and

the last two antinomies. This will have the advantage of allowing something to be said on one of Kant's most important claims, that his philosophy shows how we can believe that everything in nature happens according to law without having to abandon the conviction that the human will is free.

The Antinomy chapter begins with an attempt to delimit the sphere in which this sort of conflict arises: it is, says Kant, that of 'cosmical concepts' (*Weltbegriffe*) or 'cosmological ideas', which are relevant whenever there is a question of completing a regress from a particular empirical state of affairs to the things which condition it (every such state points beyond itself and is therefore described as 'conditioned'). Reference to the table of categories convinces Kant that there are and can be only four cosmological ideas and thus only four sets of antinomies; far more important than this is the insistence that behind the philosophising under examination lies the demand for something unconditioned, a demand which, in this case at least, seems at first sight wholly reasonable. Next, in section *2*, Kant sets out the antinomies in a systematic way, according to principles already discussed. One curiosity about the exposition is that we are given not merely a formal statement of the case on both sides, but also observations on the situation from the respective points of view. Another feature is that the arguments offered are in every case indirect: Kant represents his metaphysicians as establishing their case by showing the impossibility of the opposite view. In the third section there is a preliminary comment on the general position from Kant's own standpoint. It is argued that assertion of the four thesis propositions on the one hand, and of the four antithesis propositions on the other, amounts in each case to the advocacy of a whole philosophy. In one place (B 493−4/A 465−6) Kant calls the contrast one between 'dogmatism' and 'empiricism', in another (B 499/A 471) one between 'Platonism' and 'Epicureanism' (he has already evidently moved far from Clarke and Leibniz). Kant adds that if we had to chose between the two on grounds of interest alone, taking account of our needs as agents, we should certainly prefer Platonism; without such reference our state would be one of 'continuous vacillation' (B 503/A 475) between the two. In section *4* Kant argues that we cannot escape the difficulties by pleading the limited nature of our intellects. The blunderings of reason in this field must depend on a mistake of principle, and 'that very concept which puts us in a position to ask a question must also qualify us to answer it' (B 505/A 477). In other words, the predicament produced by the antinomies is philosophical, and must hence admit of a philosophical solution.

Section 5 is short and on the face of things rather puzzling: it says that whenever we attempt to make use of a cosmological idea we hit on something which is either too large to be comprehended by the understanding or not large enough. If for example we say that the world has no beginning we introduce a possibility which is beyond our comprehension, since we can never grasp the eternity which must have elapsed. But if we fix on a definite beginning, that does not satisfy the understanding either, for (B 515/A 487)

> since the beginning still presupposes a time which precedes it, it is still not unconditioned; and the law of the empirical employment of the understanding therefore obliges us to look for a higher temporal condition.

The significance of these remarks come out in what is said later about the regulative function of ideas. Kant's solution to the antinomy begins in section 6, continues in sections 7 and 8, and is set out in detail in section 9. The way to avoid the antinomies, we learn, is to recognise that they arise only if we fail to accept Kant's own transcendental idealism. If appearances were things in themselves, the dialectic of pure reason would be without a solution; and of course it is this assumption that the parties to the conflict unwittingly make. But once the critical point of view is adopted the whole question of the regress from conditioned to what conditions it is transformed. We are now able to see that the true function of ideas of reason is not constitutive but regulative, and to think of them not as designating objects, sensible or supersensible, but as delineating ideals to be pursued in empirical enquiry. The unconditioned is not given or implied in the given; it is *set as a task*, a task which can never be completed but for whose completion we must strive unceasingly. As for the antinomies themselves, they dissolve when we realise that in no case are the pairs of propositions concerned true contradictories. The proofs the metaphysicians offer, which are, as we saw, in every case disproofs of the opposite position, miss their mark once this is established, for it turns out that in the first two cases both contentions are false, whilst in the third and fourth they may be, but are not known to be, true.

The point on which I should like to direct attention is the last point here. Why does Kant put forward radically differing solutions to what he calls the 'mathematical' and 'dynamical' antinomies? I have already explained that formally what goes for the first two antinomies must go for the other two as well: on the supposition that the world of the senses is the only world and that it exists absolutely, both parties to the conflict must be dismissed. As Kant puts it in a passage previously quoted (B 571/A 543), neither nature nor freedom would remain on these terms. But there is a difference between the two sets of cases when it comes to offering solutions. Substituting n for m in the case of the mathematical antinomies means that we are at once presented with a third possibility, not considered hitherto: the world need be neither infinite nor finite in extent, since it could be and in fact is indefinitely extensible. A phenomenal world exists only in so far as it is constructed, and the construction can proceed, forwards and backwards, as far as we like to take it. But substituting n for m in the debate about free and natural causality produces no such compromise. If we stick to the world of the senses and understand it in Kantian fashion there is simply no possibility of finding an uncaused cause, for any cause we come across must itself be conditioned in its existence by something further. In the sense world, properly understood, everything happens according to laws of nature, with the result that the antithesis of the third antinomy is not false but true. It follows that if Kant is to save the thesis he must do it by arguing that, though not true of the sense world, it may be true of some other sphere which is separate from the latter but stands in connection with it. The argument is helped out by the point already explained about cause and effect not needing to possess homogeneity, as the parts of matter and objects in the physical world evidently must. It remains, for all that, desperately weak, as long at least as Kant stays within the proper confines of Rational Cosmology.

Let me try to elaborate. The suggestion we are invited to consider is that the phenomena of the space-time world, as well as being connected by natural causality, may also in some cases be conditioned by intelligible causes or a single intelligible cause. Now Kant himself points out (B 573/A 545) that an intelligible ground of that sort 'concerns only thought in the pure understanding' and 'does not have to be considered in empirical enquiries'. It is, in short, a mere logical possibility when looked at from the empirical point of view. What converts it into something better is apparently that it is substantiated by moral facts. 'That our reason has causality', Kant writes in a well-known passage (B 575–6/A 547–8),

> or at least that we represent it to ourselves as having causality, is evident from the *imperatives* which in all matters of conduct we impose as rules on our active powers. '*Ought*' expresses a kind of necessity and of connection with grounds which is found nowhere else in the whole of nature. . . . This '*ought*' expresses a possible action the ground of which cannot be

anything but a mere concept; whereas in the case of a merely natural action the ground must always be an appearance.

The idea of an intelligible cause gets content from the fact that we do, or think we do, certain things just because we recognise that we ought to do them; if we are right in our claims it turns out that ideas of reason 'have in actual fact proved their causality in respect of the actions of men' (B 578/A 550). But what has this to do with Rational Cosmology? In the debate between Newton and Leibniz from which we are assuming that the antinomies took their start, one question for discussion was whether *the investigation of nature* requires the postulation of a self-activating cause. Newton said there must be such a cause, Leibniz that there could not be one. To suggest, as Kant does in his solution to the third antinomy, that man in so far as he acts morally may be viewed as an intelligible ground of certain natural phenomena seems to be quite irrelevant to this issue. Kant might have been justified in appealing to the fact of moral obligation in this context if he could establish that the hypothesis of intelligible causality had something independently in its favour. But if we abstract from what he says about morality and consider the rest of his case, we find only the contention that man, 'who knows all the rest of nature solely through the senses, knows himself also through pure apperception', and is 'thus to himself, on the one hand phenomenon, and on the other . . . a purely intelligible object' (B 574–5/A 546–7). Even if this were correct it would hardly bear on cosmological questions. But in any case it is not correct: as the Deduction and Paralogisms make plain, man does not *know* himself through pure apperception in any capacity, whether as phenomenon or noumenon, though the spontaneity of his thought does entitle him to call himself an intelligence (B 157–8 note; B 403–4/A 345–6).

These strictures may be considered too severe. Kant himself distinguishes sharply between freedom as a pure transcendental idea and freedom in the practical sense. He defines the first as 'the power of beginning a state spontaneously' (B 561/A 533) and the second as 'the will's independence of coercion through sensuous impulses' (B 562/A 534). According to his argument practical freedom would not be possible unless transcendental freedom were; in the solution of the third antinomy he professes only to show that there is nothing to rule transcendental freedom out. His intention, he says at the end, has not been to establish the reality or even the possibility of freedom; we cannot in any case 'from mere concepts *a priori* know the possibility of any real ground and its causality'

(B 586/A 558). The sole aim of the argument was to show that 'causality through freedom is at least *not incompatible with* nature' (ibid.), and for this the story about the two realms and the logically possible intelligible ground of (some) phenomena is enough.

That it is not, and thus that the solution to the third antinomy is gratuitous apart from the reference to moral facts, I propose to show by reference to two further points. Consider first why Kant's solution to the fourth antinomy carries so little conviction. The fourth antinomy is concerned with necessary and contingent being; to dissolve it Kant argues that, while everything in nature must be said to be contingent, there might be outside nature some necessary being which is the non-empirical condition of all things empirical. The suggestion is not that such a being must be postulated, or even that it is a real possibility; indeed in one passage (B 590/A 562) Kant says that 'such an absolutely necessary being, as conceived by the understanding, may be in itself impossible'. The whole point of talking about it, apparently, is to set limits to the pretensions of the understanding, 'lest it should presume to decide about the possibility of things in general, and should declare the intelligible to be *impossible*, merely on the ground that it is of no use in explaining appearances' (ibid.). A necessary being of this sort is surely too impalpable to bring much comfort to the tender-minded, quite apart from the question whether the whole idea is coherent. Kant hints at something better towards the end of his discussion (B 592/A 564), when he connects the idea with what he calls 'the pure use of reason, in reference to ends'. This refers, I take it, to practical reason, for which the existence of a necessary being is an indispensable postulate. Here again an idea which is quite insubstantial in itself is alleged to be fleshed out by reference to moral needs and moral experience. And here again the question must be raised whether Kant is justified in making this appeal to morality in a context where, as he put it himself, 'the necessary being must . . . be regarded as the highest member of the cosmical series' (Observations on the thesis, B 486/A 458). The God about whose existence Rational Cosmologists disputed was supposed to belong to the world of things in space and time either as a part or as its cause; the God whom the Kantian moralist postulates is primarily relevant not to nature but to men's hearts. To offer us the second when we ask about the first is not on the face of things satisfactory.

A second consideration that may be relevant is the following. If the fourth antinomy can be solved to the satisfaction of both parties by the argument that thoroughgoing contingency in nature does not rule out non-natural necessity (though equally it does not call for it), why should not a similar solution be attempted for the second antinomy? Officially, as we know, Kant wants to say that in this case thesis and antithesis are both false: we can neither claim that nothing exists in the world save the simple and what is composed of the simple, nor that there nowhere exists in the world anything simple. Once we take account of the special status of the space–time world we see that we confront an indefinitely extending regress from larger to smaller parts. This is supposed to amount to a dismissal of both parties, but might be said to favour supporters of the antithesis rather than supporters of the thesis, since it rules out all hope of finding anything simple in the course of empirical enquiry. If Kant is right, the notion of ultimately simple parts is inapplicable to the physical world. It might, however, be argued that it could have application in another world altogether, a world different from that we experience in space and time but not un-connected with it. What we encounter as indefinitely divisible matter might indeed consist of metaphysically simple parts; atomism in the strict sense would on this view be false, but a form of monadism could take its place. There are bits of the first edition version of the Paralogisms where Kant almost toys with such an idea himself, as when he says (A 358) that what lies behind outer appearances 'may yet, when viewed as noumenon . . . , be at the same time the subject of our thoughts', i.e. be of the nature of spirit and hence simple. If this is persisted with the sharp contrast between mathematical and dynamical antinomies breaks down.

Kant might reply that this overlooks his point about the regress in the first and second antinomies being from like to like: monads would not be homogeneous with items presented in space and time, could not be encountered in the advance of experience and would hence be empirically irrelevant. But intelligible causality in the third antinomy and the necessary being of the fourth antinomy are explicitly declared to have no importance for the empirical enquirer; they are not invalidated because of that. A more telling objection is that the hypothesis of monadism in the context of the second antinomy is entirely gratuitous; there is nothing against it in point of logic, but equally there is nothing to be said for it. I have tried to argue that precisely the same must be said of the hypothesis of a necessary being as set out in the solution to the fourth antinomy; here again there is simply no reason for us to take it seriously, unless we are allowed to bring in moral considerations. If the one hypothesis is to be ruled out, why not the other? Whether we accept or reject them, it looks as if the two must stand or fall together. But if they do, that means that mathematical and dynamical antinomies cannot be dealt with on radically different lines.

Kant never pretended that the *Critique* itself offered any solution to the ancient philosophical problem of natural necessity versus free causality; at most it cleared the way for such a solution by demonstrating that the natural world has no absolute existence but is a mere phenomenon. If nature was a mere phenomenon some other being or order of beings might lie behind it, and free causality might be real in this further world even if it could get no grip on the world of nature. So far as the *Critique* is concerned, this is no more than a bare possibility; to convert it into something more we have to desert the realm of theory for that of practice, and the result of our doing so is that any conclusion we come to will itself have practical rather than theoretical force. To say that the will is free is to make not a metaphysical but a moral claim. My quarrel with Kant is not over this conclusion but with the means by which he reaches it. As a first step he must get his reader to entertain the thought of a non-natural order separate from, though connected with, the natural order we know in ordinary experience. To some extent he may have thought the trick could be done by labelling the natural order 'phenomenal': phenomena presuppose noumena, and the possibility of something noumenal is given in the very application of the term 'phenomenal'. If he did use this argument, we can only regret it. But if we ask what more he had to offer, the answer must be remarkably little. Unless he is allowed to bring in his reference to morals at what may be called the mere metaphysical stage, he cannot hope to persuade us that the possibility in which he is interested is worth bothering about. It is logically possible that the supersensible substrate of what we experience as matter takes the form of simple spiritual beings. But it is not a possibility over which many of us lose much sleep.

A further difficulty which Kant faces concerns the question how his presumed intelligible causes can have any empirical effect. As we have stressed all along, the supposed non-natural order is not wholly separate from the order of nature, but is rather to be seen as its condition; changes in the first must hence produce changes in the second. The trouble here is that Kant is committed to the thesis that whatever happens in nature does so as a result of the operation of natural causes, a position which leaves no room for an intelligible cause to make any practical difference. Kant's solution to the difficulty is to say that what from one point of view can be seen as a set of natural events following inevitably on antecedent circumstances in accordance with natural laws can from another be taken as a set of actions rationally decided on. When we are thinking about what to do we adopt the second point of view, when our concern is with what is the case we adopt the first. But if what ensues in the order of nature has to develop in a certain way from what was there before, and if an action is, on its external side, the introduction of a change in the order of nature, it looks as if the possibility of beginning a new phenomenal series as a result of intelligible causal activity must be ruled out. If there are intelligible causes they can accordingly do nothing. Kant might reply that no-one believes this when it comes to moral practice: if someone tells a malicious lie we simply don't accept a story about its being due to 'defective education, bad company, . . . the viciousness of a natural disposition insensitive to shame', and so on (B 582/A 554). It is true that we do not. But if Kant is right in arguing that the order of nature is determined through and through by causes which are themselves antecedently determined, may it not be irrational of us to take this view?

§ 37 *Speculative Theology and the Transcendental Ideal*

The last main section of the Dialectic, entitled 'The Ideal of Pure Reason', deals with mistaken metaphysical inferences in the area of theology. Powerfully argued and expressed with a lucidity which is rare in Kant, its main contentions are widely familiar and will not need repetition here. Instead, I shall address myself to a variety of subsidiary tasks. First, I shall refer to, and hope to clarify, certain difficulties in Kant's general treatment of the subject of speculative theology. Next, I shall comment on some crucial points in his criticisms of the individual proofs of God's existence. Finally, I shall give a brief critical account of the 'moral' theology which Kant wanted to put in the place of the 'speculative' theology he set out to discredit. Although not very much is made of this in the first *Critique*, it is highly important to bear it in mind if only to guard against the illusion that Kant's aims in this part of his work were entirely negative. It is also worth going into Kant's supposed moral proof and the moral belief to which it gives rise as subjects of independent philosophical interest.

Why does Kant present his discussion under the title 'The Ideal of Pure Reason'? At the very beginning of his chapter he reminds us once more of the distinction between pure concepts of the understanding, which can be exhibited *in concreto* in so far as empirical concepts can be subsumed under them, and ideas of reason, which cannot be so exhibited because 'they contain a certain completeness to which no possible empirical knowledge ever attains' (B 596/A 568). He then goes on as follows:

> But what I entitle the *ideal* seems to be further removed from objective reality even than the idea. By the ideal I understand the idea, not merely *in concreto*, but *in individuo*, that is, as an individual thing, determinable or even determined by the idea alone.

The idea '*in concreto*' would be the idea embodied in reality, the idea '*in individuo*' the idea specifying itself as an individual reality. This suggests that the ideal must necessarily be seen as a chimera, but Kant does not treat it as such. Instead, after a favourable reference to Plato, already praised in an earlier passage (B 370/A 313 ff.) for having introduced the term 'idea', he goes on to say that ideals as well as ideas are prominent in the activities of human reason. They may lack the creative power which Plato ascribed to ideas, but nevertheless 'have *practical* power (as regulative principles), and form the basis of the possible perfection of certain actions' (B 597/A 569). Thus corresponding to the idea of human wisdom in its complete purity is the Stoic ideal of the supremely wise man; this can serve as an archetype for judging particular cases. We have to concede that no ideal of this sort has objective reality; we have further to agree that the very idea of embodying such an ideal in an example, for instance by trying to present the wise man in a romance, must fail miserably. But these admissions do not remove the central point that ideals of this sort 'supply reason with a standard which is indispensable to it, providing it, as they do, with a concept of that which is entirely complete in its kind, and thereby enabling it to estimate and to measure the degree and defects of the incomplete' (B 597–8/A 569–70). We should, however, make a sharp distinction between ideals of reason of the sort described and an inferior type of ideal with which they may be confused. The painter may appeal to the ideal of, say, pure feminine beauty, the physiognomist to that of the pure Highland countenance. Each, however, is making do with an amalgam of qualities drawn from diverse experiences and put together on no particular principle; all he has in mind is a shadowy picture which is incommunicable to others. By contrast ideals of reason one and all rest on, and are indeed shaped throughout by, determinate concepts. And this is true above all of the supreme example of the species, the transcendental ideal.

To understand this passage we have to go back to the inaugural *Dissertation* of 1770. There Kant put forward for the first time the thesis that the human intellect is equipped with pure concepts of its own, and went on to discuss their uses, 'critical' and 'dogmatic' (*Dissertation*, section 9). As regards the latter he claimed that

> the general principles of pure understanding, such as are dealt with in ontology or rational psychology, issue in some exemplar, which is conceivable only by pure intellect, and is the common measure of all other things as far as real. This exemplar— *Perfectio Noumenon*—is perfection either in a theoretical or in a practical sense.

Later in the same passage Kant explained that

> In every kind of existence in which quantity is variable the maximum is the common measure and principle whereby we have knowledge. The maximum of perfection, which is called by Plato an idea (as in his 'idea' of the state), we now entitle an ideal. It is the principle of all that is contained under the general notion of any perfection, in so far as smaller degrees are supposed not to be determinable save by limiting the maximum. God, however, while as ideal of perfection he is the principle of knowledge, is at the same time, as really existing, the principle of the coming into existence of all perfection whatsoever.

I take this to imply that in 1770 Kant was still prepared to subscribe to the thesis he had argued in the *Beweisgrund* essay of 1763, that we can specify the characteristics, and indeed the existence, of a supremely real being on the basis of purely rational considerations. Reflection on Plato's doctrines in the meantime had, however, induced him to give a fresh twist to the thesis on its purely metaphysical side, and to add to it by stressing its ethical implications. He now spoke as if the prime use for the concept of the highest reality was to measure the reality of lesser things. And he argued further that to possess such a concept is to have an adequate basis for moral judgments. In the *Dissertation* itself Kant's main interest was to exploit this discovery to the detriment of all empirical theories of ethics, from Epicurus onwards. What was wrong with all such writers was that they tried to derive morality from examples. As the point was put in the later *Grundlegung* (Paton translation, 76; Berlin edition IV 408), they failed to see that you can always ask of a proffered example whether it is fit to be an example. 'Even the Holy One of the gospel must first be compared with our ideal of moral perfection before we can recognise him to be such' (ibid.). What Kant here calls 'our ideal of moral perfection' is what he had called more portentously '*Perfectio Noumenon . . .* in a practical sense' in the *Dissertation*. He had in the meantime freed his ethics of any suggestion that basic ethical concepts have a special connection with the concept of God: our ideal of moral perfection is now supposed to be determined purely by reference to moral ideas. But these ideas remain purely rational in character, and the general theory Kant carries forward into his mature philosophy thus retains substantial links with the view sketched in his inaugural lecture, on the ethical side at least.

That view is also preserved in an attenuated way on the metaphysical side too, as we can see from the title of section 2, 'The Transcendental Ideal (Prototypon Transcendentale)'. Reason, it turns out, is in possession of a peculiar concept which it has to have if it is to make judgments of determinate existence, the concept of an *ens realissimum* or of a thing which is supremely actual. The argument in support of this conclusion goes roughly as follows. If things are to have determinate existence they must each be qualified by one of every pair of possible contradictory predicates: a thing must be a or not-a, b or not-b, etc. That means that to know a thing determinately I must have the idea of the sum of all possibility. But instead of treating this as a mere agglomeration of diverse predicates I can, if I think about it, rationalise it and cut it down. I can see without difficulty that some predicates, namely those which are derivative from more basic ones, need not be there at all; I can also exclude negative predicates, on the ground that they can be formed from their positive counterparts. In this way I can come by the thought of what might be called a set of basic possibilities, and can see that appeal must be made to this thought whenever I try to characterise a thing determinately. To make matters simpler still, I can think of these basic possibilities as each being realised in a single thing, which is completely determinate in so far as it possesses all of them. If I do this, the idea of this single reality will function in my thought as a transcendental ideal, and it will be possible for me to look on it as a prototype or archetype, compared with which all other things are ectypes or 'imperfect copies' (B 606/ A 578), since it is from it that they derive the material of their possibility and to it that they approximate in various degrees.

Kant produces this extraordinary theory in the *Critique* with little or no explanation. He warns us that in any case we have no right to hypostatise the object of the idea: for the process described to go on it is not necessary that there be something supremely actual, only that we have the thought of such a thing. And in his final paragraphs he appears to be suggesting that the whole notion, though natural, is nonetheless the product of illusion. It is a case once more of confusing what is true in the restricted area of experience with what is or would be true of things generally. I have to have the notion of a whole of experience in order to make empirical judgments, but cannot conclude in consequence that knowledge of things in themselves would presuppose the existence of an all-embracing reality. What Kant fails to mention here is that at an earlier stage of his career he had himself in effect argued that it would. From the time he wrote his first metaphysical essay, the *Nova Dilucidatio* of 1755, he held that God's existence could be proved on the ground that God was what was supremely actual, and that nothing would be possible unless something were supremely actual. Not only does possibility in general presuppose actuality; it further presupposes what may be called a primary actualisation of basic possibilities in a single supremely real being. The proof is worked out most fully in the *Beweisgrund* of 1763, which revealingly appeared under the title 'The Only Possible Ground of Proof of God's Existence'; it is taken as valid in the 1764 Prize Essay on natural theology and morals (see Berlin edition II 296), and it appears to survive in the 1770 *Dissertation*. It is clear that for a long time Kant set great store by this proof. Yet when he comes in the *Critique* to examine the different attempts made to prove God's existence he passes over it in silence. He announces in B 618/A 590 that there are only three possible ways of proving God's existence by means of speculative reason: the physico-theological, where we start from the specific constitution of the world; the cosmological, where we argue from the existence of anything whatever; and the ontological, where we abstract from experience and base our case exclusively on *a priori* reasoning from mere concepts. The criticisms of the ontological proof he produces in the *Critique* are anticipated in all important respects in the discussions of the *Beweisgrund*. There, however, the ontological argument of the *Critique* is referred to as the 'Cartesian' argument, and the term 'ontological proof' itself is reserved for Kant's own *a priori* argument from possibility. In these circumstances it is remarkable that the argument is not so much as mentioned in the *Critique*.

But though not mentioned, it is all the same adverted to, in the curious section with which we have been concerned. The seemingly pedantic discussions of these pages recall a kind of thinking which Kant had by this time come to think radically misguided, but which all the same had at one time seemed to him correct, even compulsive. What we see here, in effect, is Kant trying to come to terms with his own metaphysical past, without being altogether open about what he was doing. We see him showing how one who worked with dogmatic assumptions, as Kant himself had at least until 1770, could be led into formulating the notion of the Ideal and from that into giving it existence. Unlike most critics of metaphysics Kant had suffered badly from the disease himself; as a young man and in middle life he had tried to work out new metaphysical ideas of his own. His suggested proof of God's existence from the bare fact of possibility was a shining example of such attempted innovation. In the light of his mature insights it was something which Kant could only regret; it may be because he thought this side of his philosophical work so totally mistaken that he said that none of his books and essays from before 1770 should be reissued. Whatever the truth about this, it seems clear that it is his own *a priori* argument of pre-critical days which underlies the discussion here. Kant no longer believes that the argument can be made good, but characteristically suggests that it should be kept in a weakened form. We need the idea of the *ens realissimum*, if we do not need the *ens realissimum* itself. What is supposed to be established here on this point is taken for granted in the rest of the chapter on the Ideal.

Does Kant offer a coherent account of the *ens realissimum*, and does he show what this concept has to do with the concept of God? He puts forward a general prescription for constructing a set of basic predicates, without specifying in any detail how the construction is to proceed. Would a list of such predicates include any which applied exclusively to material things? The answer is 'yes' if material predicates are truly basic, 'no' if they can be shown to be derivative. When it comes to connecting the *ens realissimum* with God everything turns on how this question is answered, yet Kant himself does nothing to help us to an answer. His concept of a sum of basic possibilities is thus at best schematic. There is also the problem why attention should be transferred from such a sum to an entity in which the possibilities are supposed to be realised in a perfect degree; the very notion of such an entity is logically suspect, since it would not so much possess its predicates as consist of them. It would not, for example, be qualified by wisdom, but would have to be identical with wisdom itself, as well as with much else. Only if this condition is satisfied could it be claimed that in it wisdom exists in the highest degree. But can it be satisfied? Kant's failure to discuss this mars his otherwise impressive treatment of the subject of speculative theology.

§ 38 *Kant's Critique of Speculative Theology*

I come now to what Kant has to say about individual proofs, but shall preface this with a brief consideration of the question whether his division of possible proofs is exhaustive. As mentioned already, he maintains that every attempted speculative proof must base itself either on the particular constitution of the world or on the indeterminate existence of anything whatever or on mere concepts, and connects these with the physico-theological, the cosmological and the ontological arguments respectively. Reflection on the history of philosophy shows that other ways of proving God's existence have certainly been tried. Thus Aquinas argued in his First Way that the fact of motion can be explained only if there is a first mover who is not moved by anything, and in his Fourth Way that if there are things which are more or less good, true or noble, there must be something which is truest, best and noblest, adding in each case 'and this we call God'. Descartes in the third *Meditation* said that the very fact that I find myself possessed of the idea of God proves that God really exists, once account is taken of the content of the idea, which is such that no finite being could invent it. Other philosophers have argued that the very fact that men have notions of right and wrong, with a conscience that brings them to bear on their conduct, itself testifies to God's existence, and yet others have claimed that we can know that God exists because God can be and sometimes is an object of direct experience.

That these alternatives have been attempted would not disconcert Kant. When Aquinas took the fact of motion as the basis of his first proof he argued from a particular feature of reality, namely that some things in the world are perceived to move. When Descartes claimed that the occurrence in me of the idea of God itself pointed to God's existence he was again setting out from a particular fact. Neither philosopher in this context was offering a form of the physico-theological argument—Aquinas reserved this for the Fifth Way, and Descartes did not believe that the argument was valid at all—but both were using procedures which were like those followed in that proof. The objections Kant had to make to physico-theology could be transferred in principle to the Thomist argument from motion and the Cartesian argument from the occurrence of the idea of God. They would also hold in the same way against the argument from moral experience. For the theist to call attention to moral experience is for him to fix on a particular fact about the world, a fact which, it is alleged, can be explained only if God made it so. One suspects that Kant's attitude to those who tried to use this argument would be similar to his attitude to those who advance the design argument: he would think of them as having their hearts in the right place, but would say that their case was quite unsatisfactory from the intellectual point of view. It should be noted in this connection that the moral proof which Kant himself puts forward is utterly different from what I am here calling the argument from moral experience, since it starts not from a fact about the world but from a situation in which an agent feels the force of moral obligation, and claims to result not in a truth which is the same for everyone, but in a conviction which is personal to the man concerned.

I shall say more on this last point later (section 39). Meantime, it should be noticed that the argument used in Aquinas' Fourth Way is like that discussed in the last section, and would doubtless be treated by Kant along the same lines. As for the suggestion that God can be experienced directly, it is clear that Kant would not have accepted it. In part this may be due to no more than prejudice: it is well known that Kant had a horror of what he called *Schwärmerei*, and was inclined to think of mystical experience as a morbid state, akin to the experience of spiritualist media. He could, however, have argued more seriously that no fact could be established by bare intuition, since 'with us men' all knowledge demands conceptual as well as interpretative elements. There could be an argument from religious experience, if that meant one basing itself on the fact that people have, or say they have, experiences of a special kind. But such an argument would run parallel to the supposed proof from moral experience considered above, and would be open to the same objections. If it could establish God's existence at all, it would not be directly, but by inference.

Kant's criticism of speculative theology is meant to do no more than its name implies, namely to discredit all attempts to produce metaphysical proofs of God's existence. It is certainly not meant to discredit the conviction that God exists, and indeed it prepares the way for Kant's own special moral proof. It need not be taken as hostile to religion. It is true that Kant nowhere in the *Critique* explicitly considers the possibility that the basic tenets of religion neither need nor could find proof, religion being a set of practices which make sense only on the supposition that there really is a God. This way of thinking, which we associate today with the names of Kierkegaard and Wittgenstein, might be taken to imply that the task of philosophy is to explicate the God of religion, the God who is a proper object of worship, rather than the God of metaphysical philosophers, the abstract being of beings. Kant began his career as a metaphysician, and perhaps never lost the metaphysical urge. Even so, the God of his moral theology is in many respects nearer to Kierkegaard's than he is to, say, Wolff's. If not quite the God of Abraham, Isaac and Jacob, he is an object of fear and awed respect, something to be felt in the heart rather than known by the bare intellect.

In dealing with the individual proofs Kant quite naturally starts with the *a priori* 'ontological' argument. This is on the obvious ground that if the *a priori* proof succeeds no other proof need be considered: we do not have to look round for empirical considerations in support of what we know to be analytically true. The ontological argument alleges that the proposition that God exists is analytically true, though its supporters add that it is the only existence proposition which answers this description. In the case of finite beings essence does not imply existence, in the case of the infinite being which is God it does. We have only to get clear what the term 'God' means to see that God exists. We mean by 'God' the being which possesses all perfections, and existence must be among these. A God who lacked existence would on this account be less than perfect, and accordingly to say that God does not, or may not, exist is to utter a self-contradiction.

Kant dismisses this whole line of thought with the celebrated declaration (B 626/A 598) that 'being is obviously not a real predicate; that is, it is not a concept of something that could be added to the concept of a thing'. A real predicate here must contrast with a grammatical predicate; 'exists' or 'is real' can certainly function as predicates from the grammatical point of view. But why is existence not a real predicate, and what is it if it is not? Kant's answer to the first question is awkwardly expressed but broadly correct. If I tell you that fairies exist I do not add anything to your concept of a fairy, or more exactly to the sum of characteristics you associate with being a fairy; if I tell you that fairies are all under two feet high I do (or may do) just this (it depends on how knowledgeable you are about fairies). Consider in this connection the differences between saying that God exists and saying that God is malignant. The thought of a God who exists is, in content, precisely identical with the thought of a God who does not exist; there is no difference between the two in idea, however much practical difference the existence or non-existence of God may make. But the thought of a God who is malignant is certainly different from the thought of a God who is without that attribute. Thomas Hardy's God, who took pleasure in tormenting people, is obviously different in idea from the benevolent deity of Christianity. And this is true whether or not anything answers in reality to either idea.

Kant does not give a very satisfactory account of what being is if it is not a real predicate. In the passage quoted he explains it as follows:

> It is merely the positing of a thing, or of certain determinations, for itself or for themselves. Logically, it is merely the copula of a judgment. The proposition, 'God is omnipotent', contains two concepts, each of which has its object. The small word 'is' adds no new predicate, but serves to posit the predicate in its relation to the subject. If we now take the subject (God) with all its predicates (among which is omnipotence) and say 'God is' or 'there is a God', we attach no new predicate to the concept of God, but only posit the subject itself with all its predicates, and indeed posit it as being an *object* which stands in relation to my *concept*.

This quotation shows that Kant was not fully clear about his own logical innovations. To make his point he must argue that there is all the difference in the world between predicating and 'positing'. Predicating is attributing a character to a subject; 'positing' is saying that a character or a group of characters is instantiated. When Kant says that 'the small word "is" serves to posit the predicate in its relation to the subject' he obscures this crucial distinction. It may that there could be no predication if there were not prior positing, and thus that the 'is' of existence underlies the 'is' of predication, but this will not warrant conflating the two. Nor is Kant's talk about positing 'the subject itself with all its predicates' at all fortunate. It is not the subject which is posited, but the characteristics it comprehends, since to posit in this connection is essentially to declare that something general as an instance. Kant came nearer to getting this point right in the *Beweisgrund* (II 74) where he argued that there was an impropriety in the expression 'God is an existing thing' and said it should be replaced by

> Something existent is God; that is, there belong to an existing thing those predicates which are collectively signified by the term 'God'.

However, his discussion both in the *Beweisgrund* and in the *Critique* was marred by failure to raise the question whether 'God' was to be understood as a concept or a proper name. He assumes without argument in the passages quoted that it should be taken as a concept, and thus provides for a reading of 'God exists' as 'deity is instantiated' (or 'deity is instantiated uniquely'). But he clearly needed to consider further the problems this reading involved.

In discussing the ontological argument Kant clearly has Descartes' version in mind (cf. B 630/A 602). Descartes himself had noticed an objection to the argument which ran as follows (*Descartes' Philosophical Works*, translated Haldane and Ross, I 181):

> Although I cannot really conceive of a God without existence any more than a mountain without a valley, still from the fact that I conceive of a mountain with a valley it does not follow that there is such a mountain in the world; similarly, though I conceive of God as possessing existence, it would seem that it does not follow that there is a God which exists.

Descartes tries to escape this conclusion by saying that the two cases are quite different, since 'from the fact that I cannot conceive God without existence, it follows that existence is inseparable from him, and hence that he really exists'. Against this Kant says bluntly that if I say there is no God, I simply set aside the concept with all its properties, and do not contradict myself at all. If I assume that God's notion includes his existence, then I cannot think God and deny his existence without falling into self-contradiction. But this does not prevent me from as it were simultaneously cancelling subject and predicate in the proposition, by declaring the concept in question to have no instance. In this respect the case of God is no different from any other. Nor for that matter would things be altered if, instead of simple existence, some other sort of existence were in question, necessary existence, for example. If God's nature includes necessary existence, then if he exists he exists necessarily: there is no question of his ceasing to exist. But it does not follow from this that God has to be real; it could be that nothing corresponded to the whole idea.

One respect in which Kant is less than satisfactory is in failing to mention that, for Descartes and other supporters of the ontological proof, the case of God is unique in so far as it is only here that essence implies existence. Kant parades the famous instance of the real and imaginary dollars (B 627/A 599); he says there is no difference in idea between the two, but a lot of difference in fact. Descartes would not have denied this claim. But though Kant is less than fair at this point, he would not admit that his unfairness made any difference to his main contention. As far as he is concerned, there is no more contradiction in denying the existence of God than in denying the existence of a hundred dollars. Some writers sympathetic to the ontological proof, e.g. Hegel, write as if denying the existence of God would involve denying the existence of every-thing: God as they see it is identical with the Absolute, and the Absolute exists if anything exists (for this line of thought, compare

H. H. Joachim's commentary on Spinoza's *Ethics*). The trouble with this in the present context is that it seems to appeal not to the ontological but to the cosmological argument, understood in a peculiar way. Clearly Kant would not allow any such appeal, since in his view the dependence is the other way round: the cosmological argument presupposes the ontological. Whether it does must be the next point for discussion.

Kant's most radical contention about speculative proofs of God's existence is that, in the end, they all rest on *a priori* considerations: there is no such thing as an empirical proof of God which stands on its own feet. Even if you are allowed to argue in the accepted metaphysical way (i.e. on the assumptions of transcendental realism and common dogmatism), you cannot complete your proof without bringing in the principle of the ontological argument. It follows that if the ontological proof collapses all speculative proofs collapse. It also follows that there is no tenable half-way position, such as that of Aquinas, who rejected the ontological argument in the form proposed by St Anselm, but thought that God's existence could be known with certainty on the basis of a variety of arguments of the cosmological and physico-theological kind.

The cosmological argument, says Kant, begins from the indeterminate empirical premise that something exists (because I at least exist) and, using the principle that if anything contingent exists so does something necessary, goes on to assert the existence of something necessary. It then has to say what this something is, and the only suitable candidate for the post is God or, as Kant prefers to put it, the *ens realissimum*. Hence it concludes that the *ens realissimum* or God exists, ultimately as necessary condition of my own contingent existence.

Kant rightly believes that the first part of the argument involves all sorts of doubtful assumptions, but at first sets these aside to concentrate on the final stage. What he wishes to claim is that there can be no advance from 'Something necessary exists' to 'God exists' without invoking the principle of the ontological proof. Why not? Kant's attempts to explain the point are not wholly lucid. He begins by saying that supporters of the cosmological argument make the transition by asking themselves what characteristics a necessary being would have, discover that such a being 'must be completely determined through its own concept', and conclude that, since only the *ens realissimum* satisfies this description, only the *ens realissimum* can count as a necessary being. What they do not see is that they are

(B 635/ A 607)

here presupposing that the concept of the highest reality is completely adequate to the concept of absolute necessity of existence; that is, that the latter can be inferred from the former.

If 'the concept of the *ens realissimum* is a concept, and indeed the only concept, which is appropriate and adequate to necessary existence, I must also admit that necessary existence can be inferred from this concept'. But this of course is precisely what the ontological proof maintained, and so 'the so-called cosmological proof really owes any cogency which it may have to the ontological proof from mere concepts' (ibid.).

Kant now proceeds to give what he believes to be a formal statement of the fallacy involved in this argument, set out 'in correct syllogistic form' (B 636/ A 608). What he calls the '*nervus probandi*' of the cosmological proof is the proposition that 'every absolutely necessary being is likewise the most real of all beings'. If this is true, so must be its converse. Its actual converse is that some *entia realissima* are absolutely necessary beings. But (B 636–7/ A 608–9)

> one *ens realissimum* is in no respect different from another, and what is true of *some* under this concept is true of *all*. In this case, therefore, I can convert the proposition *simpliciter*, not only *per accidens*, and say that every *ens realissimum* is a necessary being. But since this proposition is determined from pure *a priori* concepts alone, the mere concept of the *ens realissimum* must carry with it the absolute necessity of that being; and this is precisely what the ontological proof has asserted and what the cosmological proof has refused to admit, although the conclusions of the latter are indeed covertly based on it.

This is unsatifactory in a number of ways, not least because the idea of an *ens realissimum* is such that only one individual can answer to it. But Kant's point can be put more simply. The proof requires the assumption that we can move from 'something necessary exists' to 'God exists', and therefore that nothing is a necessary being except God. It follows that those who put it forward must claim *both* that if anything is a necessary being, it is God, *and* that if anything is God it is a necessary being. The biconditional is indispensable if we are to do justice to the word 'only' in the proof. But, says Kant, the second component in the conjunction is what the ontological argument sought to prove. The cosmological proof thus depends on the tenability of its ontological predecessor, and is useless without that.

Is this famous refutation justified? It must be confessed that its very neatness arouses suspicion. An objector might insist that existence is already taken care of in the first step in the argument, which at this stage is unchallenged, and that thereafter it is a matter of equating concepts and nothing more. To see how this would work out consider the case of an eccentric theist who thought of God not as the only necessary being, but as the only perpetually intermittent being; the only being, that is to say, that was continually coming into and going out of existence, world without end. By some argument whose premises we need not examine now this person has established that there exists something which is perpetually intermittent. He now argues that this means that God exists, on the ground that what is perpetually intermittent is God and what is God is perpetually intermittent. Must we take his second assertion here as the expression of a proposition about existence? In one way it is, since it says what sort of existence God enjoys (he keeps blinking in and out). But it is not, as it stands, a straightforward existence claim; it does not say that anything actually exists. If this is correct, it is open to the defender of the cosmological argument to say that his covert assumption that whatever is God is a necessary being should not be read as declaring that God actually exists through the necessities of his own nature, but that if God exists, he will enjoy necessary existence, which presumably means that he will continue from eternity to eternity and be in no danger of being divested of existence as finite beings are.

I suggested above that the ontological argument cannot be defended by saying that what God has in virtue of his own nature is not existence, but necessary existence. To conceive of God as possessing necessary existence is only to imply that, *if* God exists, he has a special kind of existence. Kant's defenders want to say that the proper way to understand the claim that the peculiar predicate 'necessary existence' belongs to God is to take that claim as merely hypothetical. If it is legitimate for them to make this riposte, it is equally legitimate for those who support the cosmological proof to deny that they assume the principle of the ontological argument in moving from something necessary to God. They assume only that God has a certain nature, not that he necessarily exists.

To accept this defence is, of course, to admit that Kant's criticisms of speculative theology are less devastating than they seem. But that is not to say that recognition of the point made would have induced Kant to withdraw all objections to the cosmological proof. The truth is that we have been proceeding so far on a false assumption, that the first step in the argument, the one in which we move from 'something contingent exists' to 'something necessary exists', is uncontroversial. Kant had allowed it to stand in order to present his main criticism, but once this is done he returns to say that the first step too conceals 'a whole nest of dialectical assumptions' (B 637/A 609). It involves in the first place a use of the causal principle beyond the bounds of possible experience, when 'the principle of causality has no meaning and no criterion for its application save only in the sensible world' (ibid.). We cannot build any *synthetic* conclusion on the purely intellectual concept of the contingent, and even if we could (by producing some version of the Principle of Sufficient Reason, for example) we should not know how to proceed. Further, the attempt to argue to a first cause, on the ground that an infinite series of causes is impossible, breaks down, as the argument of the antinomies showed. As far as the sensible world is concerned, we know that an unconditioned existent is impossible: everything phenomenal is conditioned by something beyond itself. And though the solution of the fourth Antinomy maintained that there might be an unconditioned existent in some non-sensible world, nothing in the cosmological argument gives any ground for postulating it. To show that something is not impossible is very different from showing that it is a real possibility. To meet these points we should have to dispute some of Kant's most fundamental philosophical convictions: we should have, for instance, to show that there is nothing in the demand that every pure concept be capable of schematisation, or to establish that the concept of cause could have some other schema than that of regular succession. I do not say that this is impossible in principle, only that it is a major philosophical task whose significance is not appreciated by dogmatists. Until it is tackled with success the cosmological argument must remain an object of profound suspicion.

The only remaining way of proving God's existence on the speculative level is to appeal to the physico-theological proof, Kant's name for what others call the argument from design. This is a proof for which Kant has what may be thought a strange respect. He writes of it (B 651/A 623) that of all the traditional proofs

> it is the oldest, the clearest, and the most accordant with the common reason of mankind

and goes on to say that

> It enlivens the study of nature, just as it itself derives its existence and gains ever new vigour from that source. It suggests ends and purposes, where our observation would not have detected them by itself, and extends our knowledge of

nature by means of the guiding-concept of a special unity, the principle of which is outside nature. This knowledge again reacts on its cause, namely, upon the idea which has led to it, and so strengthens the belief in a supreme Author that the belief acquires the force of an irresistible conviction.

That nature works as if it were the product of design is something which we assume at many levels, as the *Critique of Judgment* makes clear. It underlies our general enterprise of bringing natural phenomena under a *system* of scientific laws; it has a bearing on our judgments about natural beauty; it is involved in our attempts to make sense of living things. The remarkable orderliness of nature was something which impressed Kant, just as it had impressed Newton, from an early stage of his philosophical development; in his *Universal Natural History* of 1755 he had argued that the very fact that nature behaves as if it were a mechanism through and through is enough to prove God's existence. But he came to think that both this and other teleological considerations could be appealed to less and less as a basis for scientific theology. The argument from design, treated as a strict argument, was in fact hopelessly deficient. It concluded from a supposed fact about the order of nature to an assertion of the need for a creator of natural things; on its own terms it was entitled at most to a supreme architect. It endowed its designer with unlimited powers, when it should have claimed only that he must have powers in proportion to the effect produced. And it depended first on the cosmological argument, in so far as it used the causal principle and made the move from something contingent to something necessary, and then on the ontological proof, in so far as that was involved in the cosmological. Since these arguments were, in Kant's eyes, deficient beyond hope of repair, there was nothing really to be said for the argument from design (even if we subtracted the point about the ontological proof there would not be much). The only purpose the design argument could serve was to prepare us for a different sort of argument altogether, the moral argument. 'Physico-theology' could act as a propaedeutic for 'ethico-theology', presumably by making us better disposed to accept the latter. But since for Kant ethico-theology is entirely adequate in itself, the fact that physico-theology plays this role is not of major significance.

§ 39 *The Moral Proof of God's Existence*

'I maintain', wrote Kant in the concluding comment to his discussion of the proofs with which we have been concerned (B 664/ A 636), that all attempts to make a purely speculative use of reason in reference to theology are entirely fruitless and of their inner nature null and void; that the principles of its employment in the study of nature do not lead to any theology whatsoever; consequently that there can be no theology of reason at all unless one takes moral laws as its basis, or uses them as a clue.

The possibility that belief in God should rest not on reason but on revelation was not taken seriously by Kant, though he does make a passing reference to 'revealed theology' (B 659/A 631). Like other men of the Enlightenment he thought that if we were to continue to cherish convictions about God they must in some way have rational warrant. The famous phrase about abolishing knowledge to make room for faith is misleading in this respect. The faith Kant was talking about was not blind but rational; the assurance he thought we had of God's existence was different in kind from the assurance we have about everyday matter of fact, but not for that reason incapable of justification. Despite all that Kant said about the incompetence of speculative reason when it addressed itself to questions about God, it remains true that he thought that there was a tenable proof of God's existence, the moral proof. Speculative theology was ruled out, but moral theology could take its place. Kant sketches his moral proof of God's existence and outlines his moral theology in a chapter near the end of the *Critique of Pure Reason*, the 'Canon of Pure Reason', especially in section 2. In the following section he has an intriguing discussion of the important but difficult subject of moral belief. Both topics are considered at greater length and with more sophistication in the other two *Critiques*, primarily in the Dialectic of the *Critique of Practical Reason*, but also in the Methodology of the *Critique of Judgment*. Here the most that can be attempted is to give a summary account of his main position and offer some general comment.

How can someone who claims that there are three and only three ways of trying to prove God's existence by speculative means and believes that he has demonstrated that they one and all break down, go on to assert that God's existence can all the same be a matter for rational belief? It is clear in the first place that any proof he offers will have to be of a very special kind. It will not be possible for it to start from any fact about the world, as the cosmological and physico-theological arguments do, nor from the content of ideas, as did the ontological argument. In his pronouncements on the subject in the *Critique of Pure Reason* Kant speaks of moral theology as based on, or basing itself on, moral laws. He cannot mean that the moral theologian looks round the world, observes that there are moral practices apparently governed by rule, and takes his stand on that fact. An argument of that kind, or again one from the occurrence of moral feelings and sentiments, would be speculative; as was pointed out earlier, it would be similar in principle to the argument from design. What Kant must say is rather that the moral proof of God's existence starts from the practical moral situation, in which an individual feels the force of moral obligation and acknowledges the authority of the moral law. This is not a fact, but something personally experienced. The person concerned is in a special kind of predicament, one in which he finds himself constrained to admit that he ought to take a certain kind of action whether he wants to or not. He knows that he has to obey the injunctions of morality; the problem is whether, if he does so, he will produce a better world. Inclining the will is wholly within his power; altering the actual state of affairs so that things are more as they should be is not. The moral agent acts in circumstances which are not generally of his own choosing and over which he can at best exercise a very limited control. He is forced to rely on the co-operation of others if he is to carry out his aims successfully; he acts in a natural setting which he does not fully understand and whose vagaries he can only partially anticipate. At any moment an unkind fate can bring it about that his best and most carefully thought-out efforts produce results the opposite of those he intended. What guarantee has he that this kind of thing will not happen regularly? It is at this point, Kant suggests, that he needs to assume the existence of a moral God, one who, as it were, harmonises the spheres of fact and value, and so assures the moral man that if he follows the dictates of conscience the results produced will be for the best in the long run. Such a God has no relevance to the state of *being under* obligation, or it could not be claimed that morals is autonomous. But the thought that he exists may even so play an important, indeed an indispensable, part when it comes to *carrying out* obligations; without it the moral agent might be too discouraged in the face of an alien nature and with the sight of the wicked flourishing to persist in his moral endeavours.

The first thing to notice about this proof, if proof it can be called, is that it is itself a piece of practical thinking: it originates in a practical situation and is undertaken in response to a practical difficulty. This feature is of immense importance for the subject we are considering. Speculative arguments for God's existence purport to start from premises which are universally acknowledged and to terminate in a truth which is the same for all of us, intelligent or unintelligent, vicious or virtuous. Kant's moral proof, by contrast, cannot even begin until some individual finds himself in the situation described. If there were to be someone who was genuinely deaf to the call of moral obligation, or totally indifferent to the question whether the world could be made better or not, he could not even understand what the proof was about. Still less could he take the conclusion of the argument on trust, as something which was well-founded though on grounds which were not known to the person concerned. Moral belief in God is not something that we can acquire second-hand, as we can acquire the belief that there are quasars. It is a conviction which has to be achieved on a personal basis and retains an irremovable personal dimension. As Kant himself puts it (B 857/A 829), we must not say '*It is* certain that there is a God', but '*I am* certain that there is a God'. All knowledge can be communicated; if God's existence were a matter of knowledge we could hope to learn it from another. But it cannot be so learnt. We could indeed learn to say the words 'There is a God', and even to utter them in the favourable tones which we reserve for truths of major import. What we could not do is make them come alive, since they do this only in a personally experienced practical context.

What about the reasoning in the proof itself? In the second edition preface to the *Critique* (B xxxiff.) Kant claimed that the subtle arguments of philosophers on the immortality of the soul, the freedom of the will and the existence of God had never succeeded in 'reaching the public mind or in exercising the slightest influence on its convictions' (B xxxii), with the result that dispensing with them would have no practical effect. The plain man was convinced of their correctness by quite different arguments, which were 'universally comprehensible'. The consciousness of freedom 'rests exclusively on the clear exhibition of duties, in opposition to all claims of the inclinations', while (B xxxiii)

> the belief in a wise and great Author of the world is generated solely by the glorious order, beauty and providential care everywhere displayed in nature.

How Kant could have made this last remark after his strictures on 'physico-theology' is not apparent. What we must ask now is whether, if we substitute a version of the argument outlined above for what is here said, it can still be claimed that it is not a matter of 'subtle speculation', but of a proof with an immediate appeal.

The answer here depends on what precisely goes into the proof. In the statement given above I have made it turn on distinguishing between accepting an obligation and producing a certain result in the world; it seems clear from many passages (see in particular section *87* of the *Critique of Judgment*, on Spinoza as a virtuous atheist) that the fundamental problem with which Kant is concerned in this part of his work is that of successful moral action. It might however be said with some plausibility that neither the problem nor the solution offered are in this form immediately intelligible: the plain man would of course like to see the world made better, but is hardly conscious of the doubts on which the above case rests. But Kant himself states the position in different and simpler ways. In the *Critique of Pure Reason* (B 832/A 804 ff.) he plays on the contrast, with which the plain man would certainly be familiar, between doing what will render yourself worthy of being happy and actually being happy. When I ask what I ought to do, the answer is (B 837/A 809) 'Do that through which thou becomest worthy to be happy'. But when I go on to enquire what then I may hope, the answer is that I may hope for nothing unless (B 840–1/A 812–3)

> reason connects with the moral law, which is a mere idea, an operative cause which determines for such conduct as is in accordance with the moral law an outcome, either in this or in another life, that is in exact conformity with our supreme ends.

The hope that morality will eventually bring happiness can be counted on 'only if a Supreme Reason, that governs according to moral rules, be likewise posited as underlying nature as its cause' (B 838/A 810). Kant does not say that recognition of this fact warrants belief in God, but argues rather that to postulate God is, in the circumstances, inseparable from the obligation which reason imposes on us (see B 839/A 811). What is essentially the same argument is presented in a less popular way in the *Critique of Practical Reason* (V 125 ff.), where it is claimed that I have a duty to promote the highest good, that the latter involves both morality and happiness in proportion to morality, and that consequently I can do my duty only if I can count on a necessary connection between the two elements, something which only a moral God could assure. I am thus under a moral necessity to assume the existence of God, though 'this moral necessity is subjective, i.e. a need, and not objective, i.e. duty itself' (V 126).

Of these arguments, the last is plainly fallacious: if I have a duty in connection with the highest good, it is to promote it as far as lies within my power, not to promote it *simpliciter*. I cannot have a duty to do what is outside my capacity, despite the dictum that '*ought* implies *can*'. The alleged moral necessity for belief in God is thus highly dubious. As for the version in the first *Critique*, this has more imaginative appeal, and refers to a duty which is less controversial. But the duty to make myself worthy of happiness is one which I can carry out for myself, since it depends on nothing more than the perfecting of the will. I cannot make myself absolutely perfect by my own efforts, but I can make myself more perfect. Actually Kant invokes God here not in connection with any duty but in connection with the question what I may hope for if I do my duty and make myself more worthy to be happy; this being so, it is difficult to see how he can claim that belief in God is inseparable from the obligation. I could have this particular obligation, and feel confident that I could fulfil it, without taking account of God at all. And if it is said that I could not be confident of fulfilling my duties generally and thereby producing a better world without facing Kant's question (thus reverting to the argument as originally stated), this is indeed correct, but does not mean that we are immediately committed to Kant's position. We might think in the first place that the problem he poses, though plausible at first sight, is based on the unreal assumption that successful action is never possible, when it quite obviously is. Do I really have to show, in order to act with moral confidence, that there is no ground for thinking that an unkind fate may thwart all my efforts and turn what I hoped would be good to ill account? It is true, of course, that I act in a world of which my knowledge is limited and over which I have far less control than I should like; because of these facts the general possibility of any one of my acts turning out unfortunate can certainly not be ruled out. But the existence of this possibility is not enough to sustain Kant's case. It is, after all, only a general possibility, like the possibility that the most carefully made mathematical calculations will be found to contain a mistake. We do not need, nor can we have, any absolute guarantee against it, any more than we need or can be given protection against the Cartesian Demon.

Even on Kant's own terms, it is difficult to see in detail what belief in God is supposed to do for the moral man. Generally, it enables him to feel confident that his moral efforts will not be in vain; but how is that to be made specific? Is God to ensure that other men are more co-operative than they might naturally be, and thus that successful moral action will not be thwarted, or not be systematically thwarted, by unknown human obstacles? Is he to guarantee that nature is intelligible in detail and so more easily predictable? Or does he operate on a different level altogether, adjusting natural happenings so that they accord with moral requirements? The trouble about the last suggestion, which would fit in with the phrase already quoted about the Supreme Reason 'underlying nature as its cause', is that God could not operate as a special providence in the world as we know it without abrogating the rule of natural law and so rendering our experience unintelligible. In his essay 'Idea for a Universal History' of 1784 Kant developed an argument to show that Nature or Providence might be taken as pursuing a secret plan in history as a result of which good would come out of evil. Man on this account is prone to selfishness and un-sociability, but this fact in itself gets him into situations in which he is forced to develop his talents and co-operate, however unwillingly, with others. The development of states with a lawful civic con-stitution is the first unintended consequence of this state of affairs, the development of a federation of states on a world scale, each sub-ject to international law, can be expected to be another. But even if all this is true, what comfort can it give to the doubting moral agent? The assurance the latter wants is that his own moral efforts will not be in vain; the assurance Kant offers him as a philosopher of history is that other people's selfish actions may unwittingly turn out to have good results. So far from encouraging the virtuous to persist in their moral aims, this could tempt them to abandon them altogether, secure in the conviction that God will make everything right in the end.

In a passage already quoted Kant spoke of God as determining an appropriate outcome for moral conduct 'either in this or in another life' (B 840–1 / A 812–13). It looks as if this last phrase must be the key to his general doctrine. Given Kant's main assumptions God is in no position to interfere in the present world in a way which would dispel moral doubts. There, what will be will be, either as a result of the workings of nature or of men's deliberate actions. The latter may conduce to a further result which is morally desirable, but it will not be a result produced by men's own efforts, and so must be deemed irrelevant to the problem with which Kant confronts us. It follows that, to be effective, God must adjust the balance between just and unjust in another life. In this life the wicked flourish as the green bay tree, or at any rate are liable to do so, whilst the righteous, though they deserve to be happy, do not often find happiness. But all this could be changed if there is a life after death: evil men may finally then pay the penalty for their misdeeds, and good men be rewarded for theirs. We know that Kant believed there to be a close connection between postulating God's existence and postulating the immortality of the soul. For what he says about moral belief in God to make sense he needs at least an after life, since it is only then that God could fulfil the moral man's hope.

If this was what Kant was suggesting, it must be said at once that it would not satisfy some moral agents; it might not satisfy any. Moral activities take place in the world of experience, and it is the moralisation of this world that the moral man would like to see. He requires assurance that, if he fulfils his obligations, he has a good chance of bringing about a better state of affairs, which means that human life either immediately or in the future will be less evil than it was. He may not be consoled by the thought that in some future life God will proportion happiness to virtue; not least because he has no idea how much of him will survive in such a life. Will he still be moral, if he lacks a body and therefore sensuous desires? Of what sort of happiness will he be capable in these circumstances? The fact that no clear answers can be offered to these questions makes highly dubious Kant's claim that, as a moral agent, he 'inevitably' believes in the existence of God (see B 856/A 828). Kant himself may have seen nothing unfitting in the scheme of ideas suggested, but then he had a highly individual attitude to the whole phenomenon of morality, looking on it as an object of wonder, even awe. Less ardent moralists can still feel unhappy at the small extent to which their world is moralised, without believing that they could not act morally except on the assumption that there is a God. If this is correct the moral proof fails.

§ 40 *Meaning and Truth in Moral Belief*

It may even so be worth discussing briefly Kant's concept of *moral belief*. Two questions in particular arise about it, both relevant to Kant's central concern with the possibility of metaphysics. The first has to do with the meaning to be attached to the words 'There is a God' when God is an object of moral belief; broadly what we are after, here, is how the moral man can have an intelligible conception of God. The second has to do with the logical character of the conclusion of the moral argument, and in particular with the question whether we are intended to take it as true.

The first question is important because of what Kant argued in the Analytic. In one passage there (B 178/A 139) we read that 'concepts are altogether impossible, and can have no meaning, if no object is given for them, or at least for the elements of which they are composed'. This seems to commit Kant to a sort of atomistic empiricism. In fact his general account of meaning is not so extreme as these words suggest, since he is ready to allow that pure concepts too can have meaning, provided that they can be schematised. He also says in the Transcendental Deduction that it is one thing to know an object and another to think it, the implication here being that even in their unschematised form the categories are available for the purpose of forming concepts. I have already discussed in section 15 above the tremendous difficulties which this doctrine involves. Taken apart from their schemata, pure categories are too indeterminate to provide any precise idea. If I know only that something has the existence thought in the pure category, I know that it exists, but not as a physical object does nor yet as does a person, nor yet again as a number, and so on through all forms of determinate existence. To have a concept which is determined exclusively through pure categories is thus not of much use.

It remains true for all this that Kant thought the basic metaphysical concept of God would have to be constructed on the basis of pure categories, with the help perhaps of reason's idea of the unconditioned; no other materials were at hand for the purposes of the construction. But Kant was also clear that the thin abstraction which would result could hardly be thought to have real meaning outside the confines of the Schools. In particular, it would not suffice to meet the requirements of the moral man. The latter needs to conceive of God in clear and palpable terms; God must, in a way, be permanently present in his thoughts, and can hardly do that if the idea remains on the metaphysical level. The difficulty is solved by thinking of what God would have to be if he were to be a suitable object of religion (see *Critique of Practical Reason*, v 130 note). Many attributes we ascribe to God are also appropriate to creatures, for example power and knowledge; the difference in their case is simply that we think that God has them in the highest degree. But there are some qualities which are ascribed to God 'exclusively and without qualification of magnitude', all of them moral.

> He is the only holy, the only blessed, and the only wise being, because these concepts of themselves imply unlimitedness. By arrangement of these he is thus the holy lawgiver (and creator), the beneficent ruler (and sustainer), and the just judge. These three attributes contain everything whereby God is the object of religion, and in conformity to them the metaphysical perfections of themselves arise in reason (ibid.).

The God postulated in response to a 'need' of practical reason is basically a moral being, indeed *the* moral being; that is why he must be treated reverentially. He is entitled to our reverence because he embodies, though is not the source of, the moral law. Compared with him we are imperfect moral beings, subject to constant temptation and liable to default on our obligations at any moment. But the fact that we are moral beings at all gives us access to his nature, and so answers the question how there can be an intelligible conception of God. Kant would not deny that to think of God as the holy lawgiver, the beneficent ruler and the just judge is to conceive of him in terms of our own experience. He might well say that plain men must conceive of God on these or similar lines if he is to serve the purpose for which he is postulated, namely to exercise a real influence on men's lives. But he would deny that there was anything illegitimate in their doing so, on two grounds. First, the conception of God which emerges here does not claim any scientific status, since it is required not to explain anything, but merely to facilitate action; as Kant put it in the *Critique of Practical Reason* (v 138,140), it is a conception which belongs not to physics or metaphysics, but to morals. Second, behind the imaginative thinking of the plain man lies the solid ground of moral experience, which is open to all men even if there are some who 'through lack of good sentiments . . . may be cut off from moral interest' (b 858/a 830). To gain the grasp of God needed to keep us on the path of righteousness we require no special learning; we require only to reflect on what we know in our hearts.

I turn now to the question of the logical status of the pronouncements that are internal to moral belief, particularly that of the key pronouncement that there really is a God. Is it intended to convey a *truth*? There can be no doubt that Kant's official answer is 'yes'. The discussion of 'Opining, Knowing and Believing' in section *3* of the Canon of Pure Reason is introduced in a passage (b 850/a 822) where Kant says that all three are grades, or stages (the German word is *Stufen*), of 'holding for true' (*fürwahrhalten*). Opining is holding for true in circumstances where we are neither subjectively certain nor believe ourselves to have compelling grounds for our assertion. Belief is a holding for true which is subjectively certain though objectively insufficient. Knowledge is a holding for true which is both subjectively and objectively sufficient. In the previous section (b 833/a 805) Kant had said that the question 'What may I hope?'

> is at once practical and theoretical, in such fashion that the practical serves only as a clue that leads us to the answer to the theoretical question.

He had also declared (b 837/a 809) that

> just as the moral principles are necessary according to reason in

its practical employment, it is in the view of reason, in its theoretical employment, no less necessary to assume that everyone has ground to hope for happiness in the measure in which he has rendered himself worthy of it.

A section in the *Critique of Practical Reason* (v 142) has the heading 'On Assent arising from a Need of Pure Reason'; the German here is again *'fürwahrhalten'*. The same word is used in the title given to section *91* of the *Critique of Judgment*, rendered by Meredith as 'The Type of Assurance produced by a Practical Faith'.

Despite this array of evidence, Kant clearly felt qualms about the whole subject. We have noticed already the passage in which he says that I must not say that *it is* morally certain that there is a God, but only that *I am* morally certain. The conviction that God exists is a personal conviction, not a piece of knowledge that can be communicated. In the *Critique of Practical Reason* he explicitly addresses himself to the question, 'How is it possible to conceive of extending pure reason in a practical respect without thereby extending its knowledge as speculative?' (v 134 ff.). His answer is that through reflection on moral practice

> the theoretical knowledge of pure reason does obtain an accession, but it consists only in this—that those concepts which for it are otherwise problematical (merely thinkable) are now described assertorically as actually having objects, because practical reason inexorably requires the existence of these objects for the possibility of its practically and absolutely necessary object, the highest good.

The connection with morality makes the basic ideas of reason real, without making them available for purposes of knowledge, for (v 135)

> the three aforementioned ideas of speculative reason are not themselves cognitions; they are nevertheless transcendent thoughts in which there is nothing impossible.

We do not gain any intuition of things supersensible through the possession of these concepts, nor any indication of how to apply them for speculative purposes. The sphere of 'theoretical reason and of its knowledge with respect to the supersensuous in general' is extended 'inasmuch as knowledge is compelled to concede that there are such objects'; it is not extended to the extent of giving encouragement to metaphysical speculation. As Kant had put it in the first *Critique*, 'moral theology is . . . of immanent use only' (B 847/A 819). The point of developing it is not to fill the gap left by the discrediting of the traditional proofs, at least not in so far as those who put forward these proofs pretended to knowledge. It is to give assurance to the moral agent, to encourage him to act rather than to improve his understanding of what is the case.

If we take these points seriously, the proper conclusion to draw is surely that the words 'There is a God', said in a moral context, not only do not express knowledge in Kant's technical sense, but cannot even be considered as true. They have to do with an attitude which involves the holding of ideas, but their force is more that of an injunction than that of an assertion. In one candid passage in the second *Critique* (v 143) Kant wrote:

> Granted that the pure moral law inexorably binds every man as a command (not as a rule of prudence), the righteous man may say: I will that there be a God.

That there is a God is, if the moral proof is accepted, something of which we can be well assured; all the same it is an utterance that belongs to the will rather than the intellect. That this is so can be seen from the consideration that if we take the words out of their practical context, they become little more than empty sounds. To conclude in these circumstances that reference to the activities of practical reason results in any sort of extension to theoretical reason, even the carefully limited sort which Kant allows, is a mistake. Practical reason gives reality to certain ideas for practical purposes only; as far as the passion for speculation is concerned it leaves everything as it was. We are not even authorised on the strength of its existence to assert that there are supersensible objects, except in the appropriate practical context. That we should make that existence the basis of renewed metaphysical claims is entirely contrary to Kant's central convictions.

I stress these points in connection with a topic which was briefly mentioned at the beginning of this book, that of whether Kant should be seen as an absolute opponent of metaphysics or as a purveyor of a metaphysics of his own, what is sometimes called 'practical-dogmatic metaphysics'. It is often argued, correctly as it seems to me, that Kant was a man of the Enlightenment with a difference. He shared the passion for reason which was so common in his age, but interpreted its function in a highly individual way. The standard philosophy of the Enlightenment was a mixture of scientism, materialism and utilitarianism; Kant was suspicious of all three. One object of the *Critique* was to sever the root of materialism, as Kant himself put it (B xxxiv), another to expose the limitations of scientific knowledge whilst vindicating its reality in its own sphere. As for utilitarianism, it suffered from the enormous disadvantage of failing to recognise the unique and unconditional character of moral demands; it pretended to be a philosophy of reason, but in fact acknowledged reason only in the guise of prudence. To say these things is to say that Kant's general philosophical outlook was deeply anti-naturalist. But it could be this without being the expression of an alternative kind of metaphysics. To believe that there are questions other than those of the scientist is not necessarily to believe that the metaphysician must answer them. Certainly Kant could not allow his philosophy to end in metaphysics without embracing the grossest form of inconsistency. Nor does it seem to me that he ever clearly suggests that it should so end. The postulates of practical reason may perhaps be described as metaphysical convictions, but they should not be understood as metaphysical truths. They contain no information about another world, but have as their sole and proper function to direct human action in this world. They function more like commands or injunctions than statements, and for that reason their existence does nothing to threaten the anti-metaphysical conclusions of the main part of the *Critique*. That Kant should have thought that the world was one thing for the spectator or investigator and another for the agent may indeed seem odd; the story about phenomena and noumena goes only a little way towards diminishing the oddity. But whether we like it or not, that seems to have been his fundamental view. If it was, the neo-Kantian reading of his philosophy, which saw him as combining a modified empiricism in theory of knowledge with an ethics of pure will, may prove broadly right after all.

§ 41 *The Regulative Function of Ideas of Reason*

Concern with Kant's positive opinions in the theological field has led me to consider matters which Kant discusses in part at the very end of the *Critique*, in part in subsequent works. In following this course I have had to pass over an important chapter in the Dialectic itself, the appendix on the regulative function of ideas of reason. We must now return to consider this.

Let me begin by summarising the general position as Kant has presented it. At the beginning of the Dialectic he said that there was a distinction in the 'higher cognitive faculty' (the intellect) between two sets of powers, those that belong to *understanding* and those that belong to *reason*. Understanding is the intellect in so far as it co-operates with the senses, or works upon empirical data, reason the intellect in so far as it aspires to go beyond the empirical sphere altogether and arrive at knowledge of a non-empirical reality. Understanding possesses a special set of pure concepts of its own in the shape of the categories, and on the strength of these is able to lay down principles which govern the construction of the experienced world. Reason also turns out to have its own pure concepts, the ideas, each of them specifications of the fundamental notion of the unconditioned, and its ambition is to argue on the basis of these ideas to the existence and properties of a series of non-empirical existents, the soul, the world as an absolute whole, God. That it should proceed in this way is represented by Kant as wholly natural: the ideas in question occur spontaneously in our thought, and there is no prima facie reason to think that nothing will correspond to them. On the contrary, there are powerful motives, connected with moral needs, which impel us to try to move from the sphere of the sensible to that of the supersensible, and therefore make us want to believe that a certain form of speculative metaphysics is true.

By the time he has reached the end of the chapter on the Ideal Kant's reader is supposed to see that these bold ambitions must be disappointed. Taken as being constitutive, that is as referring to actual things, the ideas simply give rise to a series of fallacious inferences. The conviction that over and above the phenomena of consciousness there is and must be a superior subject self is shown in the Paralogisms to be nothing but misinterpretation of the logical requirement that all experiences be experiences for a single 'I'. The belief that the conditioned things of everyday life can be understood only if we see them as pointing to an unconditionally existing and self-complete cosmos is plausible when first considered on the assumption of transcendental realism, but is then invalidated by the discovery of the antinomies. With the adoption of the point of view of transcendental idealism it becomes clear that the inferences its exponents attempt either fail completely or succeed without ruling out the alternatives they meant to exclude. Finally, the claim that God is a true reality in the ordinary sense of the words, i.e. that he exists as surely as, or more surely than, any finite existent, is discredited by the exposure of the dialectical assumptions underlying all possible speculative proofs. God is a true reality, but only for the man who engages in moral activity and only for the purposes of that activity.

If ideas of reason thus do not designate existent things, what is their function? A cynic might see them as nothing more than the product of confusion, but Kant will not accept this solution. 'Everything that has its basis in the nature of our powers', he writes (B 670–1 / A 642–3), 'must be appropriate to, and consistent with, their right employment—if only we can guard against a certain misunderstanding and so can discover the proper direction of these powers'. The right employment of the faculty of reason, considered as concerned with what is the case, is to regulate the operations of the understanding. Reason is not a source of knowledge on its own account; not a single one of its ideas is constitutive, and there is no special realm which it opens up to us. On the other side it must not be seen as rivalling, or sharing, the work of the understanding: it is not its business to conceptualise the data of the senses. It moves rather on a higher logical level, issuing injunctions to which the understanding must conform in carrying out its conceptualising task. The effect of these is to demand that whatever we know be cast in systematic form, that empirical laws and principles be not a mere aggregate, but be parts of a self-differentiating whole. The understanding may not be able to comply with such a demand in the absolute sense; it depends, after all, on what turns up in experience whether or not we find systematic unity in our system of concepts. But seek for such unity we must, if Kant's doctrine is correct. If we fail to do so we may have knowledge or experience of a sort, but not science. It is thus in the important activity of achieving scientific understanding that ideas of reason are vitally involved.

To make good this point Kant must show that reason is involved in science not simply in a logical capacity but also more substantially. It is a logical requirement that we connect any concepts we have as closely as we can, that we arrange lower under higher concepts, co-ordinating sub-species under species, species under genera, and so on. Conforming to this requirement is certainly not all that Kant had in mind, since we could do so without stirring ourselves at all actively. What he was thinking of was rather the positive search for system as manifested in ongoing scientific activity, the refusal to be content with what has been achieved and the determination to find principles which show that nature is at once remarkably simple and extraordinarily variegated. We aspire, for example, to reduce fundamental powers to as small a number as possible, not just in the interests of logical neatness, but because we are convinced that the world is constructed on principles which are essentially simple. But this conviction does not prevent us from looking for ever new manifestations of those powers: as well as pursuing unity we also constantly pursue diversity. Again, we assume in our positive enquiries that 'no species or sub-species . . . are the nearest possible to each other' (B 687/A 659): there is a continuum of species, making it possible to look for intermediate species to an indefinite extent.

The comment may be made that, in so far as we engage in these activities or make these assumptions, we simply adopt certain methodological procedures. To explain science we need to refer to methodology as well as logic, but not to principles of reason. Kant himself does not distinguish methodology from logic: he describes the principle that 'entities are not to be multiplied beyond necessity' as logical (B 677/A 649), and gives the same account of his 'law of specification', that 'the variety of things is not arbitrarily to be reduced' (B 684/A 656). But he claims that in each case there stands behind the 'logical' principle a 'transcendental' counterpart. Reason here does not so much request as require. It lays it down, as a presupposition, that nature must be regarded as if it were a peculiar unity in diversity, a self-differentiating system whose parts can accordingly be handled on scientific lines. It is his conviction that scientists behave as if this were true, without making an empirical issue of the matter. It is not just a question of a methodology, since a methodology may and should be changed if it fails to lead to desired results. Here we have to do with convictions which are deeply entrenched, indeed spring from the nature of reason itself. The procedures we follow in endlessly searching for system are determined by ideas, and become unintelligible when these are left out of account.

But what, after all, do ideas *do* in this context? We have seen already that they cannot underpin science by providing it with a metaphysical basis, for the simple reason that they are not constitutive. Possession of the ideas adds nothing whatsoever to our knowledge of what is the case. What it does, if Kant is to be believed, is set up, and lend a certain intelligibility to, certain ideals. We are to proceed in our enquiries, Kant says, as if the material we encounter were itself originated by a single intelligent cause, which thus as it were accommodates nature to our understanding. We do not positively know that there is such a cause, still less what its properties in fact are; we have no objective assurance that the data experience provides will be tractable. But we could not continue our enquiries unless we were convinced that there was at least a hope of success; we do have at least this degree of subjective assurance. We are also able to form the idea, admittedly indeterminate in detail, of a being which could ensure that success will be possible. Putting these two facts, if facts they are, together Kant argues that in pursuing the search for systematic scientific knowledge we give a certain reality to the most important of reason's ideas. We let it perform a regulative function, and direct the operations of our understanding.

One difficulty in this vague theory is to know how much it claims to have established. In one remarkable passage near the beginning of his discussion (B 679/A 651) Kant, after denying that the 'systematic unity' which we presume is 'necessarily inherent in objects' could be arrived at 'through observation of the accidental constitution of nature', goes on to claim that

> The law of reason which requires us to seek for this unity is a necessary law, since without it we should have no reason at all, and without reason no coherent employment of the understanding, and in the absence of this no sufficient criterion of empirical truth.

What this seems to say is that, unless ideas operated as they do, we could not make any judgments. It seems clear, however, that we could make judgments provided that we could conceptualise our data under the general restrictions of the categories; to prove that was the whole point of the Analytic. Categories, and concepts generally, have a central role in Kant's scheme which makes them absolutely indispensable; without them there would be no experience at all. Kant cannot be saying that ideas too are necessary for the very possibility of experience, for this would undermine the whole distinction between ideas and categories. It would make nonsense of his claim in the introduction to the Dialectic (B 393/A 336) that, in the case of the ideas, no objective deduction is strictly possible.

Confusingly, Kant argues in the section headed 'The Final Purpose of the Natural Dialectic of Human Reason' (B 697/A 669ff.) that it is not only possible but also necessary to produce a transcendental deduction of the ideas, 'if they are to have the least objective validity' and 'are not to be mere thought-entities (*entia rationis ratiocinantis*)'. He admits that the deduction to be offered will be very different from that which is available in the case of the categories (B 698/A 670). In fact it turns out not to be a deduction at all, but simply a redescription of the role of ideas already sketched, along with a series of references to individual ideas. There is a difference, Kant says, between something being given to my reason as an object absolutely and as an 'object in the idea' (ibid.). When I am dealing only with the latter I presuppose something not for its own sake, but in relation to something else; it is on the latter that my attention is really directed, and I do not need to characterise the object in the idea further than it requires. So it will be a sufficient deduction of the 'three transcendental ideas' (B 699/A 671) if it can be shown that

> although they do not directly relate to, or determine, any

object corresponding to them, they nonetheless, as rules of the empirical employment of reason, lead us to systematic unity, under the presupposition of such an object in the idea.

He proceeds to show in principle how this would work out. In psychology we must

connect all the appearances, all the actions and receptivity of our mind, *as if* the mind were a simple substance which persists with personal identity (in this life at least), while its states, to which those of the body belong only as outer conditions, are in continual change.

In cosmology

we must follow up the conditions of both inner and outer natural appearances in an enquiry which is to be regarded as never allowing of completion, just as if the series of appearances were in itself endless, without any first or supreme member.

The idea of a first or supreme member endlessly beckons us on, but constantly eludes our grasp. Finally in theology

we must view everything that can belong to the context of possible experience as if this experience formed an absolute but at the same time completely dependent and sensibly conditioned unity, and yet also at the same time as if the sum of all appearances (the sensible world itself) had a single, highest and all-sufficient ground beyond itself, namely a self-subsistent, original, creative reason.

But what must be borne in mind in all three cases is that the purpose of the exercise is to facilitate empirical understanding. We presuppose the ideas not for their own sake, but because their postulation helps us to make sense of the phenomena. Accordingly, we are not required to account for the ideas in themselves, or to make their content specific. We can get by with the vaguest of general thoughts, and indeed could not improve on that if we tried (quotations all from B 700/A 672).

I suggest that Kant's appeal to particular ideas is of little or no significance. The psychological idea either does no work at all, or prejudices us in our empirical investigations, by underrating the importance of the body in the explanation of psychical phenomena. The cosmological idea does not appear as such: so far as anything important is implied under this head it is the old story, already expounded in the antinomies, about reaching the unconditioned being 'set as a task'. This has to do with the ceaseless prosecution of empirical enquiry, but not with its proceeding in any particular direction. As for the theological idea, what Kant says about it is only that it is necessary to explain what might be described as the human passion for system. In fact, it is the human passion for system writ large. Looked at critically, the whole Kantian theory about the positive role of ideas of reason turns out to be an essay on the importance and uniqueness of the notion of system in the overall search for knowledge. I do not say that Kant was wrong to insist on this idea: on the contrary, he seems to me to have shown great acumen in realising that there is a further problem about the orderliness of nature over and above that which was handled in the Analytic. If we like to put it so, the application of principles of the understanding must be governed by one or more principles of reason. But we need not put it in this manner: Kant himself used a different way of speaking when he came to tackle the problem afresh in the introduction to the *Critique of Judgment*, preferring there to attribute the assumption of 'formal purposiveness' in nature to 'reflective judgment' rather than to reason. Nor if we follow his earlier practice here and continue to speak in terms of reason's ideas is there any obligation to connect these ideas with the three metaphysical notions of God, Freedom and Immortality. The pretence that the Appendix to the Dialectic finds a respectable role for the very same notions which were subjected in its earlier chapters to such trenchant criticism is only a pretence. Even Kant cannot maintain seriously that the idea of the *ens realissimum* plays a part in the thinking of the scientist. The latter may think it an uncovenanted mercy that appropriate data continue to turn up in the course of his work; he may reflect that things could have been otherwise, or simply go forward in the blind animal faith that they will always do so. But whether he does or not, to say that his practice commits him to belief in God ('doctrinal belief', as it turns out: see B 853–5/A 825–7) is surely very extravagant. Kant himself admits that the assumption of an object in the idea is only a relative assumption (B 704/A 676): the thing concerned is supposed to exist only so far as its existence would help us to explain, or render intelligible, appearances. Twice in two pages (B 705/A 677, B 707/A 679) he insists that we cannot appeal to the 'concepts of reality, substance, causality, even that of necessity in existence' in order to fill out its content. It looks as if belief on these terms is at best very thin. But in any case, as in the parallel case of the moral belief which amounts to confidence that not all our moral strivings will be fruitless, it comes too easily. It seems that all scientists would be believers on this way of thinking.

Kant begins the Dialectic by talking about something he calls 'transcendental illusion' (B 349/A 293 ff.). The faculty of reason, he tells us, has fundamental rules and principles of its own, 'and these have all the appearance of being objective principles' (B 353/A 297).

> We therefore take the subjective necessity of a connection of our concepts for an objective necessity in the determination of things in themselves. This is an illusion which can no more be prevented than we can prevent the sea appearing higher at the horizon than at the shore, since we see it through higher light rays, or to cite a still better example, than the astronomer can prevent the moon from appearing larger at its rising, though we are not deceived by this illusion.

More detail about this is given in the Appendix. In his first account of the 'indispensably necessary, regulative employment' of the ideas (B 672/A 644) Kant says that it consists in

> directing the understanding towards a certain goal upon which the routes marked out by all its rules converge, as upon their point of intersection. This point is indeed a mere idea, a *focus imaginarius*, from which, since it lies quite outside the bounds of possible experience, the concepts of the understanding do not in reality proceed; nonetheless it serves to give to these concepts the greatest unity combined with the greatest extension. Hence arises the illusion that the lines have their source in a real object lying outside the field of empirically possible knowledge —just as objects reflected in a mirror are seen as behind it.

In the latter case the illusion that the things seen in the mirror are in front of us is indispensable if we are to see what lies behind us. Similarly the transcendental illusion cannot be avoided, though it need not deceive us, 'if we are to direct the understanding beyond any given experience (as part of the sum of possible experience) and thereby to secure its greatest possible extension' (B 673/A 645).

Is it true that we cannot avoid transcendental illusion? It depends on whether the ideas to which Kant ascribes a positive function in connection with science are the very same ideas which are misused by metaphysicians. If they are, what Kant has to say will at least be plausible, particularly for those who share his view that men have moral motives for hankering after the supersensible. But if we argue, as has been argued here, that there is little or no connection between the idea of system, with its attendant principles of homogeneity, specification and affinity (B 685/A 657), on the one hand, and the ideas of God, Freedom and Immortality, on the other, the illusion vanishes, or at least loses its power. To make intelligible to ourselves that particular data will be amenable to scientific treatment we can, if we choose, think of them as all proceeding from a supreme intelligence which benevolently accommodates nature to our understanding. Alternatively, we can see the situation in the terms of Kant's other image, as a *focus imaginarius* or ideal goal that draws us on and in so doing contributes to the endless extension of our knowledge. But it is surely clear that we do not have to think in either way, since in each case what is involved is a picture, an imaginative way of representing the facts. Pictures of course can be compulsive, but that is not to say that they are indispensable. I suspect that the hold these pictures exercised on Kant's imagination had a lot to do both with his own past as a metaphysician and with his continuing preoccupation with morals. For one who thought as he did it was natural to present the problem of system in scientific enquiry in a way which involved the idea of God; it was natural for one so situated to suppose that there must be something answering to the idea. But if this is true, it does not follow that others who recognise the importance of the problem must follow Kant's example; as more recent discussions have shown (compare here the work of Keynes and Russell) the problem can be put in quite other terms. The 'illusion' Kant speaks of could hence have constituted a real threat in Kant's own day, without posing any problem for philosophers now.

§42 *How is Critical Philosophy Possible?*

No consideration of the central arguments of the *Critique of Pure Reason* could be complete without some reference to a crucial question to which Kant gives little or no attention, that of how the *Critique* itself is possible. Kant enquires at length how there can be such things as pure mathematics and pure physics, how metaphysics can exist as a natural disposition and how, if at all, it is possible as science (cf. B 20–2). As we know, his defence of the possibility of pure physics is at the same time a vindication of a certain kind of metaphysics, 'metaphysics in its first part', as he had described it in his second preface (B xviii),

> the part that is occupied with those concepts *a priori* to which the corresponding objects, commensurate with them, can be given in experience.

Despite the criticisms to which Kant subjects metaphysics 'in its second part' (B xix), he never wavered in his conviction that a metaphysics of experience could be definitively established, and indeed that the *Critique* had laid the foundations for it. Thanks to the *Critique* we were in a position to offer undoubted proofs of principles such as those of substance and causality, though in doing so we had to recognise that it was only in relation to possible experience that they were valid or even meaningful. We could not prove these principles dogmatically, by reference to what is supposedly self-evident, nor could we find adequate justification for them by scrutinising empirical facts. What we could do was in each case to construct a transcendental argument to show that, unless they were presupposed, experience as we have it would not be possible at all.

I have discussed Kant's notion of transcendental proof in an earlier section (section 19), and do not propose to revert to it now. My purpose in mentioning it here is only to suggest that, because he gave attention to *some* questions about the possibility of philosophical knowledge, Kant may have believed that he had answered *all* relevant questions about it. If that was his view, it was seriously mistaken. A critique of pure reason, as Kant himself recognised explicitly in a later work (first introduction to the *Critique of Judgment*; Haden translation, p. 3), is an enquiry into the possibility of philosophy as a system; it is not itself a part of that system. To explain the possibility of some item or items in the system will not be to explain the possibility of critical enquiry itself. Even if the first can be undertaken satisfactorily we are left with the problem of the second. We need to show how pure reason can pronounce not just on mathematics and physics and metaphysics, but also on itself. We need to examine the logical status of its pronouncements, to say whether they are supposed to amount to knowledge, and if so to specify the type of knowledge involved. It will not do in this connection to confine ourselves to explicit conclusions, or to these and to proofs which are explicitly offered; we need also to ask ourselves about the premises of the arguments, and the presuppositions which lie behind them.

The general object of the *Critique of Pure Reason* is to circumscribe the sphere of possible knowledge. By an elaborate argument Kant seeks to establish that we can have knowledge in some areas and not in others. We can have knowledge in mathematics, pure and applied; we can arrive, in science and in daily life, at many different kinds of truth about things phenomenal; given suitable definitions, we can formulate true analytic propositions. What we cannot do is know what lies beyond the bounds of possible experience. All our knowledge is ultimately rooted in intuitions as well as in concepts, and the only form of intuition available to us is sense-intuition. It follows that knowledge, in its human form at least, is basically bound to sense. But what of the claim that it is? Is that supposed to represent a bit of sense-knowledge? Is it the result of insight on reason's part into its own nature and limitations, and if so how is that insight achieved? And if we say that it does constitute a part of the self-knowledge of reason (cf. B ix), what self is here concerned? Does reason here know itself as it appears to itself, or as it really is?

We can pursue this last question further. Kant in the Analytic, especially in its first edition form, produces a complicated story about the operations of the Understanding, the Imagination and the Senses. He tells us that the Imagination synthesises the manifold of sense, and that the Understanding brings the synthesis to concepts. Is the synthesising supposed to be done by the phenomenal self, the self which is an object of everyday knowledge? If so, why is the operation not empirically discernible, and thus something about which we can consult the empirical psychologist? Or do we have to say that an independently real self, which somehow lies behind the self of everyday discourse, is responsible for what is here described? If we do, shall we not be faced with the curious fact that we do after all possess some knowledge of something which is not phenomenal? How shall we mark off this knowledge of 'reality' which is legitimate from other purported knowledge of the same general kind which is not? How shall we avoid admitting that the main results of the Analytic are arrived at by a species of intellectual insight which they themselves claim to be unavailable to human beings?

It is to say the least unfortunate that Kant does not address himself to these and similar questions. A sympathetic commentator can do no more than ask himself what defence, if any, Kant might have found to the criticisms here implied.

One move which he might, but probably would not, have made is to say that we do not have to take the central contentions of the Analytic absolutely literally. Kant speaks in the language of faculty psychology, and introduces into his pages a cast of actors most of whom were already familiar to contemporaries. He is constantly saying that Understanding does this and Reason that; in adopting such terms he follows in the footsteps of predecessors such as Locke and Hume, to say nothing of Plato and Aristotle. But he need not have put his points in this language. For him as for others to speak of Understanding is simply a short way of referring to certain abilities and, perhaps, dispositions possessed not by 'the mind', whatever that is, but by persons. The operations of the Understanding are carried out by live human beings. Moreover, the syntheses Kant speaks of are potential or retrospective rather than actual and present. We do not have to suppose that, in order to have coherent experience, a person must actually there and then put together diverse 'representations' or diverse bits of experience; it will be enough if he has reason to believe that different items are capable of being connected under some concept, or shows after use of the concept that it does serve to connect them. It has been argued above that the work done by the concept of synthesis in the first edition of the *Critique* is taken over by that of judgment in the second. The claim cannot, of course, be made out in entirety: the second edition Deduction begins by discoursing on '*Verbindung*' ('combination'), which is simply the native German equivalent of the borrowed word '*Synthesis*', and ends with an important distinction between two kinds of synthesis, intellectual and figurative. If Kant had begun to demythologise his theory, he had not got very far with the process. Even so, I believe that to present his argument as one concerning the conditions of successful judgment is both true to his own intentions and independently illuminating. One particular advantage it offers as in connection with our present problem, since no-one in fact is inclined to ask what is concerned in judgment, the real or the phenomenal self. Judgments are made by men, in their capacity as thinkers. The judging subject is neither real nor phenomenal but an abstraction, an abstraction from the concrete person who moves and has his being in the experienced world.

Even if all this were true, it would not dissolve all difficulties, since Kant is apparently committed to further claims to philosophical self-knowledge. Take for example the well-known passage at the beginning of Transcendental Logic (B 75/ A 51), where he writes that

Our nature is so constituted that our intuition can never be other than sensible; that is, it contains only the mode in which we are affected by objects. The faculty, on the other hand, which enables us to think the object of sensible intuition is the understanding. To neither of these powers may a preference be given over the other. Without sensibility no object would be given to us, without understanding no object would be thought. Thoughts without content are empty, intuitions without concepts are blind. It is therefore just as necessary to make our concepts sensible, that is, to add the object to them in intuition, as to make our intuitions intelligible, that is to bring them under concepts. These two powers or capacities cannot exchange their functions. The understanding can intuit nothing, the senses can think nothing.

In an earlier section (section 3 above) I tried to show that Kant's doctrine of the heterogeneity of sensing and thinking is not postulated arbitrarily, but is shown by him to connect with other features of human experience, for example our ability to separate actuality and possibility and our inability to say, on the strength of possessing a concept alone, whether or not that concept has instances. As I hope I made clear, Kant's frequent appeals to the notion of intellectual intuition are to be explained by his wish to point up the importance of a crucial feature of the human intelligence, that it is through and through discursive. But what of the basic proposition that the human intelligence is discursive: how are we supposed to know that? Is it by some sort of insight into the nature of our own minds? When Kant says that 'our intuition *can* never be other than sensible', and again when he adds that 'these two powers or capacities *cannot* exchange their functions', it looks as if he must be claiming more than empirical knowledge of the essential knowing self. Experience will establish that things are so or so, but hardly that they can never be other than they are. But if Kant *is* claiming insight here, it will be intellectual insight into the necessary structure of fact, precisely the thing whose possibility he denies in other parts of the *Critique*.

I am inclined to think that, despite apparent evidence to the contrary, Kant does intend us to take the proposition that ours is a discursive intelligence as a contingent empirical truth, or rather as a philosophical conclusion from a whole series of such truths. His pronouncements about the capacities of the senses and the understanding are consequential on observation of the actual working of sense and thought. How the two work becomes plain in ordinary concrete experience. There is nothing esoteric or recondite in the reflection that I do not know what something is like because I have never had experience of it, nor in the observation that thinking as hard as one can about something will not of itself bring that something into existence. People know in particular cases that there is a fundamental difference between sensing and thinking, even if they are not familiar with the philosophical proposition that the two are heterogeneous. They realise that it is one thing to think of something in the abstract, for example a deeply satisfying personal relationship, and another to possess it in the concrete, though they may not be able to pass from this to the philosophical thesis that ours is a discursive intelligence. What Kant does in the *Critique* is build on facts we all take as obvious in our non-philosophical moments, such facts as that we can make mathematical judgments, discriminate objective from subjective successions, make determinate statements about what is happening in ourselves, generally distinguish the real from the apparent. As thus stated, these are facts of a highly general kind; behind each of them lies a vast number of more particular facts. It is these which form the ultimate basis of Kant's philosophy. It would certainly not be true to say that Kant did nothing but rehearse such facts, or even their more general counterparts, as if to do so were in itself philosophically enlightening. He is interested in them not for themselves, but in relation to philosophical theories; both theories he wants to refute, as when he discusses vulgar idealism, and theories he wants to advance himself. Unlike Wittgenstein, he is not content to leave everything as it is, if only because of his ambition to show that facts are not isolated, but often hang together in mutual support. But he is like Wittgenstein in believing that, in the last resort, all a philosopher can do is say that the facts are thus and thus; he has no separate source of knowledge or independent insight of his own.

Kant's attitude to the judgments of the ordinary man is on the face of things strangely ambivalent. In the field of practice ordinary human reason is thought of as making sound judgments from the start. As Kant put it in the *Grundlegung* (IV 404, Paton translation 72), 'there is no need of science or philosophy for knowing what man has to do in order to be honest and good'. The unsophisticated mind has 'as good hope of hitting the mark as any that a philosopher can promise himself', indeed a better hope, since the latter 'can easily confuse his mind with a mass of alien and irrelevant considerations'. Philosophy is required here only because innocence is liable to corruption at the hands of the inclinations; its essential purpose is to recall human reason to what it knows already. Things are very different when we move over to the sphere of theoretical reason. Even within the field of sense-experience the judgments of the plain man are subject to correction; the truth about the phenomenal world is known not to ordinary human reason but to science. It is really for the scientist to pronounce on what is empirically there. And when science gives way to philosophy the judgments of the unsophisticated become open to still greater errors. 'In theoretical judgments', wrote Kant in the same passage,

> when ordinary reason ventures to depart from the laws of experience and the perceptions of sense, it falls into sheer unintelligibility and self-contradiction, or at least into a chaos of uncertainty, obscurity and vacillation.

The philosophy of the uninstructed mind is either an affair of incoherent speculation or an unconvincing defence of common sense;

it is because human reason is here so weak and so easily confused that the whole critical enterprise was necessary. The instincts of the plain man in the field to which speculative philosophy falsely lays claim are sound: in this area of 'universal human concern' (B xxxiii) he knows as much as anyone does. What he lacks is the weapons by which to defend himself against the attacks of sceptics or the sophisms of men of bad faith. The *Critique of Pure Reason* provides him with these weapons, or at least lets him know that they exist.

What this leaves out is an account of the foundations on which critical philosophy itself rests. It seems to me that Kant could claim superior acumen for the philosopher, together perhaps with greater synoptic powers, but that he could not say that he has a source of knowledge all his own. He cannot argue that the mind is a discursive instrument, requiring to operate on data given from without, when it considers itself as an object of experience, but suddenly and inexplicably acquires intuitive powers when it investigates itself in philosophy. But in any case he does not need to. It will be enough if he bases his philosophy on the wide judgments of fact we spoke of above, judgments whose correctness is substantiated repeatedly and which accordingly are not liable to be challenged by scientific advance. He can take his stand at a point where what the plain man says coincides with what is said by the scientist or the philosopher. The effect of his doing so will of course be to import into his theory an element which is contingent. Kant sometimes writes as if philosophy could be respectable only if it could represent itself as a purely *a priori* science. But in practice he is prepared to allow that there are all sorts of contingent elements in his own philosophy. It is just a fact that we have these and no other forms of sensible intuition, these and no other forms of judgment, these and no other categories (B 145–6). Similarly, it is just a fact that we have a discursive and not an intuitive understanding, and again a will which, because of its connection with sensibility, is subject to moral obligation rather than automatically does what is right (cf. *Critique of Judgment*, section 76). In these respects theoretical and practical philosophy do not diverge. Each must be based on the undoubted realities of the human situation, and cannot succeed unless it is.

Kant and the Synthetic *A Priori*

At the end of section 2 above I quoted Professor Strawson's dictum that 'Kant really has no clear and general conception of the synthetic *a priori*'. As Strawson sees it, the class of Kantian synthetic *a priori* judgments comprises a variety of items, thrown together on no other principle than that they can be appealed to in support of Kant's thesis of transcendental idealism. I said before that I thought that, if justified, this criticism would be damning. I must now try to indicate to what extent it is justified.

According to Kant, men make, or attempt to make, synthetic *a priori* judgments in a number of different spheres: in pure mathematics, in 'pure physics' or 'pure natural science', in metaphysics, in ethics. Of these we can set aside the last without examination, on the ground that practical and theoretical judgments are different both in their form and, more important, in their purpose. Practical judgments have to do with the will, not with knowledge; they take the form of prescriptions which are correct or incorrect, rather than of statements which are true or false. Questions about how we know them hardly make sense, since strictly we do not know them at all. Again, we can disregard for our present purposes the alleged synthetic *a priori* judgments of metaphysics, since these in Kant's view are either wholly unjustified or to be identified with judgments of 'pure physics'. The metaphysics which Kant thinks legitimate concerns the form of the phenomenal world; the synthetic *a priori* principles to which it makes appeal are those discussed and defended in the Analytic of Principles. By contrast, the synthetic necessary 'truths' which traditional metaphysicians purvey are wholly without foundation, as the discussions of the Dialectic have made clear.

This leaves us with the cases of pure mathematics and pure physics, and the question we must now face is whether Kant has a clear and general conception of the synthetic *a priori* as far as they are concerned. The answer is that he does not. Kant contrives to bring the two groups of judgment together in a formal respect only. In each case, as he explains, the judgments in question are treated as possessing necessity, without its being the case that their contradictories are self-contradictory. Hence in each case we need to ask what it is that 'mediates' or connects subject and predicate. But though the two types of judgment are alike in this respect, the way in which Kant explains the 'mediation' differs significantly in the two cases. Mathematical judgments are synthetic *a priori*, he tells us, because mathematical concepts can be constructed in pure intuition; the judgments of pure physics answer the same description thanks to their bearing on the possibility of experience. In speaking about the constructibility of concepts in pure intuition Kant is referring to a procedure which, in his view, mathematicians must invoke if they are to *arrive at* their conclusions; his contrast between the philosopher's and the mathematician's treatment of a simple geometrical problem (B 744/A 716) is highly instructive in this respect. But when, in the Analytic of Principles, Kant appeals to the notion of the possibility of experience in connection with the judgments there discussed, he is not concerned with how we *arrive at* certain conclusions, but with how we *validate* them. His contention is that we have to assign a special status to a principle like that of causality if we are to explain a particular feature of our experience. But this is not to say that reference to possible experience will throw any light on how we *come by* such principles.

I pointed out earlier (see section 5 above) that Kant formulated his ideas about mathematical procedure and the constructibility of mathematical concepts some years before he produced his first version of the thesis of transcendental idealism. The charge that he was interested in mathematical judgments exclusively because of their bearing on this thesis will accordingly not stand up. However, the very fact that Kant approached the problem of mathematical knowledge in this way might lead one to expect that there would be important differences in his treatment of pure mathematics on the one hand and pure physics on the other. In fact, these two parts of his philosophy have little, if anything, to do with one another. The two sets of judgments in question do not form species of a common genus.

What of the judgments of 'pure physics' themselves? Here Kant's view is far more defensible. Admittedly, it is not easy to accept the title under which Kant groups the judgments concerned: the principles of the understanding have no special connection with physics, or even with natural science in general. They are more abstract than that, specifying as they do the formal properties of whatever is to be part of shared experience. This relatively unimportant defect apart, however, they constitute an intelligible class of judgments, marked off by a distinctive criterion in the form of the test of absurdity (see section 8 above) and validated by a procedure which is clear in particular cases, even if it is not wholly satisfactory when considered in the abstract (see section 19). It is important to remember in this connection that Kant does not merely speak about these principles in general terms; he lists and defends *all* the principles which he believes fall under this head. To suggest in these circumstances that he is merely putting together a hotch-potch of items which have no connection with one another, or are chosen only because they can be appealed to in support of trans-cendental idealism, is quite unconvincing. Indeed, as was briefly argued in section 26, there are grounds for thinking that the three principles dealt with in the Analogies are not only individually indispensable, but further are such that the use of any one of them calls for the use of the two others. If we are to have a unitary temporal system, we need to provide for objective statements in connection with each of the three 'modi' of time, and this means invoking the principles of Substance, Causality and Reciprocity *together*. That Kant himself did not recognise this fact is not enough to rule it out. Nor should we be put off by his failure to enquire into the relation between believing that the world is such that mathema-tics can be applied to it and believing that it falls within, or manifests, a single spatio-temporal order, since the indications are that further reflection would show that the connection between the different Kantian principles is closer than he makes them out to be, not looser.

Kantian principles of the understanding form a class with a some-what restricted membership: if we accept everything that Kant claims in this part of his work we find ourselves with five principles in all. It could be, of course, that Kant has failed to enumerate all the principles which fall into the class, as Hegel and others have argued. Whether he has or not, the view that a distinct type of principle is here in question is one to which he gives strong support. If we choose to describe such principles as 'synthetic *a priori*', that elusive phrase will have at least one intelligible use. What Kant says here may not amount to a defence of the synthetic *a priori* in general. But it seems to me that, in the Analytic, he does succeed in singling out under this description a set of judgments which have more in common than that they can be exploited in the interest of wider Kantian conclusions. Even if transcendental idealism had to be abandoned altogether, the questions of the precise status of such judgments and of the justification for accepting them would remain of continuing philosophical interest.

Index